The Muses' Library

★

COLLECTED POEMS
OF
SIR THOMAS WYATT

Tho: Wiat knight.

HOLBEIN: PORTRAIT OF SIR THOMAS WYATT

By gracious permission of H.M. The Queen

COLLECTED POEMS
OF

SIR THOMAS
WYATT, 1503?-
1542

edited
with an introduction
by

KENNETH MUIR

LONDON
ROUTLEDGE AND KEGAN PAUL LTD

953

First published in 1949
by Routledge and Kegan Paul Ltd
68–74 Carter Lane, London, E.C.4

Second impression 1955
Third impression 1960
Fourth impression 1963
Fifth impression 1966

Printed in Great Britain
by Butler & Tanner Limited
Frome and London

CONTENTS

v

ACKNOWLEDGEMENTS

THE Holbein portrait of Wyatt is reproduced by gracious permission of H.M. The King.

My thanks are due to the following: the Trustees of the British Museum, the Duke of Norfolk, the Librarian of Corpus Christi College, Cambridge, Miss Ruth Hughey (for sending me her transcripts of the Arundel MS.), Mr. R. C. Wilton, Mr. W. G. Doyle-Davidson, Professor Bruce Dickins, Professor Bonamy Dobrée, Mr. Arthur Creedy, Professor H. Orton, Mr. R. M. Wilson, Miss A. G. Foster and the Leeds City Librarian and his staff.

Acknowledgements are also due to the following authors (or to their representatives) and their publishers for permission to quote from their books: W. J. Courthope (Macmillan), Sir E. K. Chambers (Sidgwick and Jackson), Dr. E. M. W. Tillyard (Oxford University Press), Professor H. E. Rollins (Harvard University Press), Professor J. M. Berdan (Macmillan Co.), Professor F. M. Padelford (Heath), and *The Times Literary Supplement*.

Mr. Hallett Smith's admirable essay, 'The Art of Sir Thomas Wyatt' (The Huntington Library Quarterly, IX. 4.) reached me too late for me to make use of it.

KENNETH MUIR

Leeds University

INTRODUCTION

INTRODUCTION

INTRODUCTION

BY

KENNETH MUIR

I

THOMAS WYATT (or Wiat) was born at Allington Castle, on the River Medway, in 1503. The estate had been presented to his father, Sir Henry, as a reward for his sufferings in the Tudor cause during the previous reign. Wyatt made an early appearance at Court at the christening of Princess Mary in 1516. Soon afterwards he proceeded to St. John's College, Cambridge. In 1520, he married Elizabeth, the daughter of Lord Cobham. She bore him a son, also called Thomas, and a daughter, Bess; but she afterwards proved unfaithful and Wyatt refused to live with her.

Wyatt held various posts at Court and distinguished himself at a Christmas tournament in 1525. His diplomatic career began in the following year, when he accompanied Sir Thomas Chene's embassy to France and carried despatches home to England. Wolsey was informed that Wyatt had 'as much wit to remember and remark everything he seeth as any young man hath in England'. In the following year the poet accompanied Sir John Russell on a mission to the Pope, and while travelling in Italy he was captured by Spanish troops. While negotiations for his ransom were in progress, he contrived to escape. Between 1528 and 1532 he served as Marshal of Calais. On his return to England, he was made Commissioner of the Peace for Essex and he deputized for his father as Chief Ewer at the coronation of Anne Boleyn.

This task he must have performed with mixed feelings. According to one story, recorded by Nicholas Sanders, Anne had been Wyatt's mistress; and on hearing of Henry VIII's intention of marrying her Wyatt had informed the Privy Council that his former mistress was not a suitable wife for the King. Henry decided not to believe the story and Wyatt was banished from Court; but this confession proved to be his salvation at the time of Anne's downfall. This not very credible story is largely substantiated by other writers, though Harpsfield more plausibly declares that on Wyatt's revelation Henry ordered him to keep the secret. These Catholic writers were glad to collect scandals about Anne in addition to the murkier revelations at her trial, and the stories may possibly have been invented to explain Wyatt's imprisonment in 1536. Professor Berdan has argued that the story of Wyatt's relations with Anne has no basis in fact; that his imprisonment at the time of Anne's fall was a coincidence which gave rise to the gossip; and that the poems which have been thought to refer to Anne are translations from the Italian. Certainly Wyatt's imprisonment in May 1536 was directly due to a quarrel with the Duke of Suffolk, and only indirectly, if at all, connected with Anne's downfall: for, five years later, when Wyatt was again arrested, he told his judges that he did not impute his earlier imprisonment to the King, but to the Duke of Suffolk. It is also true that the sonnet (No. 7) which ends with the lines—

> *There is written, her faier neck rounde abowte*
> Noli me tangere, *for Cesars I ame;*
> *And wylde for to hold, though I seme tame.*

is translated from Petrarch. Another poem, entitled in Tottel 'Of his loue called Anna', contains the line—

> *It is mine Anna god it wot.*

But the more authentic text of the manuscript reads—

> *It is myn aunswer god it wot.*

The title, 'Anna', has been added by a later hand. A poem in the Devonshire MS. (No. 114), not certainly Wyatt's, describes how the poet's mistress wrote these words in his book—

> *I am yowris you may well be sure,*
> *And shall be whyle my lyff dothe dure.*

On a later page in the same manuscript someone has written the words—

> *I ama yowrs,*
> > *An.*

It has been argued that this Anne may be the A. J. who writes an answer to one of Wyatt's poems in the same manuscript, though this was clearly a man.

But even if all these poems are dismissed from the argument, Professor Berdan is not quite fair in his statement of the evidence, for he omits to mention the most striking poem. In a later sonnet Wyatt refers to two women, Brunet and Phillis—

> *sins I did refrayne*
> *Her that did set our country in a rore,*
> *Th'unfayned chere of Phillis hath the place*
> *That Brunet had.*

Wyatt altered the second of these lines, so as to avoid an indiscretion, to—

> *Brunet, that set my welth in such a rore.*

The lines are not in Petrarch. Professor Berdan, though he easily disposes of Nott's romantic theories, does little to disprove the assumption that Wyatt had relations with Anne before she became Queen: for the fact that she was then betrothed to Henry Percy does not, in view of her later promiscuity, prove very much.

She may well have had other lovers, platonic or otherwise.

If Anne was indeed Brunet, it is curious that the King, although officially disbelieving Wyatt's confession, rewarded him with a knighthood in March 1536, only a few months before Anne's exposure. We must assume that he believed Wyatt, but was determined to marry Anne notwithstanding.[1]

After a few weeks Wyatt was released—which he would not have been if he had committed adultery with the Queen after her marriage—and sent to Allington Castle to be under his father's supervision. There he stayed during the summer of 1536; but the King soon relented and Wyatt was made Steward of Conisborough Castle and Sheriff of Kent.

In March 1537 Wyatt was appointed Ambassador to Spain. He set out in the following month, passing through Lyons, where Louise Labé was at the height of her fame. Maurice Scève and other poets lived there, and in this *École Lyonnaise* is to be found the origins of the *Pléiade*. Marot himself had lived in Lyons before 1536, and Saint-Gelais's poems were first published there. Wyatt may have met both these poets on his earlier visit to France: there are traces of their influence on his work and one epigram of each has been copied into the Egerton MS.

Wyatt discharged his duties in Spain with zeal and efficiency, though his task was made difficult by the Emperor's resentment at the King's divorce. The arrival of two special envoys, Haynes and Bonner, added to the poet's trials; and Bonner, thinking himself slighted, sought to damage Wyatt's reputation by accusations to Cromwell. The latter, however, cleared Wyatt and showed his friendship by looking after his chaotic finances.

[1] The above discussion owes something to the essay by Sir E. K. Chambers.

During Wyatt's absence from England his father died; and on his return in May 1539 the poet spent some months at Allington. On the eve of his departure for England he wrote an epigram which is a good testimony to his patriotism and loyalty; and it was not long before his services were again required. He was sent on special missions to the French Court and to the Emperor, then in Flanders. He was present at the execution of his friend and patron, Cromwell, in July 1540, and he adapted one of Petrarch's sonnets to express his grief (No. 173). Other poems written about this time lament the desertion by his friends. He retired to Allington and there wrote his version of the Penitential Psalms, in expectation, perhaps, of the blow which fell the following January. He was arrested and all his goods confiscated. His accuser was his old enemy, Bonner, now Bishop of London; and the accusations ranged from treason to immorality. Wyatt defended himself eloquently and he was released with a full pardon, Bonner's face being saved by the official statement that Wyatt had confessed and been pardoned on the Queen's intercession.

A condition of his pardon was that he should take back his wife—he was now living with one of Queen Catherine's former maids of honour, Elizabeth Darrell —and, according to the Spanish Ambassador, Henry VIII soon afterwards became intimate with Lady Wyatt's sister. But, whatever the reason, Wyatt was again restored to favour. He was sent to Calais to watch the defences; he was elected M.P. for Kent; and he was chosen to be Vice-Admiral of a fleet that was being built. Early in October 1542 he was sent to Falmouth to escort a Spanish envoy to London. On the way he caught a fever and died at Sherborne, where he lies buried.

We can piece together Wyatt's character from his letters and poems, from the speech written for his trial, and from various anecdotes and contemporary references. The letters to his son (who was executed after the failure of the Lady Jane Grey rebellion) are sermons on the subject of honesty. He distinguishes between the common conception of honesty, such as reputation for riches or for authority, and the honesty possessed by his own father, 'that was wisdome, gentlenes, sobrenes, desire to do good, frendliness to get the love of manye, and trougth aboue all the rest'. Wyatt recommends his son to 'think and imagine alwais that you are in presence of some honist man that you know', and confesses that he himself is 'a nere example unto you of my foly and unthriftnes that hath, as I wel deseruid, brought me into a thousand dangers and hazardes, enmyties, hatrids, prisonments, despits and indignations'. In his second letter, from Spain, Wyatt again warns his son against the popular conception of honesty:

'Trust me that honist man is as comen a name as the name of a good felow, that is to say, a dronkerd, a tauerne hanter, a riotter, a gamer, a waster: so are among the comen sort al men honist men that are not knowin for manifest naughtye knaues. ... Folow not therfor the comen reputation of honestye: if you wil seme honist, be honist or els seame as you are.'

It reads almost like a commentary on the character of Iago.

Parental advice is treacherous evidence of parental character; but Wyatt's praise of integrity and hatred of hypocrisy is reinforced by his refusal to set himself up as a model, and the sincerity and piety revealed in these letters is supported by what we know of Wyatt's relations with Henry VIII and Cromwell, as well as by the Satires. The first satire is a scathing attack on the arts required for success at Court; the second is a warning against the dangers of ambition; and the third

ironically advises Brian how to get rich—by marrying
a wealthy widow or by selling his daughter or sister.[1]

The quality most apparent in the Letter to the Privy
Council and in the speech he delivered, or intended to
deliver, at his trial is courage.[2] He not only answered
all the accusations made against him, he carried the
war into the enemy's camp and exposed Bonner as a
vain and malicious time-server. Bonner had accused
Wyatt of treating him with insufficient respect, and he
retorted:

'I know no man that did you dishonour, but your
unmannerly behaviour, that made ye a laughing stock
to all men that came in your company, and me sometime to sweat for shame to see you.'

Bonner accused him of living viciously among the
nuns at Barcelona, and Wyatt replied:

'Come on now, my Lord of London, what is my
abominable and vicious living? Do ye know it, or have
ye heard it? I grant I do not profess chastity; but yet I
use not abomination. If ye know it, tell it here, with
whom and when. If ye heard it, who is your author?
Have you seen me have any harlot in my house whilst

[1] Berdan remarks: 'It cannot be said that the facts of Wyatt's
life as we know them indicate that he lived on a superior plane, un-
touched by the baser motives of the common courtier. His inti-
macy with Sir Francis Bryan scarcely argues for a lonely moral
isolation.' Bryan was known as the 'Vicar of Hell'. I have no desire
to whitewash Wyatt but I believe that his own writings and Surrey's
elegy bear witness to his integrity. More evidence is provided by
Marillac, who in January 1541 wrote of Wyatt's imprisonment
(Berdan himself quotes the passage): 'Although he is more re-
gretted than any man taken in England these three years, both by
Englishmen and strangers, no man has the boldness to say a word
for him, and by these fine laws he must be judged without knowing
why.' Another witness is Cromwell: 'I think your gentle, frank
heart doth much impoverish you'. In the *Chronicle of Henry VIII*,
the author remarks that 'everybody was very fond of Wyatt'.

[2] Froude, who tends to whitewash Henry VIII, assumes that
Wyatt really admitted his guilt, and doubts whether the speech
was actually delivered. But the letter to the Privy Council covers
much of the same ground and exhibits the same spirit.

ye were in my company? Did you ever see woman so much as dine, or sup, at my table? None, but for your pleasure, the woman that was in the galley; which I assure you may well be seen; for, before you came, neither she nor any other came above the mast. But because the gentlemen took pleasure to see you entertain her, therefore they made her dine and sup with you; and they liked well your looks, your carving to Madonna, your drinking to her, and your playing under the table. Ask Mason, ask Blage—Bowes is dead—ask Wolf, that was my steward; they can tell how the gentlemen marked it, and talked of it. It was a play to them, the keeping of your bottles, that no man might drink of but yourself; and "that the little fat priest were a jolly morsel for the Signora". This was their talk; it is not my devise: ask other, whether I do lie.'

Few people accused of treason in the last years of Henry's reign escaped with their lives even though, like Wyatt, they were innocent. Wyatt was saved largely by his own eloquence and courage, though the King must have been loth to lose so faithful a servant.

The wit and irony displayed in Wyatt's defence are also to be seen in a number of stories, probably apocryphal, which have come down to us. The King is reported to have expressed apprehension that the suppression of the monasteries would be unpopular. 'True, Sire,' Wyatt is said to have replied, 'but what if the rook's nest were buttered?' Henry thereupon decided to give the nobility part of the church lands. Another story records that when the King wished for his divorce, ostensibly on the grounds that Catherine was his dead brother's wife, Wyatt exclaimed: 'Heavens! that a man cannot repent him of his sins without the Pope's leave!' But the effect on English history of such remarks, even if Wyatt made them, has been exaggerated. It is unlikely, as one biographer has pointed out, that he 'brought about the Reformation by a *bon mot* and hastened the fall of Wolsey by a seasonable story'.

II

One of the most curious delusions in English literary history, and one which has lasted down to our own day, has been the assumption that Surrey is a better poet than Wyatt. The death of Wyatt's son on the scaffold made it politic for Tottel to minimize the father's share in the *Songes and Sonettes*, for although Surrey had also been executed for treason the Howard family had been restored to favour by 1557. An earl, moreover, is more important than a knight. Surrey's lines were smoother than Wyatt's and his versification was admired in much the same way as that of Denham and Waller was admired by Dryden. Wyatt's, on the other hand, seemed to be harsh, clumsy, and unmusical. The eighteenth century naturally found more to admire in Surrey than in Wyatt and as late as 1816 a critic could pronounce emphatically that Wyatt was not a poet at all. Courthope was the first to give a reasonably just appreciation of Wyatt's work; and Mr. Tillyard was the first to state clearly that Wyatt was a much greater poet than Surrey. Yet Mr. Berdan, the author of the standard work on *Early Tudor Poetry* (1920), damns Wyatt with faint praise, and Professor Rollins in his splendid edition of Tottel's Miscellany seems to regard Wyatt's importance as being mainly historical.

It is no part of my purpose to disparage Surrey's work; but it is necessary to insist that much of it is written in the intractable Poulter's Measure, that the metrical variations in his blank verse were more likely to be involuntary than purposeful, and that whereas he is flattered by selections in anthologies, Wyatt is not.

Mr. Berdan declares that the age does not reach its maturity until the writers of the second half of Henry VIII's reign. He takes Surrey to be the culmination of early Tudor poetry and declares that he unites the four dominating impulses of the literature of the age. Wyatt, on the other hand, in Mr. Berdan's opinion, not only chose poor models among the Italian authors, 'he also selected poor examples of their work'. He is accused (justly) of writing lines that cannot be scanned and of exhibiting few traces of the Humanistic influence. He is only allowed the merit of experimenting in stanza forms and of writing ten or eleven lyrics which possess strength and grace.

Wyatt has been undervalued [1] because critics have lacked the strength of mind to differ from their predecessors or because they have been obsessed by his historical importance as the importer of the sonnet and as the *fons et origo* of all Elizabethan poetry. It is worth remembering in this connection that about twenty-five years elapsed between the publication of Wyatt's poems and the writing of the first Elizabethan sonnet-sequence, *Astrophel and Stella*. Sidney may have been encouraged by the experiments of Surrey in the sonnet form, but both he and Spenser went to foreign models. The sonnet was virtually re-introduced into England two generations after Wyatt's first translations from Petrarch.

The intrinsic poetic merit of Wyatt has little to do with his historical importance. His finest poems [2] are not, as far as we know, translations. They apparently belong to all periods of his life and they have an ease of movement and of versification which is much less apparent in the translations. It has been argued that

---

[1] Except by Padelford, Tillyard and Chambers, as will be apparent from the extracts given below, and by Miss Foxwell, who praises him for the wrong reasons.

[2] e.g. 37–8, 57–8, 65–6, 71, 73–4, 77, 82, 91, 103, 111, 113, 130, 132, 143, 157.

the translations were early, experimental work; but many of the lyrics in the Devonshire MS. were also written early and, though some of them are feeble enough, they are smoother in versification than most of the sonnets. Other critics have suggested that the metrical deficiencies of the sonnets are due to the difficulty of the form and the need to keep as closely as possible to the original. Against this it must be said that Wyatt frequently departs from his originals when it suits him; and that though one might expect awkward inversions for the sake of the rhyme, there seems to be no particular reason why Wyatt, in writing sonnets, should lose the secret of the iambic pentameter. One might expect inexpert quatrains and forced rhymes—but not unmetrical lines. Miss Foxwell thinks that Wyatt based his versification on Pynson's edition of Chaucer; but the metrical awkwardness is common to all Wyatt's contemporaries, and there is no need to search for a particular source. Sir Edmund Chambers has argued that the sonnets 'ought to be regarded as mere exercises in translation or adaptation, roughly jotted down in whatever broken rhythms came readiest to hand, and intended perhaps for subsequent polishing at some time of leisure which never presented itself'. The difficulty of this theory is that these translations are given pride of place in the Egerton Manuscript, which was Wyatt's own. Nine out of the first fourteen poems, beautifully transcribed, are translations from Petrarch. It is difficult to avoid the assumption, since the poems are probably not in chronological order,[1] that Wyatt set a higher value on these translations than on the many fine ballets in the Devonshire MS., which were excluded from the Egerton.[2] The

[1] Miss Foxwell assumes that they are.
[2] A few leaves have been torn from E, and these may have contained poems which are now to be found only in Tottel or in the other manuscripts.

latter underwent a certain amount of revision and Wyatt's ear seems to have been satisfied with lines which have offended most of his critics.

It may be suggested that critics expect smoothness in the sonnet form and complain of irregularities which they would accept in other forms of lyrical verse. The haunting cadence of the line—

Into a straunge fashion of forsaking

has been justly praised; but if such a line turned up in a sonnet it would be regarded as harsh. To read Wyatt's sonnets after Shakespeare's or Daniel's is to have one's ear teased by irregularities and puzzled by the position of the accents. But if they are read after Donne's Divine Sonnets, they will be found more acceptable. Wyatt has been badly served by metrists who have tried to torture his lines into regular patterns. If the sonnets are read naturally, with due regard to Romance punctuation, most of them have a music of their own which, like Donne's, helps to convey the emotion. Mr. Berdan scans the first line of one sonnet (No. 4):

The longe love | that in my thought doeth harbar.

But it is difficult to believe that Wyatt intended the third and fifth of these stresses, and improbable that the accent was intended to fall so definitely on the last syllable of the line. It is more satisfactory to scan the line—

The longe love that in my thought doeth harbar.

In any case, even though the last syllable of the line is lengthened, the rhyming is imperfect, and the whole sonnet is profoundly unsatisfactory. Professor D. W. Harding's explanation is as good as any. He suggests that 'whether or not Wyatt fully understood the principles of the Italian verse on which he modelled them, it looks as if he was experimenting in most of them with lines of a fixed number of syllables, with little regard for accent—as if the old pausing verse was being complicated and spoilt by mechanical fixity in the number of syllables'.[1]

In the same article, Professor Harding argues convincingly that Wyatt in many of his poems 'positively chose the pausing line compounded of dissimilar rhythmical units'. It is difficult to believe that 'a writer who shows such exquisite management of rhythm in some of his verse could have been reduced by the mere difficulty of manipulating language to such elementary failures of metrical writing as the critics think they see in other parts of his work'. Wyatt lived at the end of one tradition and he was the main originator of another. 'It is impossible to believe that Wyatt could not quite easily have made his irregular lines regular had he wished.'

None of the sonnets, not even the late ones which are comparatively smooth, can be ranked among Wyatt's best poems. But 'You that in love finde lucke and habundance' (No. 92), for which no source has yet been discovered, has strength and mastery, and if one compares 'If waker care, if sodayne pale coulor' (No. 95), adapted from Petrarch's 'S'una fede amorosa', with the earlier and closer translation of the same original (No. 12), one is forced to conclude that the awkwardness apparent in many of the early sonnets was caused, apart from the reason suggested above, by the double difficulty of being faithful to the original and of writing the first English sonnets. Wyatt doubtless overvalued his translations because they were more difficult achievements than the songs which came to him as naturally as the leaves to a tree.

Most of the sonnets, then, are of minor importance. The Rondeaux are even less satisfying, though even

[1] *Scrutiny* (December 1946).

among these there are poems which have more than an historical interest. The gay invective of 'Ye old mule' (No. 35) and the playful indignation of 'What no, perdy' (No. 45) show that Wyatt eventually taught himself to master this form also. It is quite unfair to compare Wyatt's experiments either with the French rondeaux from which some of them were imitated or with the brittle trifles of Austin Dobson. He was not trying to write *vers de société*.

Wyatt's version of the *Penitential Psalms* (adapted from the prose paraphrase of Aretino) can best be regarded as a single poem; for the prologues link the seven psalms together and relate them all to the story of David and Bathsheba. The Psalms, as we have them, are Wyatt's first draft; and if he had lived he would doubtless have revised them. Both the *ottava rima* of the prologues and the *terza rima* of the psalms themselves are used with some skill; and Wyatt often deserts Aretino for the Vulgate or for an English translation. It may even be said that Wyatt contrived to make better metrical versions of the psalms than either Sidney or Milton. But it is difficult to agree with Miss Foxwell's praise of his achievement or to substantiate her claim that 'he touches at times the mystical vision which to Blake was the only domain of poetry and the only reality of life'.

The satires, written before the Psalms, have more intrinsic value. Though two are derived, directly or indirectly, from Horace (*Serm.*, II. 5, 6) and one from Alamanni, Wyatt contrives to anglicize them completely. They seem to be native poetry, owing more to Chaucer than to the nominal sources; and Wyatt, in satirizing Court life, draws on his own experience— even though the grapes were sour. As Nott remarked of one passage, the classical allusions lose nothing by being accommodated to the circumstances of Wyatt's own time. Wyatt, like Pope in his *Imitations from*

Horace and Johnson in *The Vanity of Human Wishes*, was not slavishly bound by his originals.

Critics have disagreed about Wyatt's use of *terza rima*, the first example in English. Saintsbury and Mr. Tillyard complain of the way in which the sense overflows the tercet, but Mr. Berdan argues that Wyatt was using the form in the manner of the *cinquecento* poets. Although we tend to lose consciousness of the tercet in reading the satires, Mr. Tillyard goes too far when he compares Wyatt's use of the form to blank verse. It is no more like blank verse than Thomson's blank verse in *Liberty*, in spite of the intrusion of accidental rhymes, resembles stanzaic verse. Wyatt realized, perhaps, that to preserve the form too rigidly would destroy the admirable conversational tone at which he was aiming. In spite of a certain stiffness in the lines, he displays an excellent poise. The tone is perfect, with just the right amount of indignation, and with the didacticism tempered with humour.

But Wyatt's reputation rests, or should rest, on his lyrics or ballets. There are more than 120 of them altogether, the worst of them crabbed and ineffective, a few in the halting verse of his immediate predecessors and contemporaries, and some fifty of them being the best lyrics written in English before the great Elizabethans. Critics have complained of the monotony of Wyatt's subject-matter, the unkindness of his mistress, and they tend to exaggerate his debt to foreign models. It is perfectly true that a large proportion of his lyrics are concerned with his lucklessness in love. The first poem in the Egerton MS. sets the tone for the whole collection—

> *Behold, love, thy power how she dispiseth!*
> *My great payne how litle she regardeth!*
> *The holy oth, wherof she taketh no cure*
> *Broken she hath; ...*

Wyatt accuses his real or imaginary mistress of cruelty, of deceit and doubleness, of disdain, of guile and newfangleness. It might well be thought from his poems that Wyatt was hopelessly in love at one time with a proud and disdainful beauty and at another time with a faithless wanton. But it should be remembered that he was writing within a certain convention, derived perhaps from the troubadours, of bondage in love.[1] To say that Wyatt usually keeps within the convention means no more than that he was composing love poems. The convention is exemplified in the prologue to *The Courte of Venus*, a contemporary collection of songs which included some of Wyatt's:

> And here foloweth, wherin you may rede
> To the court of Venus a greate nomber
> Their harts they say be as heauy as lead
> Their sorowful wo, I am sure you wil tender
> For if that I were mayden vncumber
> And had such myght as she hath mone,
> Out of their payne they should be letting gone.

It would be wrong, however, to pretend that Wyatt's complaints were unrelieved. The poem in three parts (No. 87) contains a refutation of those who slander love—

> Love is a plaisaunt fire
> Kyndeled by true desire;
> And though the payne
> Cause men to playne,
> Sped well is oft the hiere!

In another poem (No. 138) he mocks at the whole convention of the scorned lover and writes on the text of 'Gather ye rosebuds while ye may'—

> Therefore fere not t'assaye
> To gadre ye that maye
> The flower that this daye

[1] Cf. Chambers.

Is fresher than the next:
Marke well, I saye, this text.

Let not the frute be lost
That is desirid moste;
Delight shall quite the coste.
Yf hit be tane in tyme,
Small labour is to clyme.

In another poem in the Devonshire MS., he celebrates his escape from bondage in lines which, like so many of the poems, were probably sung—

Now ha, ha, ha, full well is me,
For I am nowe at libretye.

Some of the finest poems, on woman's fickleness, describe or imply a time when Wyatt was successful and happy in his love. The most beautiful of all, 'They fle from me' (No. 37), 'sheweth how he is forsaken of such as he somtime enioyed'; though Miss Foxwell seems to imply that the lady in 'thyn arraye' who kissed the poet

And softely saide, 'Dere hert, howe like you this?'

was merely indulging in the 'ordinary form of salutation among the upper classes of Wiat's day'.[1]

It should also be remembered that a number of Wyatt's poems do not deal with the subject of love at all. Several epigrams written in Spain (Nos. 80, 81, 97), two poems written in prison (Nos. 168, 172) and a group of poems written after Cromwell's execution (Nos. 170, 173, 176, 188, 195, 222) are sufficient examples.

The earlier critics tended to lay too much stress on

---

[1] Padelford speaks of it as a poem which 'one attributes to French influence because based upon a custom of chivalry and written in rhyme royal as well, it personifies Fortune under the figure of a lady kissing her knight, the service of whom she accepts, thus making him "Servant d'Amour" '. If it were not for the mention of rhyme royal, one would assume that Padelford was referring to 'Once as methought fortune me kissed' (No. 65).

Wyatt as translator; but both Mr. Tillyard and Sir Edmund Chambers have rightly emphasized the native element in the ballets. Although many of the stanza forms used by Wyatt had a scholastic origin, they had long been acclimatized and had been used in both secular and religious poetry for several generations. Wyatt used an astonishing variety of stanza forms, and if he invented half of them he would be 'one of the greatest verse-technicians in the history of the language'. But it seems probable from the court poems of the reign of Henry VIII which have come down to us that Wyatt used or adapted forms which were already in existence. The poems, which have been printed from Add. MS. 31922 and Royal MS. Appendix 58, include a version of one of Wyatt's poems, set to music by Cornish (No. 55). Many of the others in these manuscripts and in the Devonshire MS. by Wyatt's contemporaries and disciples, though inferior to his, exhibit many of his characteristics. There are two great differences, however: there are comparatively few complaints, and most of the poems are too thin and trivial to stand alone apart from the music. A snatch like the following—

> Adew, adew, my hartis lust,
>   Adew my Joy and my solace!
> With dowbyl sorow complayn I must,
>   Vntyl I dye, alas, alas!

or these verses by the King himself—

> Wherto shuld I expresse
> My inward heuynes?
> No myrth can make me fayn
> Tyl that we mete agayne.
>
> Do way, dere hart, not so;
> Let no thought yow dysmaye!
> Thow ye now parte me fro,
> We shall mete when we may.

When I remembyr me
Of your most gentyll mynde,
It may in no wise be
That I shuld be vnkynde.

The daise delectable,
The violet wan and blo,
Ye ar not varyable;
I loue you and no mo.

I make you fast and sure:
It ys to me gret payne,
Thus longe to endure
Tyll that we mete agayne.

or this song set also by Cornish—

Pleasure yt ys
To here, I wys,
The byrdes synge;
The dere in the dale,
The shepe in the vale,
The corne spryngyng,
Gods puruayaunce
For sustenaunce
Yt ys for man;
Then we alwayse
To hym giue prase,
And thank hym than.

require the accompaniment of the lute for their full
effect. Wyatt's songs, though written to be sung, need
no such assistance. On them he lavished all the resources of his art, blending the diverse influences of
minor Italian and French poetry with those of Chaucer
and of the Court. Critics like Mr. Berdan, who have
argued that Wyatt was often imitating where he was
not directly translating, have cast doubt on the sincerity of his lyrics. They imply that a man cannot express his own feelings in a borrowed convention and

that lyric poetry is a kind of confessional. In fact, as Mr. Eliot has pointed out, 'one of the qualities of a genuine poet is that in reading him we are reminded of remote predecessors' and 'one is prepared for art when one has ceased to be interested in one's own emotions and experiences except as material; and when one has reached this point of indifference one will pick and choose according to very different principles from the principles of those people who are still excited by their own feelings and passionately excited over their own passions'. To pretend that Wyatt was cold and impersonal or to maintain, as some critics have done, that his poems were mere exercises in versifying, would be as foolish as to suppose that all his poems were directly autobiographical. He had a profoundly passionate nature, but his poems are essentially dramatic. He used emotions he had experienced: but he made them serve the purposes of his art.[1]

It used to be thought that the extravagant conceits of the Metaphysicals were evidence of lack of feeling; but no one to-day would deny sincerity and passion to Donne, and Wyatt, as more than one critic has pointed out, has some affinities with Donne. His rugged versification, in his greater lyrics at least, conveys the force and subtlety of his emotion, while preserving the illusion of a man talking to men. His imagery is often well-worn and derivative and his fondness for conceits aroused the scorn of Warton.[2] But he breathed new life into the conventions he imported and his greatest poems possess an extraordinary intensity ('capable of making all disagreeables evaporate') which revivifies the imagery and makes the reader accept the imaginative truth of the conceits.

It has been observed that, unlike Petrarch, Wyatt

[1] 'What great poetry is not dramatic?' (T. S. Eliot).
[2] Warton also complained of the tasteless conceits of Milton's Nativity Ode.

does not describe the women with whom he is in love, except once to mention hair of 'crisped gold'—perhaps Elizabeth Darrell's. He is not concerned with the accidents of personal appearance but with the essential passion. Nor does he, as a rule, celebrate the joys of mutuality. He tells mainly of the pains of unsatisfied love, of the pride and fickleness of women, and of the period before the woman's capitulation. But it could not be said of him, as has been said of Donne, that he was an egocentric sensualist who ignored the feelings of the woman. One of his poems voices the plaint of a forsaken maid; and another, most exquisite, one expresses his sweetheart's grief (No. 38)—

> *There was never nothing more me payned,*
> *Nor nothing more me moved,*
> *As when my swete hart her complayned*
> *That ever she me loved.*
> *Alas the while!* [1]

Many of Wyatt's poems mention the accompanying lute (e.g. Nos. 51, 66, 84, 132) and many others were clearly written to be sung; but it is also apparent that Wyatt intended his poems for publication:

> *And patientely, O Redre, I the praye,*
> *Take in good parte this worke as yt ys mente,*
> *And greve the not with ought that I shall saye,*
> *Sins with good will this boke abrode is sente,*
> *To tell men howe in youthe I ded assaye*
> *What love ded mene and nowe I yt repente:*
> *That musing me my frendes might well be ware,*
> *And kepe them fre from all soche payne and care.*
>
> (No. 142)

The anonymous voices of the lyric poets of the preceding centuries are often beautiful, but they are sel-

---

[1] Unless I misunderstand her, Miss Foxwell believes that this poem is an example of Wyatt's humour.

dom individualized. Wyatt, for all his conventions, stands out as an individual voice, as a complex and passionate love poet, and as a great artist. In the age which followed he was surpassed as a love poet only by Spenser and Shakespeare.

SOURCES

Wyatt sometimes translates closely and sometimes takes only a hint from his original. The following list, compiled mainly from Miss Foxwell and Professor Rollins, is not exhaustive. Other poems are probably derived from minor French and Italian poets.

Alamanni: 196. Aretino: 200–13. Ariosto: 94. Boethius: 195. Filosceno: 79. Horace: 197–8. Marot: 15, 18–19. Pandulpho: 100. Petrarch: 1, 3–4, 7–9, 12, 20, 24–6, 28–32, 47, 56, 73, 81, 86, 96. Sannazaro: 33. Seneca: 176. Serafino: 14, 22, 39, 40, 44, 48, 60–1, 70, 76.

H. A. Mason in an article in *The Times Literary Supplement* (Feb. 27, March 6, 1953) shows that Wyatt in his version of the Penitential Psalms made use of a prose translation of Campensis, *A Paraphrasis vpon all the Psalmes of Dauid* (Antwerp, 1535). Sergio Baldi's *La Poesia di Sir Thomas Wyatt* (Florence, 1952) contains the best treatment of his sources.

CRITICAL COMMENTS

CRITICAL COMMENTS

HENRY HOWARD, EARL OF SURREY

1

On Wyatt's Translation of the Psalms

THE great Macedon, that out of Perse chasyd
Darius, of whose huge power all Asy rang,
In the riche arke if Homers rymes he placid
Who fayned gestes of hethen Prynces sang:
What holy graue, what wourthy sepulture
To Wyates psalmes shuld Christians then purchace?
Wher he dothe paynte the lyvely faythe and pure,
The stedfast hope, the swete returne to grace
Of just Davyd by parfyte penytence;
Where Rewlers may se in a myrrour clere
The bitter frewte of false concupicense;
How Jewry bought Vryas deathe full dere;
    In prynces hartes Goddes scourge yprynted depe
    Myght them awake out of ther synfull slepe.

2

On Wyatt's Death

Dyuers thy death doe diuersly bemone:
Some, that in presence of thy liuelyhed
Lurked, whose brestes enuy with hate had swolne,
Yeld Ceasars teares vpon Pompeius hed;
Some, that watched with the murdrers knife,
With egre thirst to drink thy giltlesse blood,
Whose practise brake by happy ende of lyfe,
Wepe enuious teares to heare thy fame so good.
But I, that knew what harbred in that hed,
What vertues rare were temperd in that brest,

Honour the place that such a iewell bred,
And kisse the ground, whereas thy corse doth rest,
   With vapord eyes: from whence such streames auayl
   As Pyramus dyd on Thisbes brest bewail.

3

Of the same

Wyatt resteth here, that quick could neuer rest,
   Whose heauenly giftes encreased by disdayn,
And vertue sank the deper in his brest—
   Such profit he by enuy could obtain.

A hed where wisdom misteries did frame,
   Whose hammers bet styll in that liuely brayn
As on a stithe, where that some work of fame
   Was dayly wrought, to turne to Britaines gayn.

A visage stern and myld, where bothe did grow
   Vice to contemne, in vertue to reioyce;
Amid great stormes, whom grace assured so
   To lyue vpright and smile at fortunes choyce.

A hand that taught what might be sayd in ryme,
   That reft Chaucer the glory of his wit;
A mark the which (vnparfited, for time)
   Some may approche but neuer none shall hit.

A toung that serued in forein realmes his king,
   Whose courteous talke to vertue did enflame
Eche noble hart; a worthy guide to bring
   Our English youth by trauail vnto fame.

An eye whose iudgement none affect could blinde,
   Frendes to allure and foes to reconcile;
Whose persing loke did represent a mynde
   With vertue fraught, reposed, voyd of gyle.

A hart, where drede was neuer so imprest
　　To hyde the thought that might the trouth auance;
In neyther fortune lost nor yet represt,
　　To swell in wealth or yeld vnto mischance.

A valiant corps where force and bewty met,
　　Happy, alas, to happy, but for foes,
Liued and ran the race that nature set;
　　Of manhodes shape, where she the molde did lose.

But to the heauens that simple soule is fled,
　　Which left with such as couet Christ to know
Witnesse of faith that neuer shall be ded,
　　Sent for our helth, but not receiued so.
Thus, for our gilte, this iewel haue we lost:
The earth his bones, the heauens possesse his gost.

4

RICHARD TOTTEL

That to haue wel written in verse, yea and in small
parcelles, deserueth great praise, the workes of diuers
Latines, Italians, and other, doe proue sufficiently.
That our tong is able in that kynde to do as praise-
worthely as ye rest, the honourable stile of the noble
earle of Surrey, and the weightinesse of the depe-
witted sir Thomas Wyat the elders verse, with seuerall
graces in sondry good Englishe writers, doe show
abundantly.　　　　　*Songes and Sonettes,* 1557

5

THOMAS SACKVILLE,
EARL OF DORSET

Not worthy Wiat worthiest of them all,
Whom Brittain hath in later yeres furthbrought,
His sacred psalmes wherin he singes the fall

Of David dolling for the guilt he wrought,
And Vries deth which he so dereli bought,
Not his hault vers that tainted hath the skie,
For mortall domes to heuenlie and to hie.

> Manuscript version of part of
> *A Mirror for Magistrates* (cir.
> 1560; published T. L. S. 1929.)

6

GEORGE PUTTENHAM

In the latter end of the same kings raigne sprong vp a new company of courtly makers, of whom Sir *Thomas Wyat* th'elder and *Henry* Earle of Surrey were the two chieftaines, who hauing trauailed into Italie, and there tasted the sweete and stately measures and stile of the Italian Poesie as nouices newly crept out of the schooles of *Dante, Ariosto* and Petrarch, they greatly pollished our rude and homely maner of vulgar Poesie, from that it had bene before, and for that cause may iustly be sayd the first reformers of our English meetre and stile. . . .

Henry Earle of Surrey and Sir *Thomas Wyat*, betweene whom I finde very litle difference, I repute them (as before) for the two chief lanternes of light to all others that haue since employed their pennes vpon English Poesie, their conceits were loftie, their stiles stately, their conueyance cleanely, their termes proper, their meetre sweete and well proportioned, in all imitating very naturally and studiously their Maister *Francis Petrarcha.*

The Arte of English Poesie, 1589

7

THOMAS WARTON

... Wyat, although sufficiently distinguished from the common versifiers of his age, is confessedly inferior to Surrey in harmony of numbers, perspicuity of expression, and facility of phraseology. Nor is he equal to Surrey in elegance of sentiment, in nature and sensibility. His feelings are disguised by affectation, and obscured by conceit. His declarations of passion are embarrassed by wit and fancy; and his style is not intelligible, in proportion as it is careless and unadorned. His compliments, like the modes of behaviour in that age, are ceremonious and strained. He has too much art as a lover, and too little as a poet. His gallantries are laboured, and his versification negligent. The truth is, his genius was of the moral and didactic species: and his poems abound more in good sense, satire, and observations on life, than in pathos or imagination. ...

It was from the capricious and over-strained invention of the Italian poets, that Wyat was taught to torture the passion of love by prolix and intricate comparisons, and unnatural allusions. ...

But Wyat appears a much more pleasing writer, when he moralises on the felicities of retirement, and attacks the vanities and vices of a court, with the honest indignation of an independent philosopher, and the freedom and pleasantry of Horace. ... Wyat may justly be deemed the first polished English satirist. I am of opinion, that he mistook his talents when, in compliance with the mode, he became a sonneteer; and, if we may judge from a few instances, that he was likely to have treated any other subject with more success than that of love. His abilities were seduced and misapplied in fabricating fine speeches to an obdurate mistress.

The History of English Poetry, 1778–81

8

G. F. NOTT

Wyatt, as a poet, can lay little claim to originality ... If we examine particularly the several species of composition which Wyatt attempted, we shall find him to have failed most in his Sonnets. In these he has shown great want of taste as well in the choice of his subjects, as in his manner of treating them. The Sonnets he has selected from Petrarch are for the most part the worst that Petrarch wrote. .... The same want of taste is observable in most of Wyatt's Rondeaus. ...

But Wyatt is more fortunate in his lesser odes, which often afford beautiful specimens as well of language, as of style, and turn of thought. They were composed probably on the impulse of the moment, and being written without effort are always natural, and frequently are tender and pathetic. His ode to his Lute is a piece of singular beauty; and has not been surpassed by any thing hitherto written in our language on a similar subject ...

But the style of thought and expression that is particularly characteristic of Wyatt's manner, is that of deep manly sorrow; which at the same time that it is descriptive of acute feeling, is free from querulousness. ... In these and many similar passages that might be adduced we observe a certain earnestness of expression, and a dignified simplicity of thought, which distinguishes Wyatt's amatory effusions from Surrey's, and I might add from those of every other writer in our language.

It will readily be granted that Wyatt's odes, as generally is the case with those who write much, are far from being all of equal beauty. In some, the thoughts are not expressed with sufficient care and precision; and in others, the thoughts themselves are not worth the labour bestowed upon them. Still the greater number possess considerable merit. Wyatt's feelings are those of no common mind; he knows how to complain, yet command respect; and excites pity without incurring humiliation. ...

The fate which has awaited Wyatt's Satires is somewhat remarkable, and deserves to be noticed. They are unquestionably his happiest and most finished productions. They may be ranked among the best satires in our language; and yet they never seem to have obtained either admirers or imitators; at least I do not recollect that any of our early writers have spoken of them in particular with commendation. This, I apprehend, may be easily accounted for. Wyatt had outstripped, as it were, his times. A taste for delicate satire cannot be general until refinement of manners is general likewise. ...

Wyatt had a deeper and a more accurate penetration into the characters of men than Surrey had: hence arises the difference in their Satires. ... In point of taste, and perception of propriety in composition, Surrey is more accurate and just than Wyatt ... Had Wyatt attempted a translation of Virgil as Surrey did, he would have exposed himself to unavoidable failure. ...

But though in all these points Wyatt confessedly ranks below Surrey, and though his works have not produced as general an effect upon our literature as Surrey's have done, still we owe him much. He was the first English writer who can be said to have aimed at any thing like legitimate style in prose ... he taught succeeding writers to give refinement of thought to amatory strains, and ... he led the way to genuine satire. *Essay on Wyatt's Poems* in *Works*, 1816

9

ROBERT BELL

The comparison between them on general grounds
must unhesitatingly be admitted to be largely in favour
of Surrey. He was more impassioned, and had a finer
sensibility and a more exact taste. But Wyatt possesses
high merits of another kind. His verse is more thought-
ful than Surrey's; more compressed and weighty. He
had not so graceful a way of making love; but his love,
nevertheless, has an air of gallantry and self-possession
that captivates the imagination by different ap-
proaches. His diction is less poetical than that of
Surrey; but a careful examination of his poems must
reverse the judgment which has pronounced it to be
more antiquated. He uses, comparatively, few expres-
sions that are not intelligible to the modern reader. His
vocabulary is extensive, and imparts constant novelty
to his descriptions. His versification, incidentally harsh
and refractory, is, generally, regular and sonorous. In
order, however, to obtain the full music of his lines, it
is necessary to remember that he drew largely on
French and Italian models, and that apparently de-
ficient syllables must be occasionally supplied by
adopting foreign accents. . . .

He is said to be overcharged with conceits; but, tak-
ing into consideration the sources from which he borrowed, and the age in which he wrote, it would be more
just to say that he is singularly free from conceits. . . .
His poems are never stained by indelicacies; and if his
poetical taste is not always faultless, his moral taste is
irreproachable.

Poetical Works of Sir Thomas Wyatt, 1854

10

W. J. COURTHOPE

Two very marked and contrary features distinguish Wyatt's poetry, the individual energy of his thought, and his persistent imitation of foreign models. Wyatt ... looked at Nature through his own eyes, and sought to express directly the feelings of his own heart ... The poet shows himself to be aware of the imperfection of his native language as an instrument of expression, and submits himself with humility to the superiority of the foreign masters whose manner he seeks to reproduce. In consequence of this his actual poetical achievements are of very unequal merit; he often aims at objects which he ought to have avoided, or at effects to which his resources are unequal; he is most successful when his fiery genius can find out a way for itself untrammelled by the precedents of art.

A History of English Poetry, vol. 2, 1897

11

F. M. PADELFORD

And now, it remains to show that Wyatt is not a mere imitator, an affected apprentice to foreign masters; that, though much of his work is done with a conscious model in mind, he is at times the peer of any courtly lyrist of the sixteenth century, the peer of Sidney and Shakespeare. In his best amatory verse, as well as in his noble satires, he breaks through the hypothetical world of fancy, with its artificial emotions and studied address, and with fine imagination realizes his experiences, and presents them in simple, fervent, and sincere language. At such times of penetrative insight, the nervous intensity of feeling calls up rare, subtle

harmonies of sound and rich qualities of tone, so that
the music of the verse seems inwrought with the emotion. These poems are like monologues snatched from
intense situations, like chance sparks from an anvil all
aglow. There is no stopping for introduction or set-
ting, and it is as if we were to enter the theatre at a
moment when a situation is critical, and passionate
utterance is at its height. The molten words, as if too
long repressed, overflow from highly-wrought emotion. The language is direct, familiar, and unadorned;
a case left to stand or fall by the bare truth of it. Nothing could be less accurate than the statement so often
met, that Wyatt was hardly more than an imitator of
the Italians. He has left a score or more of poems that,
in real imagination, imagination in the sense in which
Ruskin has defined it, surpasses anything that Petrarch
or his Italian imitators ever wrote. After Wyatt we
wait fifty years and more before another poet writes
amatory verse with equal imagination. Most of the
Elizabethan sonneteers surpass him in elegance, in
prettiness, in fancy, but not until Shakespeare is there
another who writes so passionately.

Early Sixteenth Century Lyrics, 1907

12

J. M. BERDAN

Anglica lingua fuit rudis & sine nomine rhythmus
Nunc limam agnoscit docte Viate tuam.

Nobilitas didicit te præceptore Britanna
Carmina per varios scribere posse modos.

(Leland, 1542)

That expresses precisely Wyatt's function. In an age,
when art in its narrow sense had been lost, in his work
the English language did find again the art of omis-

sion, did recognize his file, and did learn to write songs in various clearly differentiated forms.

For such a purpose as this, obviously, the content of the individual poems is a secondary matter. Whether or not they are autobiographical, whether or not he did love Anne Boleyn, whether or not they are translations, whether or not they express his real convictions,—none of these is particularly important. The important thing is that in his work the early Tudor found examples of a large variety of verse forms, coldly but carefully worked out. It must be granted that a poet whose primary interest is in form, rather than in content, is not great. Poetic technique, clever phrase, witty conceit go a little way, but only a little way. On the other hand, the great emotions that have aroused poets from the beginning are not present in Wyatt's work. The nature in his poems is of the lion-and-tiger sort drawn from books; beauty apparently makes little appeal; and his love serves merely as the occasion to make far-fetched comparisons. This lack of emotion is apparently one of the reasons why critics call him 'virile!' His better poems are observations of the life around him. In them he has mastered the medium, he carries the structure easily, and at the same time is definite and concrete. . . . But the most successful are those written to be sung. Such poems as *My Lute awake! Fforget not yet the tryde entent*, or *Blame not my lute*, have maintained their place in all anthologies. They deserve all the praise that has been lavished upon them. The union of strength and grace makes a rare and felicitous combination. But in spite of these, and the six or eight more like them, the proposition remains true that for his age Wyatt's value lay, not in the few pieces where the fire of his passion has amalgamated the content and the form into one perfect whole, but in the many others which may not unjustly be called experiments in stanza-forms. . . . With the exception of the heroic couplet and of blank verse, —two very important exceptions,—most of the stanzas to be used during the century are there. Of course with our ignorance of what the other writers were doing, it is uncritical to assume that all these novelties were first imported by Wyatt,—an assumption that would make him one of the greatest verse-technicians in the history of the language,—but they prove that the minds of the men in the circle to which Wyatt belonged were seriously occupied in studying the forms of verse.

That Wyatt was a leader in this circle seems probable. ...   *Early Tudor Poetry*, 1920

13

HYDER EDWARD ROLLINS

In many cases the poems are translated so closely as to suggest mere literary, or language, exercises; for the most partial enthusiast must admit that Wyatt's genius was chiefly derivative. Few of his poems show traces of humanistic influence: of those that do, two epigrams translated from Ausonius and Pandulpho, two moral songs from Seneca and Boethius, two satires suggested (though perhaps indirectly through the Italian) by Horace, and a tiresome 'Song of Iopas' indebted to Virgil make up the known total. Because Wyatt had a fondness for elaborate conceits, for grotesque imagery, his reputation has suffered greatly.

Many hard sayings, too, have been directed at his inability to write smoothly flowing lines and at his 'carelessness' about accents; but some of this criticism has been based on Tottel's text rather than on Wyatt's, and hence should be ignored. The uncertain accents, the strange pronunciations, the rough movement of his lines, are due to the practice of his time. He is no worse, he is indeed better, than his immediate contemporaries; but in any case he was the pioneer who fumbled in the linguistic difficulties that beset him and prepared the way for Surrey's smoother lines and more pleasing accentuation. As no one at the present day is in danger of underestimating Wyatt's significance in the history of English verse, so no one should be tempted to put too high a value on his intrinsic merit.

Tottel's Miscellany, 1929

14

E. M. W. TILLYARD

In neither the rondeau, the sonnet, nor the eight-lined epigram was Wyatt really at home. ... Only once in the rondeaus does Wyatt leave off writing English verses and create poetry, namely in the last lines of 'What no, perdie!' ... Like the rondeaus, the sonnets are experimental, but they extend over a longer period of time and ultimately approach nearer perfection. Wyatt did, in fact, write one or two tolerable sonnets. Technically, he almost invented the Shakespearean form. ... A sonnet to please must be either exquisite or grand. Wyatt could at times be exquisite in the lyric measures of which he was a master, but the effort of writing sonnets was always too great to allow exquisiteness. Of grandeur he was never a master: he can be powerful or poignant, but not grand. The sonnet was not his proper medium. ...

The courtly epigrams are not in general as rough in rhythm as the early sonnets, but they lack the necessary elegance. Wyatt makes a poor show when he competes with Austin Dobson. ...

Wyatt's Satires have been overpraised as literature because of their subject-matter. If we are interested in Wyatt we cannot but enjoy the account he gives of his own life at home while he was banished from court; but we need not therefore be persuaded that poetically the account can compare with his best songs. The truth is that all three Satires are experimental, written in a metre of which he was not master and through which one feels he was struggling towards something—he does not quite know what. ... Finally, it would be unfair to leave the Satires without mentioning the air of unaffected self-expression that for all their faults lends them a certain charm. ...

But piety does not necessarily cause poetry, and judged as poetry Wyatt's *Psalms* are academic exercises, penitential not merely in matter, but to those whose task it is to read them.

The Poetry of Sir Thomas Wyatt.
A Selection and a Study, 1929

15

ANONYMOUS

The reader of Mr. Tillyard's admirably chosen examples of Wyatt will almost wholly miss tasting for himself ... one feature of Wyatt which attracts some minds as strongly as it repels others ... The feature referred to is the mystery of Wyatt; and the mystery of Wyatt is simply whether he knew what he was doing or whether he did not ... At one moment he is the equal of the greatest in his command of rhythm and metre; at another he seems to be laboriously counting syllables on his fingers—and getting them wrong sometimes—and at a third he is, like some of his predecessors, floundering about for a foothold on stresses that may happen anywhere in the bog. It is more than an academic question. The doubt interferes with the reader's enjoyment of the poetry.

The Times Literary Supplement,
19 September 1929

16

E. K. CHAMBERS

About a hundred and twenty of the poems, gathered from all sources, may be classed as lyrical 'balettes'. We need not assume that they were all in fact set to music, for which some of them are rather long. But constant references to singing and the lute sufficiently indicate the origin of the *genre*. The range of metrical variation is very wide; more than seventy distinct stanza-forms are to be found in the hundred and twenty examples. The basis is nearly always iambic. Pentameters, tetrameters, trimeters, dimeters are all used, separately and in combination, in mono-rhyme and in cross-rhyme, with and without refrains. The types are those known in the neo-Latin poetry of the *vagantes* and analysed in mediæval treatises on poetics. Many of them also appear in earlier vernacular poetry. Here Wyatt is at the end rather than the beginning of a tradition. He handles it as a master, with a facility of rhythmical accomplishment to which his Elizabethan successors, although they had many qualities which he had not, rarely attained. ...

There is but little fundamental resemblance between Wyatt and Petrarch. He does not dwell upon the physical beauty of his lady; you learn little more than that her hair is of 'crispid gold'. He does not couple her in proud compare of everything that is in heaven and earth; there is but one perfunctory allusion to lilies and roses. Nor of course does he, like Petrarch, veil her in that circumambient penumbra of spirituality. He makes little use of visual imagery. His range of metaphor is restricted and rather conventional. For the most part he is content with the plainest of words, and relies for his effect upon his rhythmical accomplishment. This economy of speech gives him at times a

xlvii

singular plangency. In appeal or reproach every line tells like a hammer-stroke. . . .

Nor does Wyatt at all foreshadow the Elizabethans, with their lavishness, their passion for visible things, their ready flow of coloured utterance. One phrase rings curiously with Sidney—

> A hart I have besidis all this,
> That hath my herte and I have his.

But Wyatt's real affinities, if with any, are with John Donne. He has not Donne's depth of fiery and often turbid thought. His is a soul of lighter make. But there is something of the same characteristic poise. Wyatt, too, can be a psychologist, watching his own emotions in detachment, with a finger on the burning pulse.

Sir Thomas Wyatt and Some Collected Studies (1933) pp. 119–20, 129–30

POEMS

from the Egerton MS. 2711

1

BEHOLD, love, thy power how she dispiseth!
My great payne how litle she regardeth!
   The holy oth, wherof she taketh no cure,
   Broken she hath; and yet she bideth sure
Right at her ease and litle she dredeth.   5
Wepened thou art, and she vnarmed sitteth;
To the disdaynfull her liff she ledeth,
   To me spitefull withoute cause or mesure,
      Behold, love.

I ame in hold: if pitie the meveth,   10
Goo bend thy bowe, that stony hertes breketh,
   And with some stroke revenge the displeasure
   Of the and him, that sorrowe doeth endure,
And, as his lorde, the lowly entreateth.
      Behold, love.   15

7, 14 *the] thee*

2

WHAT vaileth trouth? or, by it, to take payn?
To stryve by stedfastnes for to attayne?
   To be iuste and true, and fle from dowblenes?
   Sythens all alike, where rueleth craftines,
Rewarded is boeth fals, and plain.   5
Sonest he spedeth, that moost can fain;
True meanyng hert is had in disdayn.
   Against deceipte and dowblenes,
      What vaileth trouth?

3

Deceved is he by crafty trayn 10
That meaneth no gile: and doeth remayn
  Within the trappe, withoute redresse
  But for to love, lo, suche a maistres,
Whose crueltie nothing can refrayn.
          What vaileth trouth? 15

3

CAESAR, when that the traytor of Egipt
  With th'onourable hed did him present,
  Covering his gladnes, did represent
  Playnt with his teres owteward, as it is writt:
And Hannyball eke, when fortune him shitt 5
  Clene from his reign and from all his intent,
  Laught to his folke, whome sorrowe did torment,
  His cruell dispite for to disgorge and qwit.
So chaunceth it oft that every passion
  The mynde hideth, by colour contrary, 10
  With fayned visage, now sad, now mery.
Whereby if I laught, any tyme or season
  It is for bicause I have nother way
  To cloke my care, but vnder sport and play.

13 *nother*] *no other*

4

THE longe love, that in my thought doeth harbar
  And in myn hert doeth kepe his residence,
  Into my face preseth with bolde pretence,
  And therin campeth, spreding his baner.
She that me lerneth to love and suffre, 5
  And willes that my trust and lustes negligence
  Be rayned by reason, shame and reverence,
  With his hardines taketh displeasur.
          4

Wherewithall, vnto the hertes forrest he fleith,
  Leving his entreprise with payn and cry;   10
  And ther him hideth, and not appereth.
What may I do when my maister fereth
  But in the feld with him to lyve and dye?
  For goode is the liff, ending faithfully.

13 *feld*] *field*

5

ALAS the greiff and dedly wofull smert!
The carefull chaunce shapen afore my shert;
  The sorrowfull teares, the sighes hote as fyer,
That cruell love hath long soked from myn hert;
  And, for reward of ouer great desire,   5
  Disdaynfull dowblenes have I for my hiere.

O lost seruis! O payn ill rewarded!
O pitifull hert, with payn enlarged!
  O faithfull mynde, too sodenly assented!
Retourn, Alas, sithens thou art not regarded;   10
  Too great a prouf of true faith presented
  Causeth by right suche faith to be repented.

O cruell causer of vndeserued chaunge,
By great desire vnconstantly to raunge,
  Is this your waye for prouf of stedfastenes?   15
Perdy you knowe—the thing was not so straunge
  By former prouff—to muche my faithfulnes.
  What nedeth then suche coloured dowblenes?

I have wailed thus, weping in nyghtly payn;
In sobbes and sighes, Alas! and all in vayn;   20
  In inward plaint and hertes wofull torment:
And yet, Alas, lo, crueltie and disdayn
  Have set at noght a faithful true intent,
  And price hath priuilege trouth to prevent.

5

But though I sterve and to my deth still morne,
And pece mele in peces though I be torne,
    And though I dye yelding my weried gooste,
Shall never thing again make me retorne.
    I qwite th'entreprise of that that I have lost,
    To whome so ever lust for to proffer moost.   30

2 *shert*] *shirt*.[1]

6

(*Fragment*)[2]

BUT sethens you it asaye to kyll,
    Try crueltie and dowblenes.
That that was yowers you seke to spill,
    Against all ryght and gentilnes;
And sethens yow will, even so I will.   5

And then, helas, when no redresse
    Can be too late, ye shall repent;
And save yourself with wordes expresse:
    Helas! an hert of true intent
Slaine have I, by vnfaithfulnes.   10

I plede and reason my selffe emonge;
    Agaynst reason howe I suffer;
But she that doethe me all the wronge
    I plede and reason my selffe emonge.

[1] Cf. Chaucer, *The Knight's Tale*: 'That shapen was my deeth erst than my sherte.'
[2] These lines are covered with religious musings of a later date. A leaf has been lost containing the earlier part of this poem. The last four lines, in a different stanza form and apparently in a different handwriting, may not belong to the poem.

7

WHO so list to hount, I knowe where is an hynde,
    But as for me, helas, I may no more:
    The vayne travaill hath weried me so sore.
    I ame of theim that farthest commeth behinde;
Yet may I by no meanes my weried mynde   5
    Drawe from the Diere: but as she fleeth afore,
Faynting I folowe. I leve of therefore,
    Sins in a nett I seke to hold the wynde.
Who list her hount, I put him owte of dowbte,
    As well as I may spend his tyme in vain: 10
    And, graven with Diamonds, in letters plain
There is written her faier neck rounde abowte:
    Noli me tangere, for Cesars I ame;
    And wylde for to hold, though I seme tame.

8

MYNE olde dere En'mye, my froward master,
    Afore that Quene, I caused to be acited;
Whiche holdeth the divine parte of nature:
    That, lyke as goolde, in fyre he mought be tryed.
    Charged with dolour, theare I me presented   5
With horrible feare, as one that greatlye dredith
A wrongfull death, and iustice alwaye seekethe.

And thus I sayde: 'Once my lefte foote, Madame,
    When I was yonge I sett within his reigne;
Whearby other then fierlye burninge flame   10
    I never felt, but many a grevous payne;
    Tourment I suffred, angre, and disdayne,
That myne oppressed patience was past,
And I myne owne life hated at the last.

Thus hytherto have I my time passed   15
   In payne and smarte. What wayes proffitable,
How many pleasant dayes have me escaped
   In serving this false lyer so deceaveable?
   What witt have wordes so prest and forceable
That may contayne my great myshappynesse,   20
And iust complayntes of his vngentlenesse?

O! small honye, muche aloes, and gall!
   In bitternes have my blynde lyfe taisted
His fals swetenes, that torneth as a ball,   24
   With the amourous dawnce have made me traced;
   And where I had my thought and mynde ataced
From all erthely frailnes and vain pleasure,
He toke me from rest and set me in error.

He hath made me regarde god muche lesse then I
      ought,   30
   And to my self to take right litle heede;
And, for a woman, have I set at nought
   All othre thoughtes, in this onely to spede:
   And he was onely counceillor of this dede,
Always whetting my youthely desyere
On the cruell whetstone tempered with fier.   35

But, helas, where nowe had I ever wit,
   Or els any othre gift geven me of nature?
That souner shall chaunge my weryed sprite
   Then the obstinate will, that is my rueler.
   So robbeth my libertie with displeasure   40
This wicked traytor, whome I thus accuse,
That bitter liff have torned me in pleasaunt vse.

He hath chased me thorough dyvers regions,
   Thorough desert wodes and sherp high moun-
      taignes,   44
Thoroughe frowarde people and straite pressions,

Thorough rocky sees, over hilles and playnes,
  With wery travaill, and labourous paynes;
Always in trouble and in tediousnes,
In all errour and daungerous distres.

But nother he, nor she, my tother ffoo,   50
  For all my flyght did ever me forsake;
That though tymely deth hath ben to sloo,
  That, as yet, it hathe me not overtake;
  The hevynly goodenes, of pitie, do it slake:
And note this his cruell extreme tyranny,   55
That fedeth hym with my care and mysery.

Syns I was his, owre rested I never,
  Nor loke for to do ; and eke the waky nyghtes
The bannysshed slepe may no wyse recouer.
  By deceipte and by force over my sprites   60
  He is rueler: and syns there neuer bell strikes
Where I ame, that I here not my playntes to renewe,
And he himself, he knoweth that I say is true.

Ffor never wormes have an old stock eaten,
  As he my hert, where he is alwaye resident;   65
And doeth the same with deth daily thretyn:
  Thens com the teres and the bitter torment,
  The sighes, the wordes, and eke the languisshe-
    ment,
That annoye boeth me and peraduenture othre:
Iudge thou that knowest th'one and th'othre.'   70

Myn aduersary, with grevous reprouff,
  Thus he began: 'Here, Lady, th'othre part:
That the plain trueth, from which he draweth alowff,
  This vnkynd man shall shew ere that I part.
  In yonge age I toke him from that art   75
That selleth wordes, and maketh a clattering knyght,
And of my welth I gave him the delight.

Nowe shameth he not on me for to complain,
   That held him evermore in pleasaunt game   79
From his desire, that myght have ben his payne;
   Yet onely thereby I broght him to some frame,
   Which as wretchednes he doth greately blame;
And towerd honor I qwickened his wit,
Where els, as a daskard, he myght have sitt.

He knoweth that Atrides, that made Troye frete,
   And Hannyball to Rome so trobelous,   86
Whome Homere honoured, Achilles that grete,
   And the Affricane Scipion, the famous,
   And many othre by much vertue glorious,
Whose fame and honor did bryng theim above,   90
I did let fall, in base dishonest love.

And vnto him, though he no dele worthy were,
   I chose right the best of many a mylion,
That, vnder the mone, was never her pere
   Of wisdome, womanhode and discretion;   95
   And of my grace I gave her suche a facon
And eke suche a way, I taught her for to teche
That never base thought his hert myght have reche.

Evermore, thus, to content his maistres,
   That was his onely frame of honestie.   100
I sterred him still towerd gentilnes,
   And caused him to regard fidelitie;
   Patiens I taught him in aduersite:
Suche vertues he lerned in my great schole,
Wherof he repenteth, the ignoraunt ffole.   105

These were the deceptes and the bitter gall
   That I have vsed, the torment and the anger;
Sweter then for to injoye eny othre in all.
   Of right good seede ill fruyte I gather
   And so hath he that th'unkynde doeth forther.
I norisshe a Serpent vnder my wyng,   111
And, of his nature, nowe gynneth he to styng.

And for to tell, at last, my great seruise:
 From thousand dishonestes I have him drawen,
That, by my meanes, in no maner of wyse, 115
 Never vile pleasure him hath overthrowen;
 Where, in his dede, shame hath him alwaies
  gnawen,
Dowbting reporte that sholde com to her eare:
Whome now he accuseth he wounted to fere.

What soever he hath of any honest custume 120
 Of her and me, that holdeth he every wit;
But lo, there was never nyghtely fantome
 So ferre in errour as he is from his wit
 To plain on vs: he stryveth with the bit,
Which may ruell him and do him pleasure and pain,
And in oon oure make all his greife remayn. 126

But oon thing there is above all othre:
 I gave him winges, wherwith he might vpflie
To honor and fame; and, if he would, farther
 Then mortall thinges, above the starry sky; 130
 Considering the pleasure that an Iye
Myght geve in erthe by reason of his love,
What shuld that be that lasteth still above?

And he the same himself hath sayed or this,
 But now forgotten is boeth that and I 135
That gave her him, his onely welth and blisse.'
 And at this worde, with dedly shright and cry:
 'Thou gave her me,' quod I, 'but by and by
Thou toke her streight from me, that wo worth
  thee!'
'Not I,' quod he, 'but price, that is well worthy.'

At last, boeth, eche for himself, concluded; 141
 I, trembling; but he, with small reverence:
'Lo, thus as we have nowe eche othre accused,

11

Dere lady, we wayte onely thy sentence.'
 She smyling: 'After thissaid audience,   145
It liketh me,' quod she, 'to have herd your question,
But lenger tyme doth aske resolution.'

121 *wit*] *whit* 134 *or*] *ere*

9

WAS I never yet of your love greved,
 Nor never shall while that my liff doeth last;
 But of hating myself that date is past,
 And teeres continuell sore have me weried.
I will not yet in my grave be buried;   5
 Nor on my tombe your name yfixed fast,
 As cruell cause that did the sperit son hast
 Ffrom th'unhappy bonys, by great sighes sterred.
Then, if an hert of amourous faith and will
 May content you, withoute doyng greiff,   10
 Please it you so to this to doo releiff:
Yf othre wise ye seke for to fulfill
 Your disdain, ye erre, and shall not as ye wene;
 And ye yourself the cause therof hath bene.

10

ECHE man me telleth I chaunge moost my devise,
 And on my faith me thinck it goode reason
 To chaunge propose like after the season,
 Ffor in every cas to kepe still oon gyse
Ys mytt for theim that would be taken wyse;   5
 And I ame not of suche maner condition,
 But treted after a dyvers fasshion;
 And therupon my dyversnes doeth rise.

12

But you that blame this dyversnes moost,   9
  Chaunge you no more, but still after oon rate
  Trete ye me well, and kepe ye in the same state;
And while with me doeth dwell this weried goost,
  My wordes nor I shall not be variable,
  But alwaies oon, your owne boeth ferme and
    stable.

5 *mytt*] *meet*

11

FFAREWELL, the rayn of crueltie!
Though that with pain my libertie
Dere have I boght, yet shall suretie
Conduyt my thoght of joyes nede.

Of force I must forsake pleasure: 5
A goode cause iust syns I endure
Thereby my woo, which be ye sure
Shall therwith goo me to recure.

I fare as oon escaped that fleith:
Glad that is gone yet still fereth,[1]   10
Spied to be cawght, and so dredeth
That he for nought his pain leseth.

In ioyfull pain reioyse myn hert,
Thus to sustain of eche a part;
Let not this song from the estert;   15
Welcome emong my plaisaunt smert.

12

YF amours faith, an hert vnfayned,
  A swete languor, a great lovely desire,
  Yf honest will kyndelled in gentill fiere,
Yf long error in a blynde maze chayned,

[1] This line makes doubtful sense. Nott proposed 'Glad that he is gone'. Perhaps it should read: 'Glad he is gone'.

13

Yf in my visage eche thought depaynted   5
  Or els in my sperklyng voyse lower or higher
  Which nowe fere, nowe shame, wofully doth tyer,
  Yf a pale colour which love hath stayned,
Yf to have an othre then my self more dere,
  Yf wailing and sighting continuelly   10
  With sorrowfull anger feding bissely,
Yf burning a farr of and fresing nere
  Ar cause that by love my self I destroye,
  Yours is the fault and myn the great annoye.

10 *sighting*] *sighing*

13

FFAREWELL Love and all thy lawes for ever:
  Thy bayted hookes shall tangill me no more;
  Senec and Plato call me from thy lore,
  To perfaict welth my wit for to endever.
In blynde error when I did perseuer,   5
  Thy sherpe repulse that pricketh ay so sore
  Hath taught me to sett in tryfels no store
  And scape fourth, syns libertie is lever.
Therefore farewell: goo trouble yonger hertes
  And in me clayme no more authoritie;   10
  With idill youth goo vse thy propertie
And theron spend thy many brittil dertes;
  For hetherto though I have lost all my tyme
  Me lusteth no lenger rotten boughes to clymbe.

14

MY hert I gave the, not to do it payn,
  But to preserue it was to the taken;
  I serued the not to be forsaken,
  But that I should be rewarded again.

14

I was content thy seruant to remayn,   5
   But not to be payed vnder this fasshion.
   Nowe syns in the is none othre reason
   Displease the not if that I do refrain.
Vnsaciat of my woo and thy desire,
   Assured be craft to excuse thy fault;   10
   But syns it please the to fain a default,
Farewell, I say, parting from the fyer:
   For he that beleveth bering in hand
   Plowithe in water and soweth in the sand.

15

FFOR to love her for her lokes lovely
My hert was set in thought right fermely,
   Trusting by trouth to have had redresse;
   But she hath made an othre promes
And hath geven me leve full honestly.   5
Yet do I not reioyse it greatly,
For on my faith I loved to surely;
   But reason will that I do sesse
      For to love her.

Syns that in love the paynes ben dedly,   10
Me thincke it best that reddely
   I do retorne to my first adresse;
   For at this tyme to great is the prese,
And perilles appere to abundauntely
      For to love her.   15

8 *sesse*] *cease* 13 *prese*] *press*

16

THERE was never ffile half so well filed,
   To file a file for every smythes intent,
   As I was made a filing instrument
   To frame othres, while I was begiled.
      15

But reason hath at my follie smyled,   5
  And pardond me syns that I me repent
  Of my lost yeres and tyme myspent;
  For yeuth did me lede and falshode guyded.
Yet this trust I have of full great aperaunce:
  Syns that decept is ay retourneable,   10
  Of very force it is aggreable;
That therewithall be done the recompence.
  Then gile begiled plained should be never,
  And the reward litle trust for ever.

17

HELPE me to seke for I lost it there,
And if that ye have founde it ye that be here
  And seke to convaye it secretely,
  Handell it soft and trete it tenderly,
Or els it will plain and then appere.   5
  But rather restore it mannerly,
  Syns that I do aske it thus honestly;
For to lese it, it sitteth me to nere:
    Helpe me to seke.

Alas, and is there no remedy,   10
But have I thus lost it wilfully?
  I wis it was a thing all to dere
  To be bestowed and wist not where.
It was myn hert: I pray you hertely
    Helpe me to seke.   15

18

YF it be so that I forsake the,
As banysshed from thy company,
  Yet my hert, my mynde and myn affection
  Shall still remain in thy perfection;

16

And right as thou lyst so order me.   5
  But some would saye in their opinion
  Revoultid is thy good intention;
Then may I well blame thy cruelte,
    Yf it be so.

But my self I say on this fasshion: 10
I have her hert in my posession,
  And of it self there cannot, perdy,
  By no meanes love an herteles body;
And on my faith, good is the reason,
    If it be so.   15

19

Thou hast no faith of him that hath none,
But thou must love him nedes by reason,
  For as saieth a proverbe notable,
  Eche thing seketh his semblable,
And thou hast thyn of thy condition.   5
Yet is it not the thing I passe on;
Nor hote nor cold is myn affection,
  For syns thyn hert is so mutable,
  Thou hast no faith.

I thought the true withoute exception,   10
But I perceve I lacked discretion
  To fasshion faith to wordes mutable;
  Thy thought is to light and variable,
To chaunge so oft withoute occasion,
  Thou hast no faith.   15

20

Goo burnyng sighes vnto the frosen hert!
Goo breke the Ise whiche pites paynfull dert
  Myght never perse, and if mortall prayer
  In hevyn may be herd, at lest I desire

That deth or mercy be ende of my smert.   5
Take with the payn wherof I have my part,
And eke the flame from which I cannot stert,
   And leve me then in rest, I you require.
      Goo, burning sighes!

I must goo worke, I se, by craft and art,   10
For trueth and faith in her is laide apart.
   Alas, I cannot therefor assaill her
   With pitefull plaint and scalding fyer
That oute of my brest doeth straynably stert.
      Goo, burning sighes!   15

21

I⊤ may be good, like it who list,
   But I do dowbt: who can me blame?
For oft assured yet have I myst,
   And now again I fere the same.
    The wyndy wordes, the Ies quaynt game,   5
Of soden chaunge maketh me agast:
For dred to fall I stond not fast.

Alas! I tred an endles maze
   That seketh to accorde two contraries;
And hope still and nothing hase,   10
   Imprisoned in libertes;
    As oon vnhard, and still that cries;
Alwaies thursty, and yet nothing I tast;
For dred to fall I stond not fast.

Assured, I dowbt I be not sure;   15
   And should I trust to suche suretie
That oft hath put the prouff in vre
   And never hath founde it trusty?
    Nay, sir, in faith it were great foly.
And yet my liff thus I do wast;   20
For dred to fall I stond not fast.
18

22

RESOUND my voyse, ye wodes that here me plain,
  Boeth hilles and vales causing reflexion;
And Ryvers eke record ye of my pain,
  Which have ye oft forced by compassion
  As judges to here myn exclamation;   5
Emong whome pitie I fynde doeth remayn:
Where I it seke, Alas, there is disdain.

Oft ye Revers, to here my wofull sounde,
  Have stopt your course and, plainly to expresse,
Many a tere by moystor of the grounde   10
  The erth hath wept to here my hevenes;
  Which causeles to suffre without redresse
The howgy okes have rored in the wynde:
Eche thing me thought complayning in their kynde.

Why then, helas, doeth not she on me rew?   15
  Or is her hert so herd that no pitie
May in it synke, my joye for to renew?
  O stony hert ho hath thus joyned the?
  So cruell that art, cloked with beaultie,
No grace to me from the there may procede,   20
But as rewarded deth for to be my mede.

18 *ho*] *who*

23

IN faith I wot not well what to say,
  Thy chaunces ben so wonderous;
Thou fortune with thy dyvers play
  That causeth joy full dolourous,
  And eke the same right joyus   5
Yet though thy chayne hathe me enwrapt,
Spite of thy hap hap hath well hapt.

19

Though thou me set for a wounder,
    And sekest thy chaunge to do me payn,
Mens mynds yet may thou not order,   10
    And honeste, and it remayn,
        Shall shyne for all thy clowdy rayn;
In vayn thou sekest to have me trapped:
Spite of thy hap hap hath well happed.

In hindering thou diddest fourther,   15
    And made a gap where was a stile;
Cruell willes ben oft put vnder,
    Wenyng to lowre, thou diddist smyle.
        Lorde! how thy self thou diddist begile,
That in thy cares wouldest me have lapped!
But spite of thy hap hap hath well happed.

24

Som fowles there be that have so perfaict sight,
    Agayn the Sonne their Iyes for to defend,
    And som bicause the light doeth theim offend,
    Do never pere but in the darke or nyght.
Other reioyse that se the fyer bright   5
    And wene to play in it as they do pretend,
    And fynde the contrary of it that they intend.
    Alas, of that sort I may be by right,
For to withstond her loke I ame not able;
    And yet can I not hide me in no darke place,   10
    Remembraunce so foloweth me of that face,
So that with tery yen swolne and vnstable,
    My destyne to behold her doeth me lede;
    Yet do I knowe I runne into the glede.

2 *Agayn*] *against* 12 *yen*] *eyes*

20

25

BICAUSE I have the still kept fro lyes and blame
   And to my power alwaies have I the honoured,
   Vnkynd tong right ill hast thou me rendred
   For suche deserft to do me wrek and shame.
In nede of succor moost when that I ame   5
   To aske reward, then standest thou like oon aferd
   Alway moost cold, and if thou speke towerd,
   It is as in dreme vnperfaict and lame.
And ye salt teres again my will eche nyght
   That are with me when fayn I would be alone,
   Then are ye gone when I should make my mone;
And you so reddy sighes to make me shright,   12
   Then are ye slake when that ye should owtestert;
   And onely my loke declareth my hert.

26

I FYNDE no peace and all my warr is done;
   I fere and hope, I burne and freise like yse;
   I fley above the wynde yet can I not arrise;
   And noght I have and all the worold I seson;
That loseth nor locketh holdeth me in prison   5
   And holdeth me not, yet can I scape nowise;
   Nor letteth me lyve nor dye at my devise,
   And yet of deth it gyveth none occasion.
Withoute Iyen, I se; and withoute tong I plain;
   I desire to perisshe, and yet I aske helthe;   10
   I love an othre, and thus I hate my self;
I fede me in sorrowe and laughe in all my pain;
   Likewise displeaseth me boeth deth and lyffe;
   And my delite is causer of this stryff.

5 loseth] looseth

21

27

THOUGH I my self be bridilled of my mynde,
  Retorning me backeward by force expresse,
  If thou seke honor to kepe thy promes,
  Who may the hold, my hert, but thou thy self
    vnbynd?
Sigh then no more, syns no way man may fynde   5
  Thy vertue to let, though that frowerdnes
  Of ffortune me holdeth; and yet, as I may gesse,
  Though othre be present, thou art not all behinde.
Suffice it then that thou be redy there
  At all howres; still vnder the defence   10
  Of tyme, trouth and love, to save the from offence;
Cryeng *I burne in a lovely desire*
  With my dere maisteres that may not followe,
  Whereby his absence torneth him to sorrowe.[1]

28

MY galy charged with forgetfulnes
  Thorrough sharpe sees in wynter nyghtes doeth pas
  Twene Rock and Rock; and eke myn ennemy, Alas,
  That is my lorde, sterith with cruelnes;

Nott punctuates and emends these lines as follows:

  'Crying I burn in a lovely desire,
      With my dear Mistress that may not follow;
      Whereby mine absence turneth me to sorrow.'

But 'maisteres' is the genitive of 'master', and it is therefore
wrong to alter the pronouns in 1.14.

And every owre a thought in redines,[1]   5
   As tho that deth were light in suche a case.
   An endles wynd doeth tere the sayll apase
   Of forced sightes and trusty ferefulnes.
A rayn of teris, a clowde of derk disdain,
   Hath done the wered cordes great hinderaunce;   10
   Wrethed with errour and eke with ignoraunce.
The starres be hid that led me to this pain;
   Drowned is reason that should me consort,
   And I remain dispering of the port.

29

Auysing the bright bemes of these fayer Iyes,
   Where he is that myn oft moisteth and wassheth,
   The werid mynde streght from the hert departeth
   For to rest in his woroldly paradise,
And fynde the swete bitter vnder this gyse.   5
   What webbes he hath wrought well he perceveth,
   Whereby with himself on love he playneth;
   That spurreth with fyer, and bridilleth with Ise.
Thus is it in suche extremitie brought:
   In frossen thought nowe and nowe it stondeth in
      flame;   10
   Twyst misery and welth, twist ernest and game;
But few glad, and many a dyvers thought;
   With sore repentaunce of his hardines:
   Of suche a rote commeth ffruyte fruytles.

11 *Twyst*] *Twixt*

30

Ever myn happe is slack and slo in commyng,
   Desir encresing, myn hope vncertain,
   That leve it or wayt it doeth me like pain,
   And Tigre-like, swift it is in parting.

[1] Nott suggests 'At every oar', translating 'A ciascun remo'.

Alas, the snow shalbe black and scalding;   5
   The See waterles; fisshe in the mountain;
   The Tamys shall retorne back into his fontain;
   And where he rose the sonne shall take lodging;
Ere that I in this fynde peace or quyetenes,
   Or that love or my lady rightwisely   10
   Leve to conspire again me wrongfully;
And if that I have after suche bitternes
   Any thing swete, my mouth is owte of tast,
   That all my trust and travaill is but wast.

31

LOVE and fortune and my mynde, remembre
   Of that that is nowe, with that that hath ben,
   Do torment me so that I very often
   Envy theim beyonde all mesure.
Love sleith myn hert; fortune is depriver   5
   Of all my comfort; the folisshe mynde then
   Burneth and plaineth as one that sildam
   Lyveth in rest, still in displeasure.
My plaisaunt dayes they flete away and passe,
   But daily yet the ill doeth chaunge into the
      wours;   10
   And more then the half is runne of my cours.
Alas, not of steill but of brickell glasse,
   I see that from myn hand falleth my trust,
   And all my thoughtes are dasshed into dust.

32

How oft have I, my dere and cruell foo,
   With those your Iyes for to get peace and truyse,
   Profferd you myn hert, but you do not vse
   Emong so high things to cast your mynde so lowe.

Yf any othre loke for it, as ye trowe,   5
  There vayn weke hope doeth greately them abuse;
  And thus I disdain that that ye refuse;
  It was ons myn: it can no more be so.
Yf I then it chase, nor it in you can fynde
  In this exile no manner of comfort,   10
  Nor lyve allone, nor where he is called resort,
He may wander from his naturall kynd.
  So shall it be great hurt vnto vs twayn,
  And yours the losse and myn the dedly pain.

33

LIKE to these vnmesurable montayns
  Is my painfull lyff, the burden of Ire,
  For of great height be they, and high is my desire,
  And I of teres, and they be full of fontayns.
Vnder craggy rockes they have full barren playns;   5
  Herd thoughtes in me my wofull mynde doeth tyre;
  Small fruyt and many leves their toppes do atyre;
  Small effect with great trust in me remayns.
The boystrous wyndes oft their high bowghes do blast
  Hote sighes from me continuelly be shed;   10
  Cattell in theim, and in me love is fed;
Immoveable ame I, and they are full stedfast;
  Of the restles birdes they have the tune and note,
  And I always plaintes that passe thorough my
    throte.

34

MADAME, withouten many wordes
  Ons I ame sure ye will or no;
And if ye will, then leve your bordes,
  And vse your wit and shew it so.

And with a beck ye shall me call,   **5**
    And if of oon that burneth alwaye
Ye have any pitie at all,
    Aunswer him faire with yea or nay.

Yf it be yea I shalbe fayne;
    If it be nay, frendes as before;   **10**
Ye shall an othre man obtain,
    And I myn owne and yours no more.[1]

35[2]

Ye old mule, that thinck yourself so fayre,
Leve of with craft your beautie to repaire,
    For it is time withoute any fable:
    No man setteth now by riding in your saddell;
To muche travaill so do your train apaire,   **5**
        Ye old mule!

With fals favoure though you deceve th'ayes,
Who so tast you shall well perceve your layes
    Savoureth som what of a Kappurs stable,
        Ye old mule!   **10**

Ye must now serve to market and to faire,
All for the burden for pannyers a paire;
    For syns gray heres ben powdered in your sable,
    The thing ye seke for you must yourself enable
To pourchase it by payement and by prayer,   **15**
        Ye old mule!

7 *ayes*] *eyes*

[1] The next poem in the Manuscript is an answer to the above in another hand and not by Wyatt.
[2] See M.L.R. 1925 for a French parallel to this poem.

36 [1]

Suche happe as I ame happed in
   Had never man of trueth I wene;
At me fortune list to begyn,
   To shew that never hath ben sene
     A new kynde of vnhappenes: 5
   Nor I cannot the thing I mene
     My self expres.

My self expresse my dedely pain
   That can I well, if that myght serue;
But when I have not helpe again   10
   That knowe I not vnles I starve;
     For honger still a myddes my foode
   Is so graunted that I deserve
     To do me good.

To do me good what may prevaill   15
   For I deserve and not desire,
And still of cold I me bewaill,
   And raked ame in burnyng fyer;
     For tho I have, suche is my lott:
   In hand to helpe that I require,   20
     It helpeth not.

It helpeth not, but to encrese
   That that by prouff can be no more;
That is the hete that cannot cesse,
   And that I have to crave so sore.   25
     What wonder is this gredy lust
   To aske and have, and yet therefore
     Refrain I must.

[1] Much of this poem is partly obliterated by later mathematical
calculations, especially lines 10, 13.

Refrain I must: what is the cause?
    Sure as they say: *so hawkes be taught*.   30
But in my case laieth no suche clause,
    For with suche craft I ame not caught;
      Wherefore I say and good cause why,
With haples hand no man hath raught
      Suche happe as I.   35

37

THEY fle from me that sometyme did me seke
    With naked fote stalking in my chambre.
I have sene theim gentill tame and meke
    That nowe are wyld and do not remembre
    That sometyme they put theimself in daunger   5
To take bred at my hand; and nowe they raunge
Besely seking with a continuell chaunge.

Thancked be fortune, it hath ben othrewise
    Twenty tymes better; but ons in speciall,
In thyn arraye after a pleasaunt gyse,   10
    When her lose gowne from her shoulders did fall,
    And she me caught in her armes long and small;
Therewithall swetely did me kysse,
And softely saide, *dere hert, howe like you this?*

It was no dreme: I lay brode waking.   15
    But all is torned thorough my gentilnes
Into a straunge fasshion of forsaking;
    And I have leve to goo of her goodenes,
    And she also to vse new fangilnes.
But syns that I so kyndely ame serued,   20
I would fain knowe what she hath deserued.

38

THERE was never nothing more me payned,
  Nor nothing more me moved,
As when my swete hert her complayned
  That ever she me loved.
    Alas the while!   5

With pituous loke she saide and sighed:
  Alas, what aileth me
To love and set my welth so light
  On hym that loveth not me?
    Alas the while!
                                                       10

Was I not well voyde of all pain,
  When that nothing me greved?
And nowe with sorrous I must complain,
  And cannot be releved.
    Alas the while!   15

My restfull nyghtes and joyfull daies
  Syns I began to love
Be take from me; all thing decayes,
  Yet can I not remove.
    Alas the while!   20

She wept and wrong her handes withall,
  The teres fell in my nekke;
She torned her face and let it fall;
  Scarsely therewith coulde speke.
    Alas the while!   25

Her paynes tormented me so sore
  That comfort had I none,
But cursed my fortune more and more
  To se her sobbe and grone:
    Alas the while!   30

29

39

PATIENCE, though I have not
   The thing that I require,
I must of force, god wot,
   Forbere my moost desire;
For no ways can I fynde   5
To saile against the wynde.

Patience, do what they will
   To worke me woo or spite,
I shall content me still
   To thyncke boeth daye and nyte,   10
To thyncke and hold my peace,
Syns there is no redresse.

Patience, withouten blame
   For I offended nought;
I knowe they knowe the same,   15
   Though they have chaunged their thought.
Was ever thought so moved
To hate that it haith loved?

Patience of all my harme,
   For fortune is my foo;   20
Patience must be the charme
   To hele me of my woo:
Patience withoute offence
Is a painfull patience.

40 [1]

PACIENS for my devise,
   Impaciens for your part;
Of contraries the gyse
   Is ever the overthwart:
Paciens, for I ame true,   5
The contrary for yew.

Paciens, a good cause why
   You have no cause at all;
Therefore you standeth awry,
   Perchaunce sometyme to fall: 10
Paciens then take him vp,
And drynck of paciens cupp.

Paciens, no force for that,
   But brusshe your gowne again;
Pacience, spurne not therat;   15
   Let no man knowe your payne:
Pacience evyn at my pleasure,
When youres is owte of mesure

Thothre was for me,
   This pacience is for you;   20
Chaunge when ye list let se,
   For I have taken a new;
Pacience, with a good will,
Is easy to fulfill.

---

[1] A note at the head of this poem in D reveals that it was written as a sequel to No. 39. 'Patiens tho I had nott &c. To her that saide this patiens was not for her, but that the contrarye of myne was most metiste for her porposse'.

31

41 [1]

Y<small>E</small> know my herte, my ladye dere,
    That sins the tyme I was your thrall
I have bene yours bothe hole and clere,
    Tho my rewarde hathe bene but small:
    So am I yet and more then all,   5
        And ye kno well how I haue serued;
As yf ye prove it shall apere
        Howe well, how long,
            How faithefulye,
        And soffred wrong   10
            How patientlye!
    Then sins that I have neuer swarfde,
    Let not my paines be ondeseruid.

Ye kno also, though ye saye naye,
    That you alone are my desire;   15
And you alone yt is that maye
    Asswage my fervent flaming fire;
    Soccour me then I you require.
        Ye kno yt ware a just request,
Sins ye do cause my heat, I saye,   20
        Yf that I bourne,
            That ye will warme,
        And not to tourne
            All to my harme
    Sending suche flame from frosen brest   25
    Against all right for my vnrest.

And I knowe well how frowerdly
    Ye have mystaken my true intent
And hetherto how wrongfully
    I have founde cause for to repent: 30

[1] The first twenty-three lines are missing in E through a lost leaf.
The rhyme-scheme is altered in the E version of stanza 3 and it is
possible that Wyatt made corresponding alterations in the missing
stanzas.

But deth shall ryd me redely
  Yf your hard hert do not relent;
    And I knowe well all this ye knowe,
      That I and myne
        And all I have   35
      Ye may assigne
        To spill or save.
Why are ye then so cruell ffoo,
Vnto your owne that loveth you so?

12 *swarfde*] *swerved*

42

WHO hath herd of suche crueltye before?
  That when my plaint remembred her my woo
That caused it, she cruell more and more
  Wisshed eche stitche, as she did sit and soo,
Had prykt myn hert, for to encrese my sore;   5
  And, as I thinck, she thought it had ben so:
For as she thought this is his hert in dede,
She pricked herd and made her self to blede.

43

IF fansy would favor,
  As my deseruing shall,
My love, my paramor,
  Should love me best of all.

But if I cannot attain   5
  The grace that I desir,
Then may I well complain
  My seruice and my hier.

33

Ffansy doeth knowe how
    To fourther my trew hert,   10
If fansy myght avowe
    With faith to take part.

But fansy is so fraill
    And flitting still so fast,
That faith may not prevaill   15
    To helpe me furst nor last.

Ffor fansy at his lust
    Doeth rule all but by gesse;
Whereto should I then trust
    In trouth or stedfastnes?   20

Yet gladdely would I please
    The fansy of her hert,
That may me onely ease
    And cure my carefull smart.

Therefore, my lady dere,   25
    Set ons your fantasy
To make som hope appere
    Of stedfast remedy.

Ffor if he be my frend
    And vndertake my woo,   30
My greif is at an ende
    If he continue so.

Elles fansy doeth not right,
    As I deserue and shall—
To have you daye and nyght,   35
    To love me best of all.

44

Alas! madame, for stelyng of a kysse,
  Have I so much your mynd then offended?
Have I then done so greuously amysse,
  That by no meanes it may be amended?
Then revenge you, and the next way is this: 5
  An othr kysse shall have my lyffe endid.
For to my mowth the first my hert did suck,
The next shall clene oute of my brest it pluck.

45

What no, perdy, ye may be sure!
Thinck not to make me to your lure,
  With wordes and chere so contrarieng,
  Swete and sowre contrewaing;
To much it were still to endure.   5
Trouth is trayed where craft is in vre;
But though ye have had my hertes cure,
  Trow ye I dote withoute ending?
    What no, perdy!

Though that with pain I do procure   10
For to forgett that ons was pure,
  Within my hert shall still that thing,
  Vnstable, vnsure, and wavering,
Be in my mynde withoute recure?
    What no, perdy!

46

The wandering gadlyng in the sommer tyde,
  That fyndes the Adder with his recheles fote,
Startes not dismayd so soudenly a side
  As jalous dispite did, tho there ware no bote,

35

When that he sawe me sitting by her side,   5
    That of my helth is very croppe and rote.
It pleased me then to have so fair a grace
To styng that hert that would have my place.

47

THE lyvely sperkes that issue from those Iyes,
    Against the which ne vaileth no defence,
    Have prest myn hert and done it none offence,
    With qwaking pleasure more than ons or twise.
Was never man could any thing devise   5
    The sonne bemes to torne with so great vehemence,
    To dase mans sight, as by their bright presence.
Dased ame I muche like vnto the gyse
Of one istricken with dynt of lightening,
    Blynded with the stroke, erryng here and there,   10
    So call I for helpe, I not when ne where,
The pain of my falt patiently bering:
    For after the blase, as is no wounder,
    Of dedly *nay* here I the ferefull thounder.

48

WHAT nedeth these thretning wordes and wasted
    wynde?
    All this cannot make me restore my pray.
To robbe your good, I wis, is not my mynde,
    Nor causeles your fair hand did I display.
Let love be judge, or els whome next we meit,   5
    That may boeth here what you and I can say.
She toke from me an hert and I a glove from her:
Let vs se nowe, if th'one be wourth th'othre.

36

49

RYGHT true it is, and said full yore agoo:
  Take hede of him that by thy back the claweth.
For none is wourse then is a frendely ffoo;
  Though they seme good, all thing that the deliteth,
  Yet knowe it well, that in thy bosom crepeth: 5
  For many a man such fier oft kyndeleth,
  That with the blase his berd syngeth.

50 [1]

WHAT wourde is that that chaungeth not,
  Though it be tourned and made in twain?
It is myn aunswer, god it wot,
  And eke the causer of my payn.
  A love rewardeth with disdain,   5
Yet is it loved. What would ye more?
It is my helth eke and my sore.

51

AT moost myschief
I suffre greif;
For of relief
  Syns I have none,
My lute and I   5
Continuelly
Shall vs apply
  To sigh and mone.

Nought may prevaill
To wepe or waill;   10
Pitie doeth faill
  In you, Alas!

[1] This poem has been entitled 'Anna' by a later hand. See textual notes.

Morning or mone,
Complaint or none,
It is all one,   15
   As in this case.

Ffor crueltie,
Moost that can be,
Hath soveraynte
   Within your hert;   20
Which maketh bare
All my welfare:
Nought do you care
   How sore I smart.

No Tigres hert   25
Is so pervert,
Withoute desert
   To wreke his Ire;
And you me kyll
For my good will: 30
Lo, how I spill
   For my desire!

There is no love
That can ye move,
And I can prove   35
   None othre way;
Therefore I must
Restrain my lust,
Banisshe my trust
   And welth away.   40

Thus in myschief
I suffre greif,
For of relief
   Syns I have none,
My lute and I   45
Continuelly
Shall vs apply
   To sigh and mone.
38

52

MARVAILL no more all tho
  The songes I syng do mone,
For othre liff then wo
  I never proved none.
And in my hert also   5
  Is graven with lettres diepe
A thousand sighes and mo,
  A flod of teres to wepe.

How may a man in smart
  Fynde matter to rejoyse?   10
How may a morning hert
  Set fourth a pleasaunt voise?
Play who that can that part:
  Nedes must in me appere
How fortune overthwart   15
  Doeth cause my morning chere.

Perdy, there is no man
  If he never sawe sight
That perfaictly tell can
  The nature of the light.   20
Alas, how should I then,
  That never tasted but sowre,
But do as I began,
  Continuelly to lowre?

But yet perchaunce som chaunce   25
  May chaunce to chaunge my tune;
And when suche chaunce doeth chaunce,
  Then shall I thanck fortune.
And if I have suche chaunce,
  Perchaunce ere it be long   30
For such a pleasaunt chaunce
  To syng som plaisaunt song.

39

53

WHERE shall I have at myn owne will
    Teres to complain? Where shall I fett
Suche sighes that I may sigh my fill,
    And then again my plaintes to repete?

Ffor tho my plaint shall have none end,   5
    My teres cannot suffice my woo;
To mone my harme have I no frend,
    For fortunes frend is myshappes ffoo.

Comfort, god wot, els have I none
    But in the wynde to wast my wordes;   10
Nought moveth you my dedly mone,
    But all you torne it into bordes.

I speke not now to move your hert
    That you should rue vpon my pain:
The sentence geven may not revert;   15
    I know suche labor were but vayn.

But syns that I for you, my dere,
    Have lost that thing that was my best,
A right small losse it must appere
    To lese these wordes and all the rest.   20

But tho they sparkill in the wynde,
    Yet shall they shew your falsed faith,
Which is retorned vnto his kynde,
    For like to like, the proverbe saieth.

Ffortune and you did me avaunce;   25
    Me thought I swam and could not drowne;
Happiest of all, but my myschaunce
    Did lyft me vp to throwe me downe.
40

And you with your owne cruelnes
    Did set your fote vpon my neck;   30
Me and my welfare to oppresse,
    Withoute offence your hert to wreke.

Where are your plaisaunt wordes, alas?
    Where your faith, your stedfastnes?
There is no more, but all doeth passe   35
    And I ame left all comfortles.

But forbicause it doeth you greve,
    And also me my wretched liff,
Have here my trouth, shall not releve,
    But deth alone my wery striff.   40

Therefore farewell my liff, my deth,
    My gayn, my losse, my salve, my sore;
Farewell also with you my breth,
    For I ame gone for evermore.

54 [1]

SHE sat and sowde that hath done me the wrong,
    Whereof I plain, and have done many a daye;
And whilst she herd my plaint in pitious song,
    Wisshed my hert the samplar as it lay.
The blynd maister whome I have serued so long,   5
    Grudging to here that he did here her saye,
Made her owne wepon do her fynger blede,
To fele if pricking were so good in dede.

[1]Cf. No. 42.

41

55

'A, ROBYN,
Joly Robyn,
Tell me how thy leman doeth,
And thou shall knowe of myn.'

'My lady is vnkynd, perde!'   5
  'Alack, whi is she so?'
'She loveth an othre better then me,
  And yet she will say no.' [1]

Responce

I fynde no suche doublenes,
  I fynde women true.   10
My lady loveth me dowtles,
  And will chaunge for no newe.

Le plaintif

Thou art happy while that doeth last,
  But I say as I fynde,
That womens love is but a blast   15
  And torneth like the wynde.

Responce

Yf that be trew yett as thou sayst
  That women turn their hart,
Then spek better of them thou mayst,
  In hop to have thy partt.   20

Le plaintif

Suche folkes shall take no harme by love,
  That can abide their torne;
But I, alas, can no way prove
  In love but lake and morne.

[1] See *Twelfth Night*, IV. 2.

Responce

But if thou will avoyde thy harme,   25
    Lerne this lessen of me:
At othre fires thy self to warme,
    And let theim warme with the.

24 *lake*] *lack*

56

SUCHE vayn thought as wonted to myslede me,
    In desert hope by well assured mone,
    Maketh me from compayne to live alone,
    In folowing her whome reason bid me fle.
She fleith as fast by gentill crueltie,   5
    And after her myn hert would fain be gone;
    But armed sighes my way do stoppe anone,
    Twixt hope and drede locking my libertie.
Yet, as I gesse, vnder disdaynfull browe
    One beame of pitie is in her clowdy loke,   10
    Whiche comforteth the mynde that erst for fere
        shoke;
And therwithall bolded I seke the way how
    To vtter the smert that I suffre within,
    But suche it is I not how to begyn.

57

THO I cannot your crueltie constrain
For my good will to favor me again,
    Tho my true and faithfull love
    Have no power your hert to move,
        Yet rew vpon my pain.   5

Tho I your thrall must evermore remain
And for your sake my libertie restrain,
   The greatest grace that I do crave
   Is that ye would vouchesave
      To rew vpon my pain.   10

Tho I have not deserued to obtain
So high Reward but thus to serue in vain,
   Tho I shall have no redresse,
   Yet of right ye can no lesse
      But rew vpon my pain.   15

But I se well that your high disdain
Wull no wise graunt that I shall more attain;
   Yet ye must graunt at the lest
   This my powre and small request:
      Reioyse not at my pain.   20

58

To wisshe and want and not obtain,
To seke and sew esse of my pain,
Syns all that ever I do is vain,
   What may it availl me?

All tho I stryve boeth dey and howre   5
Against the streme with all my powre,
If fortune list yet for to lowre,
   What may it availl me?

If willingly I suffre woo,
If from the fyre me list not goo,   10
If then I burne, to plaine me so
   What may it availl me?

And if the harme that I suffre
Be runne to farr owte of mesur,
To seke for helpe any further   15
   What may it availl me?

What tho eche hert that hereth me plain
Pitieth and plaineth for my payn?
If I no les in greif remain,
    What may it availl me?   20

Ye, tho the want of my relief
Displease the causer of my greife,
Syns I remain still in myschiefe,
    What may it availl me?

Suche cruell chaunce doeth so me threte   25
Continuelly inward to fret,
Then of relesse for to trete
    What may it availl me?

Ffortune is deiff vnto my call,
My torment moveth her not at all,   30
And though she torne as doeth a ball,
    What may it availl me?

Ffor in despere there is no rede;
To want of ere speche is no spede;
To linger still alyve as dede,   35
    What may it availl me?

21 Ye] Yea

59 [1]

Some tyme I fled the fyre that me brent,
    By see, by land, by water and by wynd;
And now I folow the coles that be quent
    From Dovor to Calais against my mynde.
Lo! how desire is boeth sprong and spent!   5
    And he may se that whilome was so blynde;
And all his labor now he laugh to scorne,
Mashed in the breers that erst was all to torne.

8 Mashed] Meshed

[1] This poem has been thought to refer to Anne Boleyn.

60

HE is not ded that somtyme hath a fall;
  The sonne retorneth that was vnder the clowd;
And when fortune hath spitt oute all her gall,
  I trust good luck to me shalbe allowd.
For I have sene a shippe into haven fall   5
  After the storme hath broke boeth mast and shrowd;
And eke the willowe that stowpeth with the wynde
Doeth ryse again, and greater wode doeth bynd.

61

THE furyous gonne in his rajing yre,
  When that the bowle is rammed in to sore
And that the flame cannot part from the fire,
  Cracketh in sonder, and in the ayer doeth rore
The shevered peces; right so doeth my desire,   5
  Whose flame encreseth from more to more,
Wych to lett owt I dare not loke nor speke:
So now hard force my hert doeth all to breke.

62

MY hope, Alas, hath me abused,
  And vain rejoysing hath me fed;
Lust and joye have me refused,
  And carefull plaint is in their stede;
  To muche avauncing slaked my spede;   5
Myrth hath caused my hevines,
And I remain all comfortles.

Whereto did I assure my thought
  Withoute displeasure stedfastly?
In fortunes forge my joye was wrought,   10

And is revolted redely.
I ame mystaken wonderly;
For I thought nought but faithfulnes,
Yet I remain all comfortles.

In gladsom chere I did delite,　　　　　　15
　　Till that delite did cause my smert
And all was wrong where I thought right;
　　For right it was that my true hert
　　Should not from trouth be set apart,
Syns trouth did cause my hardines:　　　20
Yet I remain all comfortles.

Sometyme delight did tune my song,
　　And led my hert full pleasauntly;
And to my self I saide among:
　　My happe is commyng hastely.　　　25
　　But it hath happed contrary:
Assuraunce causeth my distres,
And I remain all comfortles.

Then if my note now do vary,
　　And leve his wonted pleasauntnes,　　30
The hevy burden that I cary
　　Hath alterd all my joyefulnes:
　　No pleasure hath still stedfastnes,
But hast hath hurt my happines,
And I remain all comfortles.　　　　　　35

24 *among* = *all the time*

63

WHAT deth is worse then this,
　　When my delight,
My wele, my joye, my blys,
　　Is from my sight?
　　Boeth daye and nyght　　　　　　5
My liff, alas, I mys.
47

Ffor though I seme alyve,
  My hert is hens;
Thus, botles for to stryve
    Oute of presens   10
    Of my defens,
Towerd my deth I dryve.

Hertles, alas, what man
  May long endure?
Alas, how lyve I then?   15
    Syns no recure
    May me assure,
My liff I may well ban.

Thus doeth my torment goo
  In dedly dred;   20
Alas, who myght lyve so
    Alyve as deed,
    Alyve to lede
A dedly lyff in woo?

64

Th'enmy of liff, decayer of all kynde,
  That with his cold wethers away the grene,
This othre nyght me in my bed did fynde,
  And offered me to rid my fiever clene;
And I did graunt, so did dispaire me blynde.   5
  He drew his bowe with arrowe sharp and kene,
And strake the place where love had hit before,
And drave the first dart deper more and more.

65

Ons as me thought fortune me kyst
  And bad me aske what I thought best;
And I should have it as me list,
  Therewith to set my hert in rest.

I asked nought but my dere hert   **5**
   To have for evermore myn owne:
Then at an ende were all my smert,
   Then should I nede no more to mone.

Yet for all that a stormy blast
   Had overtorned this goodely day;   **10**
And fortune semed at the last
   That to her promes she saide nay.

But like as oon oute of dispere
   To soudden hope revived I;
Now fortune sheweth herself so fayer   **15**
   That I content me wonderly.

My moost desire my hand may reche,
   My will is alwaye at my hand;
Me nede not long for to beseche
   Her that hath power me to commaund   **20**

What erthely thing more can I crave?
   What would I wisshe more at my will?
No thing on erth more would I have,
   Save that I have to have it still.

Ffor fortune hath kept her promes   **25**
   In graunting me my moost desire:
Of my suffraunce I have redres,
   And I content me with my hiere.

28 *hiere*] *hire*

66

My lute awake! perfourme the last
Labor that thou and I shall wast,
   And end that I have now begon;
For when this song is sung and past,
   My lute be still, for I have done.   **5**

As to be herd where ere is none,
As lede to grave in marbill stone,
   My song may perse her hert as sone;
Should we then sigh, or syng, or mone?
   No, no, my lute, for I have done.   **10**

The Rokkes do not so cruelly
Repulse the waves continuelly,
   As she my suyte and affection,
So that I ame past remedy:
   Whereby my lute and I have done.   **15**

Prowd of the spoyll that thou hast gott
Of simple hertes thorough loves shot,
   By whome, vnkynd, thou hast theim wone,
Thinck not he haith his bow forgot,
   All tho my lute and I have done.   **20**

Vengeaunce shall fall on thy disdain,
That makest but game on ernest pain;
   Thinck not alone vnder the sonne
Vnquyt to cause thy lovers plain,
   All tho my lute and I have done.   **25**

Perchaunce the lye wethered and old,
The wynter nyghtes that are so cold,
   Playnyng in vain vnto the mone;
Thy wisshes then dare not be told;
   Care then who lyst, for I have done.   **30**

And then may chaunce the to repent
The tyme that thou hast lost and spent
   To cause thy lovers sigh and swoune;
Then shalt thou knowe beaultie but lent,
   And wisshe and want as I have done.   **35**

Now cesse, my lute, this is the last
Labour that thou and I shall wast,
    And ended is that we begon;
Now is this song boeth sung and past:
    My lute be still, for I have done.   40

7 *lede*] *lead grave*] *engrave*

67

I F chaunce assynd
Were to my mynde
By very kynd
    Of destyne;
Yet would I crave   5
Nought els to have
    But onlye liff and libertie.

Then were I sure
I myght endure
The displeasure   10
    Of crueltie,
Where now I plain
Alas in vain,
    Lacking my liff for libertie.

Ffor withoute th'one   15
Th'othre is gone,
And there can none
    It remedy;
If th'one be past,
Th'othre doeth wast,   20
    And all for lack of libertie.

And so I dryve
As yet alyve,
All tho I stryve
    With myserie;   25

Drawing my breth,
Lowking for deth,
  And losse of liff for libertie.

But thou that still
Maist at thy will   30
Torne all this ill
  Aduersitie;
For the repare
Of my welfare
  Graunt me but liff and libertie.   35

And if not so
Then let all goo
To wretched woo,
  And let me dye;
For th'one or th'othre   40
There is none othre,
  My deth, or liff with libertie.

68

NATURE, that gave the bee so feet a grace
  To fynd hony of so wondrous fashion,
Hath taught the spider owte of the same place
  To fetche poyson, by straynge alteration.
Tho this be straynge, it is a straynger case   5
  With oon kysse by secret operation
Boeth these at ons in those your lippes to fynde,
In chaunge wherof I leve my hert behinde.

69

I HAVE sought long with stedfastnes
  To have had som ease of my great smert;
But nought availleth faithfulnes
  To grave within your stony hert.

But happe and hit, or els hit not,   5
   As vncertain as is the wynde,
Right so it fareth by the shott
   Of love, alas, that is so blynd.

Therefore I plaid the foole in vain,
   With pitie, when I first began,   10
Your cruell hert for to constrain,
   Syns love regardeth no doulfull man.

But, of your goodenes, all your mynde
   Is that I should complain in vain:
This is the favor that I fynde,   15
   Ye list to here how I can plain.

But tho I plain to please your hert,
   Trust me, I trust to temper it so,
Not for to care which do revert:
   All shalbe oon in welth or woo.   20

Ffor fansy rueleth, tho right say nay,
   Even as the goodeman kyst his kowe;
None othre reason can ye lay
   But as who saieth, I reke not how.

70

LYKE as the Swanne towardis her dethe
   Doeth strayn her voyse with dolefull note,
Right so syng I with waste of breth,
   I dy! I dy! and you regarde yt note.

I shall enforce my faynting breth   5
   That all that heris this dedlye note
Shall knowe that you dothe cause my deth:
   I dy! I dy! and you regarde yt note.

Your vnkyndnes hath sworne my dethe,
   And chaunged hathe my plesaunte note   10
To paynfull sighes that stoppis my brethe
   I dy! I dye! and you regarde yt note.

Consumeth my lif, faileth my brethe;
   Your fawte is forger of this note,
Melting in tearis, a cruell dethe: 15
   I dy! I dy! and you regarde yt note.

My faith with me after my dethe
   Bured shalbe, and to this note
I do bequethe my verye brethe
   To cry *I dyede and you regarde yt note.*   20

71

In eternum I was ons determed
For to have lovid and my minde affermed,
That with my herte it shuld be conpermed
    In eternum.

Forthwith I founde the thing that I myght like,   5
And sought with loue to warme her hert alike,
For, as me thought, I shulde not se the like
    In eternum.

To trase this daunse I put my self in prese;
Vayne hope ded lede and bad I should not cese   10
To serue, to suffer, and still to hold my pease
    In eternum.

With this furst rule I fordred me apase,
That, as me thought, my trowghthe had taken place
With full assurans to stond in her grace   15
    In eternum.

It was not long or I by proofe had found
That feble bilding is on feble grounde;
For in her herte this worde ded never sounde,
    In eternum.   20

In eternum then from my herte I kest
That I had furst determined for the best;
Nowe in the place another thought doeth rest,
    In eternum.

1 *determed*] *determined* 9 *prese*] *press* 21 *kest*] *cast*
(dial.)

72

    SYNS ye delite to knowe
    That my torment and woo
       Should still encrese
       Withoute relese,
    I shall enforce me so   5
    That liff and all shall goo,
       For to content your cruelnes.

    And so this grevous trayne
    That I to long sustayn,
       Shall sometyme cese   10
       And have redresse
    And you also remain
    Full pleased with my pain,
       For to content your cruelnes.

    Onles that be to light   15
    And that ye would ye myght
       Se the distresse
       And hevines
    Of oon slain owte right,
    Therewith to please your sight,   20
       And to content your cruelnes.

Then in your cruell mode
Would god fourthwith ye woode
   With force expresse
   My hert oppresse   25
To do your hert suche good,
To se me bathe in blode,
   For to content your cruelnes.

Then cowld ye aske no more,
Then should ye ease my sore,   30
   And the excesse
   Of myn excesse;
And you should evermore
Defamed be therefore,
   For to repent your cruelnes.   35

22 *mode*] *mood*

73

HEVYN and erth and all that here me plain
   Do well perceve what care doeth cause me cry,
Save you alone to whome I cry in vain:
   Mercy, madame, alas, I dy, I dy!

Yf that you slepe, I humbly you require   5
   Forbere a while and let your rigour slake,
Syns that by you I burne thus in this fire:
   To here my plaint, dere hert, awake, awake!

Syns that so oft ye have made me to wake
   In plaint and teres and in right pitious case,   10
Displease you not if force do now me make
   To breke your slepe, crieng *alas, alas!*

It is the last trouble that ye shall have
  Of me, madame, to here my last complaint.
Pitie at lest your poure vnhappy slave,   15
  For in dispere, alas, I faint, I faint!

It is not now, but long and long ago
  I have you serued as to my powre and myght
As faithfully as any man myght do,
  Clayming of you nothing of right, of right.   20

Save of your grace only to stay my liff,
  That fleith as fast as clowd afore the wynde;
For syns that first I entred in this stryff
  An inward deth hath fret my mynde, my mynd.

Yf I had suffered this to you vnware,   25
  Myn were the fawte and you nothing to blame;
But syns you know my woo and all my care
  Why do I dy? Alas, for shame, for shame!

I know right well my face, my lowke, my teeres,
  Myn Iyes, my Wordes, and eke my drery chiere
Have cryd my deth full oft vnto your eres;   31
  Herd of belefe it doeth appere, appere!

A better prouff I se that ye would have
  How I ame dede; therefore when ye here tell
Beleve it not all tho ye se my grave.   35
  Cruell, vnkynd! I say farewell, farewell!

74

Comfort thy self, my wofull hert,
  Or shortly on thy self the wreke,
For length redoubleth dedly smert:
  Why sighes thou, hert, and woult not breke?

57

To wast in sighes were pitious deth;   5
   Alas, I fynd the faynt and weke.
Enforce thy self to lose thy breth:
   Why sighes thou, hert, and woult not breke?

Thou knowest right well that no redresse
   Is thus to pyne and for to speke.   10
Pardy, it is remediles:
   Why sighes thou then, and woult not breke?

It is to late for to refuse
   The yoke when it is on thy neck;
To shak it of vaileth not to muse: 15
   Why sighes thou then, and woult not breke?

To sobbe and sigh it were but vain,
   Syns there is none that doeth it reke;
Alas, thou doyst prolong thy pain:
   Why sighes thou then, and woult not breke?

Then in her sight, to move her hert,   21
   Seke on thy self thy self to wreke,
That she may knowe thou sufferdst smert:
   Sigh there thy last, and therewith breke!

75 [1]

DESIRE, alas, my master and my foo,
   So sore alterd thi selff, how mayst thou se?
Some tyme I sowght that dryvys me to and fro;
   Some tyme thow ledst that ledyth the and me.
What reson is to rewle thy subiectes so   5
   By forcyd law and mutabilite?
For where by the I dowtyd to have blame,
Evyn now by hate agayne I dowt the same.

76 [1]

VENEMUS thornes that ar so sharp and kene
   Sometyme ber flowers fayre and freshe of hue;
Poyson offtyme is put in medecene
   And cawsith helth in man for to renue;
Ffyre that purgith allthing that is vnclene
   May hele, and hurt: and if thes bene true,
I trust somtyme my harme may be my helth,
Syns evry wo is joynid with some welth.

77

To cause accord or to aggre,
Two contraries in oon degre,
And in oon poynct, as semeth me,
To all mans wit it cannot be:
     It is impossible.   **5**

Of hete and cold when I complain
And say that hete doeth cause my pain,
When cold doeth shake me every vain
And boeth at ons, I say again
     It is impossible.   **10**

That man that hath his hert away,
If lyff lyveth there, as men do say,
That he hertles should last on day
Alyve and not to torne to clay,
     It is impossible.   **15**

Twixt lyff and deth, say what who sayth,
There lyveth no lyff that draweth breth;
They joyne so nere and eke, i' feith,
To seke for liff by wissh of deth
     It is impossible.   **20**

[1] Wyatt's handwriting.

Yet love that all thing doeth subdue,
Whose power ther may no liff eschew,
Hath wrought in me that I may rew
These miracles to be so true,
    That are impossible.   25

78

THOUGH this the port and I thy seruaunt true,
  And thou thy self doist cast thy bemes from hye
From thy chieff howse, promising to renew
  Boeth joye and eke delite, behold yet how that I,
  Bannysshed from my blisse, carefully do crye,   5
'Helpe now, Citherea, my lady dere,
My ferefull trust, en vogant la galere.'

Alas the dowbt that dredfull absence geveth!
  Withoute thyn ayde, assuraunce is there none.
The ferme faith that in the water fleteth   10
  Succor thou therefor: in the it is alone.
  Stay that with faith that faithfully doeth mone,
And thou also gevest me boeth hope and fere,
Remembre thou me, en vogant la galere.

By sees and hilles elonged from thy sight,   15
  Thy wonted grace reducing to my mynde,
In sted of slepe thus I occupy the nyght;
  A thowsand thoughtes and many dowbtes I fynde,
  And still I trust thou canst not be vnkind;
Or els dispere my comfort and my chiere   20
Would she fourthwith, en vogant la galere.

Yet on my faith, full litle doeth remain
  Of any hope whereby I may my self vphold;
For syns that onely wordes do me retain,
  I may well thinck the affection is but cold.   25

But syns my will is nothing as I would,
But in thy handes it resteth hole and clere,
Forget me not en vogant la galere.

7 *en vogant la galere*=when I put out to sea

79

VNSTABLE dreme according to the place,
  Be stedfast ons; or els at leist be true:
  By tasted swetenes make me not to rew
The sudden losse of thy fals fayned grace.
By goode respect in such a daungerous case   5
  Thou broughtes not her into this tossing mew,
  But madest my sprite lyve my care to renew,
My body in tempest her succor to enbrace.
The body dede, the spryt had his desire;
  Paynles was th'one, th'othre in delight: 10
  Why then, Alas, did it not kepe it right,
Retorning to lepe into the fire,
  And where it was at wysshe it could not remain?
  Such mockes of dremes they torne to dedly pain.

80 [1]

IN dowtfull brest, whilst moderly pitie
  With furyous famyn stondith at debate,
Sayth thebrew moder: 'O child vnhappye,
  Retorne thi blowd where thow hadst milk of late.
Yeld me those lymms that I made vnto the,   5
  And entre there where thou wert generate;
For of on body agaynst all nature
To a nothr must I mak sepulture.'

3 *thebrew*] *the Hebrew*

[1] Wyatt's handwriting. 'Of the mother that eat her childe at the siege of Ierusalem'—T.

61

81 [1]

OFF Cartage he, that worthie warier
   Could ouercome but cowld not vse his chaunce;
And I like wise off all my long indeuer,
   The sherpe conquest, tho fortune did auance,
Cowld not it vse: the hold that is gyvin ouer   5
   I vnpossest. So hangith in balaunce
Off warr, my pees, reward of all my payne;
At Mountzon thus I restles rest in Spayne.

82

PROCESSE of tyme worketh suche wounder,
   That water which is of kynd so soft
Doeth perse the marbell stone a sonder,
   By litle droppes faling from aloft.

And yet an hert that sems so tender   5
   Receveth no dropp of the stilling teres,
That alway still cause me to render
   The vain plaint that sowndes not in her eres.

So cruel, alas, is nowght alyve,
   So fiers, so frowerd, so owte of fframe;   10
But some way, some tyme, may so contryve
   By mens the wild to tempre and tame.

And I that alwaies have sought, and seke
   Eche place, eche tyme for some lucky daye,
This fiers Tigre lesse I fynde her meke   15
   And more denyd the lenger I pray.

The lyon in his raging furor
   Forberis that sueth mekenes for his boote;
And thou, Alas, in extreme dolor
   The hert so low thou tredis vnder thy foote. 20

[1]Wyatt's handwriting.

Eche fiers thing lo! how thou doest exceede,
　And hides it vnder so humble a face;
And yet the humble to helpe at nede,
　Nought helpeth tyme, humblenes, nor place.

12 *mens] means*

83

AFTER great stormes the cawme retornes,
　And plesanter it is thereby;
Fortune likewise that often tornis
　Hath made me now the moost happy.

Thevin that pited my distres,　　　　　　5
　My iust desire and my cry,
Hath made my languor to cesse
　And me also the most happy.

Whereto dispaired ye, my frendes?
　My trust alway in her did ly[1],　　　　10
That knoweth what my thought intendes,
　Whereby I lyve the most happy.

Lo! what can take hope from that hert
　That is assured stedfastly?
Hope therefore ye that lyve in smert,　　15
　Whereby I ame the most happy.

And I that have felt of your paine,
　Shall pray to god continuelly
To make your hope, your helth retayne,
　And me also the most happy.　　　　　　20

[1] Mr. R. C. Harrier urges the retention of the MS reading 'in hid ly' (i.e. *in occulto*); but 'that' (l. 11) would then refer to 'trust' rather than 'heaven'.

84

ALL hevy myndes
　　Do seke to ese their charge,
And that that moost theim byndes
　　To let at large.

Then why should I　　　　　　　　5
　　Hold payne within my hert,
And may my tune apply
　　To ese my smart?

My faithfull lute
　　Alone shall here me plaine;　　　10
For els all othre sute
　　Is clene in vaine.

Ffor where I sue
　　Redresse of all my grieff,
Lo, they do most eschew　　　　　15
　　My hertes relieff.

Alas, my dere,
　　Have I deserued so,
That no help may appere
　　Of all my wo?　　　　　　　　20

Whome speke I to,
　　Vnkynd and deff of ere?
Alas, lo, I go,
　　And wot not where.

Where is my thoght?　　　　　　25
　　Where wanders my desire?
Where may the thing be soght
　　That I require?

Light in the wynde
   Doth fle all my delight;   30
Where trouth and faithfull mynd
   Are put to flyght.

Who shall me gyve
   Fetherd wynges for to fle,
The thing that doeth me greve   35
   That I may se?

Who would go seke
   The cause whereby to playne?
Who could his foo beseke
   For ease of payne?   40

My chaunce doeth so
   My wofull case procure,
To offer to my ffoo
   My hert to cure.

What hope I then   45
   To have any redresse?
Of whome or where or when
   Who can expresse?

No! sins dispaire
   Hath set me in this case,   50
In vain oft in the ayre
   To say *Alas,*

I seke nothing
   But thus for to discharge
My hert of sore sighing,   55
   To plaine at large;

And with my lute
   Sumtyme to ease my pain,
For els all othre sute
   Is clene in vain.   60

85

To seke eche where, where man doeth lyve,
The See, the land, the Rocke, the clyve,
   Ffraunce, Spayne and Ind and every where
Is none a greater gift to gyve
     Lesse sett by oft and is so lyeff and dere,   5
     Dare I well say, than that I gyve to yere.

I cannot gyve browches nor Ringes,
Thes goldsmythes work and goodly thinges,
   Piery nor perle oryente and clere;
But for all that is no man bringes   10
   Leffer juell vnto his lady dere,
     Dare I well say then that I gyve to yere.

Nor I seke not to fetche it farr,
Worse is it not tho it be narr,
   And as it is it doeth appere   15
Vncontrefaict, mistrust to barr,
   Left hole and pure, withouten pere,
     Dare I well say the gyft I gyve to yere.

To the, therefore, the same retain;
The like of the to have again   20
   Ffraunce would I gyve if myn it were.
Is none alyve in whome doeth rayne
   Lesser disdaine. Frely, therefore, lo here
     Dare I well gyve, I say, my hert to yere.

11 *Leffer*] *liefer*

86

O GOODELY hand,
Wherein doeth stand
Myn hert distrast in payne;
Faire hand, Alas,
In little spas   5
My liff that doeth restrayne.

O fyngers slight,
Departed right,
So long, so small, so rownd;
Goodely bygone,   10
And yet alone
Most cruell in my wound.

With Lilis whight
And Roses bright
Doth stryve thy color faire;   15
Nature did lend
Eche fyngers ende
A perle for to repayre.

Consent at last,
Syns that thou hast   20
My hert in thy demayne,
For seruice trew
On me to rew
And reche me love againe.

And if not so,   25
Then with more woo
Enforce thiself to strayne
This simple hert,
That suffereth smert,
And rid it owte of payne.   30

21 *demayne*] *demesne*

I

Lo, what it is to love!
Lerne ye that list to prove
    At me, I say,
    No ways that may
The grownd of grieff remove   5
    My liff alweie
    That doeth decaye:
Lo, what it is to love!

Ffle alwaye from the snare,
Lerne by me to beware   10
    Of suche a trayne
    Which doubles payne,
And endles woo and care,
    That doth retayne;
    Which to refrayne,   15
Fle alwaye from the snare.

To love and to be wise,
To rage with good aduyse,
    Now thus, now than,
    Now of, now an,   20
Vncerteyn as the dyse;
    There is no man
    At ons that can
To love and to be wise.

Suche are the dyvers throws,   25
Suche, that no man knows
    That hath not profd
    And ons have lofd;
Suche are the raging woos,
    Soner reprofd   30
    Then well remofd;
Suche are the dyvers throws.

Love is a fervent fire,
Kendeld by hote desire,
    For a short pleasure   35
    Long displeasure;
Repentaunce is the hire;
    A poure tresoure,
    Withoute mesure
Love is a fervent fire.   40

Lo, what it is to love! &c.

20 *an*] *on*

II

Leve thus to slaunder love!
Though evill with suche it prove
    Which often vse
    Love to mysuse
And loving to reprove;   5
    Such cannot chose
    For their refuse
But thus to slaunder love.

Ffle not so much the snare;
Love sildom causeth care;   10
    But by deserftes
    And crafty partes
Som lese their owne welfare;
    Be true of hertes
    And for no smartes   15
Fle not so much the snare.

To love and not to be wise
Is but a mad devise;
    Such love doeth last
    As sure and fast   **20**

As chaunce on the dise;
    A bitter tast
    Coms at the last,—
To love and not to be wise.

Suche be the plaisaunt daies,   25
Suche be the honest wayes;
    There is no man
    That fully can
Know it, but he that sayes
    Loving to ban   30
    Were folly then.
Such be the plaisaunt daies.

Love is a plaisaunt fire
Kyndeled by true desire;
    And though the payne   35
    Cause men to playne,
Sped well is oft the hiere.
    Then though som fayne
    And lese the gayne,
Love is a plaisaunt fyre.   40

Leve thus to slaunder love! &c.

13 *lese*] *lose*

III

WHO most doeth slaunder love,
The dede must alwaye prove;
    Trouth shall excuse
    That you accuse
For slaunder and reprove;   5
    Not by refuse
    But by abuse
You most do slaunder love.

Ye graunt it is a snare
And would vs not beware.   10
    Lest that your trayne
    Should be to playne
Ye colour all the care.
    Lo, how you fayne
    Pleasure for payne   15
And graunt it is a snare!

To love and to be wise,
It were a straunge devise:
    But from that tast
    Ye vow the fast;   20
On zyns tho run your dise,
    Ambs-as may hast
    Your payne to wast.
To love and to be wise!

Of all suche pleasaunt dayes,   25
Of all suche pleasaunt playes,
    Without deserft
    You have your part,
And all the worould so says;
    Save that poure hert   30
    That for more smert
Feleth yet suche pleasaunt dayes

Suche fire and suche hete
Did never make ye swete,
    For withoute payne   35
    You best obtayne
To good spede and to great;
    Who so doeth playne
    You best do fayne
Suche fire and suche hete.   40

Who now doeth slaunder love, &c.

88

I LEDE a liff vnpleasant, nothing glad,
   Crye and complaynt offerre, voydes joyfullnesse;
So chaungethe vnrest that nought shall fade;
   Payne and dyspyte hathe altered plesantnes;
Ago, long synnys, that she hathe truly made   5
   Dysdayne for trowght, sett lyght yn stedfastnes,
I haue cause goode to syng this song:
Playne or reioyse, who felythe wele or wrong.

89

YF in the world ther be more woo
   Then I haue yn my harte,
Wher so ytt is, itt doithe come fro,
And in my brest there doithe itt groo,
   Ffor to encrease my smarte.   5
Alas, I ame recepte of euery care
   And of my liff eche sorrow claymes his parte.
     Who list to lyue yn quyetnes
By me lett hym beware,
    Ffor I by highe dysdayne   10
     Ame made withoute redresse,
   And vnkyndenes, alas, hathe slayne
    My poore trew hart all comfortles.

90 [1]

TH'ANSWERE that ye made to me, my dere,
   When I did sewe for my poore hartes redresse,
Hath so apalld my countenaunce and my chere,
   That yn this case I ame all comfortlesse,
   Sins I of blame no cawse can well expresse.   5

[1] After line 10 come the following lines in the manuscript:
      Another? Why? Shall lyberty be bond?
      Ffre hart may not be bond but by desert.
A space is left for the completion of the stanza.

I haue no wrong when I can clayme no right;
   Nowght tane me fro wher I nothing haue had:
Yete of my wo I can nott so be quyte,
   Namely, sins that another may be glad
   With that that thus in sorowe makethe me sad. 10

Nor none can clayme, I say, by former graunte
   That knowithe nott of any graunt att all;
And by deserte I dare well make avaunte,
   Of faythfull will ther is no wher that shall
   Bere you more trowthe, more redy att your call.

Now good then call agayne that frendly worde   16
   That seithe your frende in saving of his payne;
And say, my dere, that itt was sayde in borde:
   Late or too sone lett that nott rule the gayne,
   Wherwith free will doth trew deserte retayne.   20

91

Most wretched hart most myserable,
   Syns the comforte is from the fled,
Syns all the trouthe is turned to fable,
   Most wretched harte why arte thow nott ded?

No, no, I lyve and must doo still,   5
   Wherof I thank god and no mo;
Ffor I me selff have all my will,
   And he is wretched that wens hym so.

Butt yete thow hast bothe had and lost
   The hope so long that hathe the fed,   10
And all thy travayle and thy cost:
   Most wretched harte why arte thou nott ded?

Some other hope must fede me new;
    Yff I haue lost, I say what tho?
Dyspayre shall nott throwghe it ynsew,   15
    For he is wretched that wenys hym so.

The sonne, the mone doth frowne on the;
    Thow hast darkenes in daylightes stede,
As good in grave as soo to be;
    Moost wretched hert, why art thou not ded?

Some plesaunt sterre may shewe me light,   21
    But tho the heven wold worke me woo,
Who hath himself shal stande vp right,
    And he is wretched that wens him soo.

Hath he himself that is not sure?   25
    His trust is like as he hath sped;
Against the streme thou maist not dure:
    Most wretched herte why art thou not ded?

The last is worst, who feres not that?
    He hath himself where so he goo;   30
And he that knoweth what is what
    Sayeth he is wretched that wens him soo.

Seist thou not how they whet their teth,
    Which to touche thee somtime ded drede?
They finde comforte for thy mischief: 35
    Moost wretched hert why art thou not dede?

What tho that currs do fal by kinde
    On him that hathe the overthro?
Al that can not opresse my minde,
    For he is wretched that wens him soo.   40

Yet can it not be thenne denyd;
    It is as certain as thy crede;
Thy gret vnhap thou canst not hid:
    Vnhappy thenne why art thou not dede?

Vnhappy, but no wretche therfore,   45
    For happe doth comme again and goo;
For whiche I kepe my self in store,
    Sins vnhap cannot kil me soo.

92 [1]

You that in love finde lucke and habundance
    And live in lust and joyful jolitie,
    Arrise for shame! Do away your sluggardie!
    Arise, I say, do May some obseruance!
Let me in bed lye dreming in mischaunce;   5
    Let me remembre the happs most vnhappy
    That me betide in May most comonly,
    As oon whome love list litil to avaunce.
Sephame saide true that my natiuitie
    Mischaunced was with the ruler of the May:
    He gest, I prove, of that the veritie.   11
In May my welth and eke my liff, I say,
    Have stonde so oft in such perplexitie:
    Reioyse! Let me dreme of your felicitie.

93

And if an Iye may save or sleye,
    And stryke more diepe then wepon longe,
And if an Iye by subtil play
    May moue on more thenne any tonge,
    How can ye say that I do wronge   5
Thus to suspecte withoute deserte?
For the Iye is traitor of the herte.

[1] Wyatt was imprisoned in May 1534 and again in May 1536.

To frame all wel I ame content
  That it were done vnwetingly;
But yet I say, who wol assent,   10
  To do but wel, do no thing whie
  That men shuld deme the contrary.
For it is said by men expert
That the Iye is traitor of the hert.

But yet, alas, that loke all sowle   15
  That I doo clayme of right to haue,
Shuld not, methinkes, goo seke the scole
  To please all folke; for who canne crave
  Frendlier thing thenne hert witsaue?
By loke to giue in frendely parte;   20
For the Iye is traitor of the hert.

And my suspect is without blame,
  For, as ye saye, not only I
But other moo haue demyd the same;
  Thenne is it not Jelowsye   25
  But subtill loke of rekeles Iye
Did raunge to farre to make me smart,
Ffor the Iye is traitor of the hert.

But I your freende shal take it thus,
  Sins you wol soo, as stroke of chaunce; 30
And leve furder for to discus
  Wither the stroke did sticke or glaunce;
  But scuse who canne, let him avaunce
Dissembled lokes; but for my parte
My Iye must stil bitray my harte.   35

And of this grief ye shalbe quitte
  In helping trowth stedfast to goo;
The time is longe that doth sitt
  Feble and weike and suffreth woo.
  Cherish him wel, continnewe soo, 40
Let him not fro your hart astart;
Thenne feres not the Iye to shewe the hert.

94 [1]

FROM thes hye hilles as when a spryng doth fall,
   It tryllyth downe with still and suttyll corse;
Off this and that it gaders ay, and shall,
   Tyll it have just off flowd the streme and forse,
Then at the fote it ragith ouer all: 5
   So faryth love when he hath tan a sorse;
His rayne is rage, resistans vaylyth none;
The first estew is remedy alone.

95

IF waker care, if sodayne pale Coulor,
   If many sighes with litle speche to playne,
   Now ioy, now woo, if they my chere distayne
For hope of small, if muche to fere therfore,
To hast, to slak my passe lesse or more,   5
   Be signe of love, then do I love agayne,
   If thow aske whome, sure sins I did refrayne
Brunet, that set my welth in such a rore,
Th'unfayned chere of Phillis hath the place
   That Brunet had: she hath and ever shal.   10
   She from my self now hath me in her grace:
She hath in hand my witt, my will and all;
   My hert alone wel worthie she doth staye,
   Without whose helpe skant do I live a daye.

5 *passe*] *pace*

[1]In Wyatt's handwriting.

96 [1]

In Spayne

So feble is the threde that doth the burden stay
　Of my pore lyff, in hevy plyght that fallyth in dekay,
That but it have elles where some aide or some socours,
　The runnyng spyndell off my fate anon shall end his
　　cours.
Ffor sins th'unhappy howre that did me to depart　5
　From my swete wele, one only hope hath staide my
　　lyff apart;
Wych doth perswade such wordes vnto my sory mynd.
　Mayntene thy sellff, O wofull spryte, some better luk
　　to fynd;
Ffor tho thou be depryffd from thy desyerd syght
　Who can the tell iff thi retorne be for thy most
　　delyght?　10
Or who can tell thy losse if thou ons maist recover
　Some pleasant howre thy wo may rape and the de-
　　fend and cover?
This is the trust that yet hath my lyff systaynid;
　And now, alas, I se' it faint and I by trust ame
　　trainid.
The tyme doth flete and I perceyve thowrs how thei
　　bend　15
　So fast that I have skant the space to marke my
　　comyng end.
Westward the sonne from owt th'est skant doth shew
　　his lyght,
　When in the west he hyds hym straite within the
　　darke of nyght;
And coms as fast where he began his path a wrye
　From est to west, from west to th'est so doth his
　　jornei ly.　20

[1] In Wyatt's handwriting, with numerous corrections. Translated from Petrarch.

The lyff so short, so fraile, that mortall men lyve here,
   So gret a whaite, so hevy charge, the body that we
     bere;
That when I thinke apon the distance and the space
   That doth so ferr devid me from my dere desird face,
I know not how t'attayne the wynges that I require,
    To lyfft my whaite that it myght fle to folow my
     desyre.   26
Thus off that hope, that doth my lyff some thing sus-
    tayne,
   Alas, I fere and partly fele full litill doth remayne.
Eche place doth bryng me grieff where I do not behold
   Those lyvely Iyes wich off my thowghtes were wont
     the kays to hold.   30
Those thowghtes were plesaunt swete whilst I enioyd
    that grace;
   My plesure past, my present payne where I myght
     well embrace;
But for becawse my want shold more my wo encresse,
   In wache, in slepe, both day and nyght my will doth
     neuer cesse
That thing to wisshe wheroff sins I did lese the syght
   I neuer saw the thing that myght my faythfull hert
     delyght.   36
Th'vnesy lyff I lede doth teche me for to mete
   The flowde, the sees, the land and hilles that doth
     them entremete
Twene me' and those shining lyghtes that wontyd to
    clere
   My darke panges off clowdy thowghtes as bryght as
     Phebus spere;   40
It techith me also what was my plesant state,
   The more to fele by such record how that my welth
     doth bate.
If such record, alas, provoke th'enflamid mynd
   Wich sprang that day that I did leve the best of me
     byhynd;

If love forgett hym sellff by lenght of absence let,
   Who doth me guyd, O wofull wretch, vnto this
      bayted net   46
Where doth encresse my care? Much better were for
   me
   As dome as stone, all thing forgott, still absent for to
      be.
Alas, the clere crystall, the bryght transparant glas,
   Doth not bewray the colour hyd wich underneth it
      has,   50
As doth th'accomberd sprite thowghtfull throws dis-
   cover
   Off fiers delyght, off fervent love, that in our hertes
      we cover:
Owt by these Iyes it shewth that euermore delyght
   In plaint and teres to seke redresse, and that both
      day and nyght.
Thes new kyndes off plesurs wherein most men reioyse
   To me thei do redowble still off stormye syghes the
      voyce;   56
Ffor I ame one off them whom plaint doth well con-
   tent:
   It sittes me well, myn absent welth meseems me to
      lament,
And with my teris for to' assay to charge myn Iyes
   tweyne,
   Lyke as myn hert above the brink is frawtid full of
      payne;   60
And for bycawse therto off those fayre Iyes to trete,
   Do me provoke, I shall retorne my plaint thus to re-
      pete.
Ffor there is nothing elles that towches me so within
   Where thei rule all and I alone nowght but the cace
      or skyn.
Wherfore I do retorne to them as well or spryng,   65
   From whom decendes my mortall wo above all othr
      thing.

So shall myn Iyes in payne accompagnie min hert,
  That were the guydes that did it lede of love to fele
  the smert.
The cryspid gold that doth sormount Apollos pryd,
  The lyvely stremes off plesaunt sterres that vnder it
  doth glyd,   70
Wherein the bemes off love doth still encresse theire
  hete,
  Wich yet so farre towch me so nere in cold to make
  me swete;
The wise and plesaunt talk so rare or elles alone
  That did me gyve the courtese gyfft that such had
  neuer none,
Be ferre from me, alas, and euery other thing   75
  I myght forbere with better will then that that did
  me bryng
With plesant word and chere redresse off lingerd payne,
  And wontyd offt in kendlid will to vertu me to trayne.
Thus ame I dryven to here and herken affter news,
  My confort skant, my large desire, in dowtfull trust
  renews.   80
And yet with more delyght, to mone my wofull cace,
  I must complaine those handes, those armes that
  fermely do embrace
Me from my sellf, and rule the sterne of my pore
  lyff,
  The swete disdaynes, the plesant wrathes and eke the
  lovely stryff
That wontid well to tune in tempre just and mete   85
  The rage that offt did make me erre by furour vndis-
  crete.
All this is hid me fro with sharp and craggyd hilles,
  At othr will my long abode my diepe dispaire full-
  filles.
But if my hope somtyme ryse vp by some redresse,
  It stumblith strait, for feble faint my fere hath such
  excesse.   90
T.W.—E   81

Such is the sort off hope, the lesse for more desyre,
    Whereby I fere and yet I trust to se that I requyre,
The restyng place of love where vertu lyves and grose,
    Where I desire my wery lyff may also sometyme take
      repose.

My song, thou shalt ataine to fynd that plesant place
    Where she doth lyve by whome I lyve; may chaunce
      thou have this grace.   96
When she hath red and seene the dred where in I sterve,
    Bytwene her brestes she shall the put, there shall she
      the reserve.
Then tell her that I come, she shall me shortly se;
    Yff that for whayte the body fayle, this sowle shall
      to her fle.   100

40 *spere*] *sphere*

97 [1]

TAGUS, fare well, that westward with thy stremes
    Torns vp the grayns off gold alredy tryd:
With spurr and sayle for I go seke the Tems
    Gaynward the sonne that shewth her welthi pryd
And to the town which Brutus sowght by drems   5
    Like bendyd mone doth lend her lusty syd.
My Kyng, my Contry alone for whome I lyve,
Of myghty love the winges for this me gyve.

98 [2]

OFF purpos Love chase first for to be blynd,
    For he with sight of that that I behold
Vanquisht had bene against all godly kynd;
    His bow your hand and trusse shold have vnfold,

[1] Wyatt's handwriting. Written May 1539.
[2] Wyatt's handwriting.

And he with me to serve had bene assind: 5
   But, for he blind and rekelesse wolde him hold,
And still by chaunse his dedly strokes bestow,
With such as see I serve and suffer wow.

1 *chase*] *chose*   8 *wow*] *woe*

99 [1]

WHAT rage is this? what furour of what kynd?
What powre, what plage, doth wery thus my mynd?
Within my bons to rancle is assind
     What poyson, plesant swete?

Lo, se myn iyes swell with contynuall terys;   5
The body still away sleples it weris;
My fode nothing my faintyng strenght reperis,
     Nor doth my lyms sustayne.

In diepe wid wound the dedly strok doth torne
To curid skarre that neuer shall retorne.   10
Go to, tryumphe, reioyse thy goodly torne,
     Thi frend thow dost opresse.

Opresse thou dost, and hast off hym no cure;
Nor yett my plaint no pitie can procure,
Fiers tygre fell, hard rok withowt recure,   15
     Cruell rebell to love!

Ons may thou love, neuer belovffd agayne;
So love thou still and not thy love obttayne;
So wrathfull love with spites of just disdayne
     May thret thy cruell hert.   20

[1] In Wyatt's handwriting with many corrections. See textual
notes. On the next page Wyatt has written the following couplet:

Ffrom thowght to thowght, from hill to hill love doth me lede,
Clene contrary from restfull lyff thes comon pathes I trede.

83

'What rage is this? what furour of what kynd?'
(Egerton MS. 2711, fol. 69v)

100 [1]

VULCANE bygat me; Mynerua me taught;
  Nature, my mother; craft norischt me yere by yere;
Thre bodyes ar my fode, my strength is in naught:
  Angre, wrath, wast, and noyse, are my children dere.
Gesse frend what I ame and how I ame wrought: 5
  Monstre of see or of lande or of elswhere?
Know me and use me and I may the defende,
  And if I be thine enmye I may thy life ende.

101

Jopas' Song

WHEN Dido festid first the wandryng Troian knyght,
  Whom Junos wrath with stormes did force in
    Lybyke sandes to lyght,
That myghty' Atlas did teche, the souper lastyng long,
  With cryspid lokkes, on golden harpe, Jopas sang in
    his song.

That same, quod he, that we the world do call and
    name,   5
  Off hevin and yerth with all contentes it is the very
    frame;
Or thus, off hevinly powrs, by more powre kept in one
  Repugnant kyndes, in myddes of whome the yerth
    hath place alone;
Firme, round, off liuing thynges the moder place and
    nourse,
  Withowt the wyche in egall whaight this hevin doth
    hold his course;   10
And it is calld by name the first moving hevin:
  The firmament is next containing othr sevyn.

¹ This 'discripcion of a gonne' is translated from the Latin of Pandulpho. The handwriting is later than the rest of the E MS.

Off hevinly powrs that same is plantid full and thikk,
  As shyning lyghtes wych we call steres that therin
  cleve and stikk;
With great swifft sway the first, and with his restles
  sours   15
  Caryth it sellff and all those eight in evin continuall
  cours.
And off this world so rownd with in that rollyng case,
  There be two pointes that neuer move but fermely
  kepe ther place:
The tone we se alway, the tothr stondes obiect
  Against the same, deviding just the round by line
  direct;   20
Wich by ymagination draune from ton to tothr
  Towchith the centre of the yerth, for way there is no
  nothr:
And thes bene calld the poles, discribd by sterres not
  bryght,
  Artyke the tone northward we se, Antartyke tothr
  hight.
The lyne that we devise from ton to tothr so   25
  As Axell is, apon the wich thevins abowt doth go;
Wych off water, nor yerth, of Ayre nor fyre have kynd:
  Therfore the substance of those same were herd for
  man to fynd.
But thei ben vncorrupt, symple and pure, vnmixt,
  And, so we say, bene all those sterys that in those
  same bene fixt;   30
And eke those erryng sevin, in cyrcles as thei stray,
  So calld by cawse against that first thei have repug-
  nant way.
And smaller by ways to, skant sensible to man,
  To busy work for my pore harp, let sing them he
  that can!
The widest saff the first off all thes nyne above,   35
  On hunderd yere doth aske of space for on degre to
  move:

86

Off wich degres we make in the first moving hevin
    Thre hunderd and thre skore in partes justly devided
      evin.

And yet there is an othr by twene those hevins tow,
    Whose moving is so sli, so slake, I name it not for
      now.   40

The sevent hevyn, or the shell, next to the sterry skye,
    All those degres that gadreth vp with agid pas so
      slye,

And doth performe the same, as elders compt hath
    bene,
    In nyne and twentye yeres complete and days almost
      sixtene,

Doth cary in his bowght the sterr of Saturne old,   45
    A thretner of all lyving thinges with drowfft and
      with his cold.

The sixt whom this containes doth staulk with yonger
    pase,
    And in twelff yere doth sum what more then tothrs
      viage wase;

And this in it doth bere the sterre of Jove benigne,
    Twene Saturns malice and vs men, frendly deffend-
      ing signe.   50

The fift berth blody Mars that in three hundred days
    And twise elefn with on full yere hath finisht all
      those ways.[1]

A yere doth aske the fourt, and houres therto six,
    And in the same the day his yie the sonne therein he
      stix.

The third that governd is by that that governth me;   55
    And love for love and for no love provokes, as offt
      we se.

[1] After line 52, at the foot of the page, the following couplet is
written, but there is no indication of where it should be inserted in
the poem:
    Nor is it lyk that man may think these sters all
    Streys their path as thei do passe within that hevinly hall.
The whole poem is in Wyatt's handwriting, with numerous corrections.

POEMS

In like space doth performe that course that did the
    tother,
  So doth the next to the same that second is in order.
But it doth bere the sterr that calld is Mercury,
    That mayni' a craffty secret stepp doth tred, as cal-
    cars try.   60
That skye is last and first next vs: those ways hath gone
  In sevin and twenty comon days and eke the third of
  one;
And beryth with his sway the diuerse Mone abowt,
  Now bryght, now browne, now bent, now full, and
  now her lyght is owt.
Thus have thei of thire owne two movinges all those
    sevin: 65
  One, wherein they be carid still eche in his sevrall
  hevin;
An othr, of hym sellffes where their bodis ben layd
  In by ways and in lesser rowndes, as I afore have
  sayd;
Saff of them all, the sonne doth stray lest from the
    straight,
  The sterry sky hath but on cowrse, that we have
  calld the eight;   70
And all these movinges eight ar ment from west to
    th'est,
  Altho thei seme to clymb alofft, I say, from est to
  west.
But that is but by force of the first moving skye,
  In twise twellff howres from est to th'est that caryth
  them bye and bye.
But mark me well also, thes movinges of these sevin 75
  Be not about that axell-tre of the first moving hevin;
For thei have theire two poles directly tone to
    tother. . . .

35 *saff*] *save*

88

POEMS
from the Devonshire MS. Add. 17492

POEMS

from the Devonshire MS. Add. 17492

102

TAKE hede be tyme leste ye be spyede,
Your lovyng Iyes can not hide,
At last the trowthe will sure be tryde,
    Therefore take hede!

For Som ther be of crafete kynde: 5
Thowe yow shew no parte of your mynde,
Sewrlye there Iyes ye can not blynde,
    Therefore take hede!

Ffor in lyke case there selves hathe bene,
And thowgt ryght sure none had theym sene,
But it was not as they did wene,   11
    Therefore take hede!

All thowgth theye be of dyvers skoolles,
And well can yose all craftye toolles,
At lengthe they prove themselfs bott foolles,
    Therefore take hede!   16

Yf theye myght take yow in that trape,
Theye wolde sone leve yt in your lape;
To love vnspyed ys but a happe:
    Therefore take hede!   20

5 *crafete*] *crafty* 7 *Sewrlye*] *Surely* 18 *leve yt in your lape* = *tell you plainly*

91

103

My pen, take payn a lytyll space
To folow that whyche dothe me chace,
   And hathe in holde my hart so sore;
But when thow hast thys browght to passe,
   My pen, I prithe, wryght nomore!   5

Remember, oft thow hast me eaysyd,
And all my payne full well apeaysyd,
   But now I know, vnknowen before,
Ffor where I trust I am dysceavyd:
   And yet my pen, thow canst no more.   10

A tyme thow haddyst as other have
To wryght whyche way my hope to crave;
   That tyme ys past: withdrawe therffore!
Syns we do lose that other save,
   As good leve off and wryght no more.   15

Yn worthe to vse another waye,
Not as we wold but as we maye;
   For ons my losse ys past restore,
And my desyre ys my decaye,
   My pen, yet wryght a lytyll more.   20

To love in vayn who euer shall,
Off worldlye payn yt passythe all,
   As in lyke case I fynd. Wherfore
To hold so fast and yet to ffall?
   Alas, my pen, now wryght no more!   25

Syns thow hast taken payn thys space
To folow that whyche dothe me chace,
   And hathe in hold my hart so sore,
Now hast thow browght my mynde to passe:
   My pen, I prithe, wryght no more!   30

6 *eaysyd*] *eased* 7 *apeaysyd*] *appeased*

104 [1]

At last withdrawe yowre cruelltie,
    Or let me die at ons;
It is to moche extremitie
    Devised for the nons
To holde me thus alive   5
In paine still for to dryve.
    Whatt maye I more sustayne,
    Alas that dye wuld faine
    And cane not dye for paine?

For to the flame wherwith ye burne   10
    My thought and mye desyre,
When into ashys it shulde turne
    My hert by feruent fyer,
Ye send a stormy rayn
That doythe it quynche agayne,   15
    And make myn eys expresse
    The tearyes that do redres
    My lyue in wrecchydnes.

Then when thes shulde haue drownde
    And ouerwhelmd my hart,   20
The heate doithe them confownde,
    Renewing all my smart;
Then doithe the flame encresse,
My tormyntt can not cease;

[1] In A and P there is a poem by John Harington which seems to
be based on the above. It begins:

> At least withdraw your creweltie
>   Or force the tyme to worke your will,
> Yt is to moche extreamytie
>   To kepe me pent in pryson styll,
>   Free from all fawte, voyd of all cawse,
>   Without all right, agaynst all lawse;
>   How can you use more crewell spight
>   Than offre wrong and promes right,
>   Yet can not accuse nor will acquyght?

My woo doithe then revive,   25
    And I remaine alyve,
    With deathe still for to stryve.

Butt if that he wolde haue my Death,
    And that ye wolde no nother,
Shortly then for to spen my brethe,   30
    Withdrawe the ton or tother:
For thus yowr cruelnes
Doithe lete it selfe doubtles,
    And it is reason why
    No man alyve nor I   35
    Of doble dethe can dy.

30 *spen*] *spend*

105

To wette yowr Iye withouten teare
    And in good helth to faine desease,
That yu therby myn eye myght bleyr,
    Therwith your other frendes to please;
And thoo ye thinke ye ned not feare,   5
    Yet so ye can not me apease;
But as ye list, faine, flater or glose,
Ye shall not wynne yf I do lose.

Prat and paint and spare not,
    Ye knowe I can me worke [1];   10
And if so be ye carre not,
    Be sure I do not reke:
And thowe ye swere it were not,
    I can bothe swere and speke;
By god and by this crosse,   15
Yff I haue the moke, ye shall haue the loss.

[1] It is possible that Wyatt wrote 'wreke'—which would both rhyme and make easier sense.

106

I LOVVE lovyd and so doithe she,
　And yet in love wee sufer still;
The cause is strange as semeth me,
　To lovve so well and want our will.

O deadly yea! O grevous smart!　　　　　5
　Worse then refuse, vnhappë gaine!
I lovve: whoeuer playd this part
　To lovve so well and leve in payn?

Was euer hart soo well agrede,
　Sines lovve was lovve as I do trowe,　　10
That in ther lovve soo evell dyd sped,
　To love so well and leve in woo?

Thes morne wee bothe and hathe don long
　With wofull plaint and carefull voice:
Alas! it is a grevous wrowng　　　　　15
　To love so well and not reioice.

And here an end of all our mone!
　With sighinge oft my brethe is skant,
Sines of myshappe ours is alone—
　To lovve so well and it ¹ to wantt.　　　20

But they that causer is of thes,
　Of all owr cares god send them part!
That they may trowe what greve it iss
　To lovve so well and leve in smart.

8 *leve*] *live*　13 *Thes*] *Thus* or *This*　21 *thes*] *this*
23 *greve*] *grief*

¹Possibly Wyatt wrote 'yet'.

107

Suffryng in sorow in hope to attayn,
Desyryng in fere and dare not complayn,
  Trew of beleffe, in whome ys all my trust,
Do thow apply to ease me off my payn,
  Els thus to serve and suffer styll I must.   5

Hope ys my hold, yet in Dyspayre to speke
I dryve from tyme to tyme and dothe not Reke
  How long to lyve thus after loves lust,
In studye styll of that I dare not Breke:
  Wherfore to serve and suffer styll I must.   10

Encrease of care I fynd bothe day and nyght;
I hate that was sumtyme all my delyght;
  The cawse theroff ye know I have dyscust,
And yet to Reffrayn yt passythe my myght:
  Wherfore to serve and suffer styll I must.   15

Love who so lyst, at lengthe he shall well say:
To love and lyve in fere yt ys no play.
  Record that knowythe, and yf thys be not just,
That where as love dothe lede there ys no way
  But serve and suffer euer styll he must.   20

Then for to leve with losse of lybertye
At last perchawnce shall be hys Remedye;
  And for hys trewthe regnith with fals mystrust,
Who wold not rew to se how wrongfullye
  Thus for to serve and suffer styll he must.   25

Untrew by trust oftymes hathe me betrayd,
Mysusyng my hope, styll to be delayd,
  Fortune allways I have the fownd vnjust;
And so with lyke rewarde now am I payd:
  That ys, to serve and suffer styll I must.   30

96

Neuer to cesse, nor yet lyke to attayn,
As long as I in fere dare not complayn;
   Trew of beleff hathe allways ben my trust,
And tyll she knowythe the cawse of all my payn,
    Content to serve and suffer styll I must.   35

1 *leve*] *live*

108

FFAREWELL all my wellfare,
   My shue ys trode awry;
Now may I karke and care
   To syng *lullay by by.*
Alas! what shall I do thereto?   5
There ys no shyffte to helpe me now.

Who made hytt suche offence
   To love for love agayn?
God wott that my pretence
   Was but to ease hys payn;   10
Ffor I had Ruthe to se hys wo;
Alas, more fole, why dyd I so?

Ffor he frome me ys gone
   And makes there at a game,
And hathe leffte me alone   15
   To suffer sorow and shame.
Alas! he ys vnkynd dowtles
To leve me thus all comfortles.

Hytt ys a grevows smarte
   To suffer payne and sorowe;   20
But most grevyd my hart
   He leyde hys feythe to borow:
And falshode hathe hys feythe and trowthe,
And he forsworne by many an othe.

All ye lovers, perde,   **25**
   Hathe cawse to blame hys dede,
Whyche shall example be
   To lett yow off yowre spede;
Let neuer woman agayn
Trust to suche wordes as men can fayn.   **30**

Ffor I vnto my coste
   Am warnyng to yow all,
That they whom you trust most
   Sonest dysceyve yow shall;
But complaynt cannot redresse   **35**
Of my gret greff the gret excesse.

109

THE hart and servys to yow profferd
   With ryght good wyll full honestly,
Refuse yt not, syns yt ys offerd,
   But take yt to you gentylly.

And tho yt be a small present,   **5**
   Yet good, consyder gracyowsly
The thowght, the mynd, and the entent
   Of hym that lovys you faythfully.

Yt were a thyng of small effecte
   To worke my wo thus cruelly,   **10**
Ffor my good wyll to be abiecte:
   Therfor accepte it lovyngly.

Payn or travell, to rune or ryde,
   I vndertake yt pleasawntly;
Byd ye me go and strayte I glyde   **15**
   At your commawndement humbly.

Payn or pleasure, now may yow plant
  Evyn whyche it plese yow stydfastly;
Do whyche yow lyst, I shall not want
  To be your servant secrettly.   20

And syns so muche I do desyre
  To be your owne assuryddly,
Ffor all my servys and my hyer
  Reward your servante lyberally.

110

WHAT menythe thys? When I lye alone,
I tosse, I turne, I syghe, I grone;
My bedd me semys as hard as stone:
      What menys thys?

I syghe, I playne contynually;   5
The clothes that on my bedd do ly
Always methynks they lye awry:
      What menys thys?

In slumbers oft for fere I quake;
Ffor hete and cold I burne and shake;   10
Ffor lake of slepe my hede dothe ake:
      What menys thys?

A mornynges then when I do rysse
I torne vnto my wontyd gysse;
All day after muse and devysse   15
      What menys thys?

And yff perchanse by me there passe
She vnto whome I sue for grace,
The cold blood forsakythe my face:
    What menythe thys?   20

But yff I sytte nere her by,
With lowd voyce my hart dothe cry,
And yet my mowthe ys dome and dry:
    What menys thys?

To aske ffor helpe no hart I have,   25
My tong dothe fayle what I shuld crave,
Yet inwardly I Rage and Rave:
    What menys thys?

Thus have I passyd many a yere
And many a day, tho nowght apere;   30
But most of that that most I fere:
    What menys thys?

11 *lake*] *lack* 13 *rysse*] *rise* 14 *gysse*] *guise* 15 *devysse*]
devise

111

    Ys yt possyble
    That so hye debate,
So sharpe, so sore, and off suche rate,
Shuld end so sone and was begone so late?
    Is it possyble?   5

    Ys yt possyble
    So cruell intent,
So hasty hete and so sone spent,
Ffrom love to hate, and thens ffor to Relent?
    Is it possyble?   10

Ys yt possyble
That eny may fynde
Within on hert so dyverse mynd,
To change or torne as wether and wynd?
    Is it possyble?   15

Is it possyble
To spye yt in an Iye
That tornys as oft as chance on dy?
The trothe whereoff can eny try?
    Is it possyble?   20

It is possyble
Ffor to torne so oft,
To bryng that lowyste that wasse most aloft,
And to fall hyest yet to lyght sofft:
    It is possyble.   25

All ys possyble,
Who so lyst beleve;
Trust therfore fyrst, and after preve:
As men wedd ladyes by lycence and leve,
    All ys possyble.   30

112

ALAS, poore man, what hap have I
    That must fforbere that I love best?
I trow yt be my desteny
    Neuer to lyve in quiet Rest.

No wonder ys tho I complayn,   5
    Not withowt cawse ye may be sure;
I seke ffor that I cannot attayn,
    Whyche ys my mortall dysplesure.

Alas, pore hart, as in thys case
  With pensyff playntes thow art opprest;   10
Vnwysse thow wert to desyre place
  Where as another ys possest.

Do what I can to ese thy smart,
  Thow wylt not let to love her styll;
Hyrs and not myn I se thow art: 15
  Let her do by the as she wyll.

A carefull carkace full of payn
  Now hast thou lefft to morne for the;
The hart ons gone, the body ys slayn;
  That ever I saw her, wo ys me!   20

Mine Iye, alas, was cawse of thys,
  Whyche her to se had never hys ffyll;
To me that syght full bytter ys
  In Recompence of my good wyll.

She that I sarve all other above   25
  Hathe payd my hyre, as ye may se;
I was vnhappy, and that I prove,
  To love above my poore degre.

113

  And wylt thow leve me thus?
  Say nay, say nay, ffor shame,
  To save the from the Blame
  Of all my greffe and grame;
  And wylt thow leve me thus?   5
    Say nay, Say nay!

  And wylt thow leve me thus,
  That hathe lovyd the so long,
  In welthe and woo among?

And ys thy hart so strong   10
As for to leve me thus?
    Say nay, Say nay!

And wylt thow leve me thus,
That hathe gevyn the my hart,
Never for to Depart,   15
Nother for payn nor smart;
And wylt thow leve me thus?
    Say nay, Say nay!

And wylt thow leve me thus
And have nomore Pyttye   20
Of hym that lovythe the?
Helas thy cruellte!
And wylt thow leve me thus?
    Say nay, Say nay!

16 *nother*] *neither*

114

THAT tyme that myrthe dyd stere my shypp,
   Whyche now ys frowght with hevines,
And fortune beate not then the lypp,
   But was defence off my dystresse,
   Then in my boke wrote my maystresse: 5
I am yowres, yow may well be sure,
And shall be whyle my lyff dothe dure.

But she her selffe whyche then wrote that
   Is now myn extreme enemye;
Above all men she dothe me hate,   10
   Reioysyng of my myserye;
   But thoughe that for her sake I dye,
I shall be hyres, she may be sure,
As long as my lyff dothe endure.

POEMS

It is not tyme that can were owt   15
  With me that once ys fermly sett;
Whyle nature kepys her corse abowt,
  My love frome her no man can lett;
  Thowghe neuer so sore they me thrett,
Yet am I hyrs, she may be sure,   20
And shallbe whyle that lyff dothe dure.

And once I trust to see that day,
  Renuare of my joy and welthe,
That she to me theyse wordes shall say:
  In feythe, welcum (to me myselffe)   25
  Welcum, my joy! welcum, my helthe!
Ffor I am thyne, thow mayst be sure,
And shallbe whyle that lyff dothe dure.

Ho me alas! What woordes were theyse?
  In comenant I myght fynd them so!   30
I reke not what smart or dysease
  I suffred, so that I myght knoo
That she were myn, I myght be sure,
And shuld be whyle that lyff dothe dure.[1]

3 *beate*] bit   15 *were*] *wear*   23 *Renuare*] *Renewer*
30 *comenant*] covenant

[1] A line has dropped out. Nott conjectured that the last three
lines should read:

    'After my passed pain and woe
    That she were mine: and might be sure,
    She should be while that life doth dure.'

On a later page of the manuscript some one has written 'I ama
yowres An'. This inscription has been used in conjunction with the
above poem to support the theory that Anne Boleyn was Wyatt's
mistress.

104

115 [1]

THE restfull place, Revyver of my smarte,
The labors salve, incressyng my sorow,
The bodys ese and trobler off my hart,
Quieter of mynd and my vnquyet foo,
Fforgetter of payn, Remembryng my woo,   5
The place of slepe, wherein I do but wake
Be sprent with teres, my bed I the forsake.

The frost, the snow, may not redresse my hete,
Nor yet no heate abate my fervent cold.
I know nothyng to ese my paynes mete: 10
Eche care cawsythe increse by twenty fold.
Revyvyng carys vpon my sorows old,
Suche overthwart affectes they do me make,
By sprent with terys my bed for to forsake.

Yet helpythe yt not: I fynd no better ese   15
In bed or owt; thys moste cawsythe my payn—
Where most I seke how beste that I may plese,
My lost labor, Alas, ys all in vayn.
Yet that I gave I cannot call agayn:
No place fro me my greffe away can take,   20
Wherefor with terys my bed I the forsake.

---

[1] The following eight-line version of the first stanza of this poem
appears in E on the same page as No. 7 but in a later handwriting:

To his bedde

O restfull place, reneewer of my smart,
  O laboors salue, encreasing my sorowe,
O bodyes ease, O troobler of my hart,
  Peaser of mynde, of myne unquyet fo,
  Refuge of payene, remembrer of my wo,
Of care coomefort, where I dispayer my part,
  The place of slepe, wherein I doo but wake;
  Bysprent with teares, my bedde, I thee forsake.

116

As power and wytt wyll me Assyst,
My wyll shall wyll evyn as ye lyst.

Ffor as ye lyst, my wyll ys bent
In euery thyng to be content,
To serve in love tyll lyff be spent,   5
And to Reward my love thus ment,
    Evyn as ye lyst.

To fayn or fable ys not my mynd,
Nor to Refuce suche as I fynd,
But as a lambe of humble kynd,   10
Or byrd in cage, to be Assynd
    Evyn as ye lyst.

When all the flokk ys cum and gone,
Myn eye and hart agreythe in one,
Hathe chosyn yow only Alone   15
To be my joy, or elles my mone,
    Evyn as ye lyst.

Joy, yf pytty apere in place,
Mone, yf dysdayn do shew hys face;
Yet crave I not as in thys case   20
But as ye lede, to follow the trace
    Evyn as ye lyst.

Sum in wordes muche love can fayn,
And sum for wordes gyve wordes agayn;
Thus wordes for wordes in wordes Remayn,   25
And yet at last wordes do optayn
    Evyn as ye lyst.

To crave in wordes I wyll exchew,
And love in dede I wyll ensew;
Yt ys my mynd bothe hole and trew,   30
And for my trewthe I pray yow rew
     Evyn as ye lyst.

Dere hart, I bydd your hart farewell
With better hart than tong can tell;
Yet take thys tale as trew as gospell;   35
Ye may my lyff save or expell
     Evyn as ye lyst.

117

Sum tyme I syghe, sumtyme I syng,
Sumtyme I lawghe, sumtyme mornynge,
As one in dowte, thys ys my ssayyng:
Have I dysplesyd yow in any thyng?

Alake, what aylythe you to be grevyd?   5
Ryght sory am I that ye be mevyd;
I am your owne yf trewthe be prevyd
And by your dyspleasure as one myschevyd.

When ye be mery than am I glad,
When ye be sory than am I sad;   10
Such grace or fortune I wold I had
Yow for to plese howeuer I were bestad.

When ye be mery, why shuld I care?
Ye are my joye and my wellfare.
I wyll you love; I wyll not spare   15
Into yowre presens as farr as I dare.

All my poore hart and my love trew,
Whyle lyff dothe last I gyve yt yow;
And yow to serve with servys dew,
And neuer to change yow for no new.   20
107

118

PACYENCE of all my smart,
  Ffor fortune ys tornyd awry;
Pacyence must ese my hart
  That mornes contynually;
Pacyence to suffer wrong   5
Ys a pacyence to long.

Pacyence to have a nay
  Of that I most desyre;
Pacyence to haue allway
  And euer burne lyke fyre;   10
Pacyence withowt desart
Ys grownder of my smart.

Who can with mery hart
  Set forthe sum plesant song,
That allways felys but smart   15
  And neuer hathe but wrong?
Yet pacyence evermore
Must hele the wownd and sore.

Pacyence to be content
  With froward fortunes trayn;   20
Pacyence to the intent
  Sumwhat to slake my payne;
I se no Remedy
But suffer pacyently.

To playn wher ys none ere   25
  My chawnce ys chawnsyd so,
Ffor yt dothe well apere
  My frend ys tornyd my foo;
But syns there ys no defence
I must take pacyence.   30

Who wold have euer thowght
   A hart that was so sett,
To have suche wrong me wrowght
   Or to be cownterfett?
But who that trustythe most   35
Ys lyke to pay the cost.

I must of force, god wott,
   Thys paynfull lyff susteyen;
And yet I know nott
   The chefe cawse of my payn;   40
Thys ys a strange dyssease:
To serve and neuer plese.

I must of force endure
   Thys drawght drawyn awry,
Ffor I am fast and sure   45
   To have the mate therby;
But note I wyll thys texte,
To draw better the nexte.

119

In faythe methynkes yt ys no Ryght
   To hate me thus ffor lovyng ye;
So fayre a face, so full off spyght,
   Who wold have thowght suche crueltye?
   But syns there ys no Remedye   5
That by no meanes ye can me love,
I shall you leve and other prove.

Ffor yff I have for my good wyll
   No reward els but cruelltye,
In faythe thereoff I can no skyll   10
   Sythe that I lovyd ye honestlye;

But take hede I wyll tyll I dye
Or that I love so well agayn,
Syns women vse so muche to fayn.

13 *or*] *ere*

120

THE knott whych ffyrst my hart dyd strayn,
  Whan that your servant I becam,
Doth bynde me styll for to Remayne
  All waies your owne, as nowe I am:
And yff ye fynde that I do ffayn,   5
  With just judgement my selffe I dam
    To haue dysdayn.

Iff other thowght in me do growe
  Butt styll to love yow stedefastly,
Yff that the profe do nott well showe   10
  That I am yowrs assueredly,
Lett euery welth turne me to woo,
  And yow to be contynually
    My chefest foo.

Yff other love or newe request   15
  Do ese my hart, but only thys,
Or yf within my weryd brest
  Be hyd one thowght that mene amys,
I do desyer that myne vnrest
  May styll encrease, and I to myss   20
    That I love best.

Yff in my love ther be one spott
  Off false deceyte or doblenes,
Or yff I mynde to slypp thys knott
  By want of fayth or stedefastnes,   25
Lett all my sarwyes be forgott,
  And when I would have cheefe redresse
    Esteme me nott.

110

But yff that I consume in payn
   Of burnynge syghes and fervent love,   30
And daly seke non other gayn
   But with my dede thes wordes to prove,
Me thynke off Ryght I shuld optayne
   That ye wulde mynde for to remove
       Yowr gret dysdayn.   35

And for the ende off thys my songe
   Vnto yowr handys I do submytt
My dedly greff and payns so stronge,
   Whych in my harte be fermly shytt:
And when ye lyst, redresse my wronge,   40
   Syns well ye knowe this paynfull fytt
       Hath last to longe.

26 *sarwyes*] *service* 39 *shytt*] *shut*

121

IT was my choyse, yt was no chaunce
   That browght my hart in others holde,
Wherby ytt hath had sufferaunce
   Lenger, perde, then Reason wold;
Syns I ytt bownd where ytt was free   5
   Me thynkes ywys of Ryght yt shold
       Acceptyd be.

Acceptyd be withowte Refuse,
   Vnles that fortune have the power
All Ryght of love for to abuse;   10
   For, as they say, one happy howre
May more prevayle then Ryght or myght,
   Yf fortune then lyst for to lowre,
       What vaylyth Right?

What vaylyth Ryght yff thys be trew?   15
    Then trust to chaunce and go by gesse.
Then who so lovyth may well go sew,
    Vncerten hope for hys redresse.
Yett some wolde say assueredly
    Thou mayst appele for thy relesse   20
        To fantasy.

To fantasy pertaynys to chose:
    All thys I knowe, for fantasy
Ffurst vnto love dyd me induse;
    But yet I knowe as stedefastly   25
That yff love haue no faster knott,
    So nyce a choyse slyppes sodenly.
        Yt lastyth nott.

Itt lastyth not that stondes by change;
    Fansy doth change; fortune ys frayle: 30
Both thes to plese the way ys strange.
    Therfore me thynkes best to prevayle:
Ther ys no way that ys so just
    As trowgh to lede, tho tother fayle,
        And therto trust.   35

17 *sew*] *sue* 34 *trowgh*] *truth*

122

So vnwarely was never no man cawght
With stedefast loke apon a goodly face
As I of late: for sodenly, me thowght,
    My hart was torne owte of hys place.

Thorow myn Iye the strock frome hyrs dyd slyde, 5
Dyrectly downe vnto my hert ytt ranne;
In helpe wherof the blood therto dyd glyde,
    And left my face both pale and wann.

Then was I like a man for woo amasyd,
Or like the byrde that flyeth into the fyer;   10
For whyll that I on her beaulte gasyd,
    The more I burnt in my desyre.

Anon the blowd stert in my face agayn,
Enflamde with hete that yt had att my hert,
And browght therwith therowt in euery vayne 15
    A qwakynd hete with plesaunt smert.

Then was I like the strawe, when that the flame
Ys drevyn therin by force and rage off wynd;
I can nott tell, alas, what I shall blame,
    Nor what to seke, nor what to fynd.   20

But wele I wote the greffe holdes me so sore
In hete and cold betwyxt hope and drede,
That but her helpe to helth doth me restore,
    Thys restles lyff I may nott lede.

16 *qwakynd*] *quickened*

123

Howe shulde I
  Be so plesaunte
  In mye semblaunt
As my fellowes bee?

Not long agoo   5
It chaunsed soo
  As I ded walke alone
I harde a man
That nowe and than
  Himself ded thus bemone: 10

Alas (*he saide*)
I am betraide
  And vttrelye ondone;
Whome I dede trust
And think so iuste   15
  Another man hathe wonne.

Mye servise due
And herte so true
  On her I ded bestow;
I never ment   20
For to repente
  Yn welthe nor yet in woo.

Love ded asyen
Her to be myn
  And not to love non nue;   25
But who can bynd
Ther ffeckell kynd
  That never wyll be tru.

Eche westerne winde
Hathe turnid her minde   30
  And blowen it clene awaye;
Therebye my welthe,
My mirth and helthe,
  Are dryven to grete dekaye.

Ffortune ded smyle   35
A righte shorte while
  And never saide me naye,
With plesaunte plaes
And joyfull dayes
  My tyme to passe awaye.   40

Allas! Ah las!
The tyme so was,
   So never shall it be,
Sins she is gone
And I alone   45
   Armeles as ye maye see.

Where is the othe,
Where is the trothe
   That she to me ded gyve?
Such fayned wordes   50
With selie boordes
   Lett no wise man beleve.

Ffor even as I
Thus wofullye
   Vnto my self complaine,   55
Yf ye then truste
Nedes lerne ye muste
   To sing my song in vayne.

Howe shulde I
   Be so plesaunte   60
   In mye semblaunt
As my fellowes bee?

124

FULL well yt maye be sene
   To suche as vnderstand
How some there be that wene
   They haue theyre welthe at hand,
     Throughe loves abusyd band;   5
But lytyll do they see
Th'abuse wherin they bee.

115

Of loue there ys a kynd
  Whyche kyndlythe by abuse,
As in a feble mynd,   10
  Whome fansy may enduce
  By loues dysceatefull vse,
To folowe the fond lust
And profe of a vayn trust.

As I my self maye saye   15
  By tryall of the same,
No wyght can well bewraye
  The falshed loue can frame;
  I saye, twixt grefe and grame,
Ther ys no lyvyng man   20
That knows the crafte loue can.

Ffor loue so well can fayn
  To favour for the whyle,
That suche as sekes the gayn
  Ar servyd with the gyle;   25
  And some can thys concyle,
To gyue the symple leave
Them sellfes for to dysceave

What thyng may more declare
  Of loue the craftye kynd   30
Then se the wyse, so ware,
  In loue to be so blynd?
  Yf so yt be assynd,
Let them enjoye the gayn,
That thynkes yt worthe the payn. 35

26 *concyle*] *conceal*

116

125

SYNS loue ys suche that, as ye wott,
  Cannot always be wysely vsyd,
I say therfore then blame me nott,
  Tho I therin haue ben abusyd;
    Ffor as with cause I am accusyd,   5
Gyllty I graunt, suche was my lott,
  And tho yt cannot be excusyd
Yet let suche folye be forgott.

Ffor in my yeres of rekles youthe
  Me thought the power of loue so gret   10
That to her lawes I bound my trouthe
  And to my wyll there was no lett.
    Me lyst nomore so far to fett
Suche frute lo as of loue ensewthe;
  The gayn was small that was to gett,   15
And of the losse the lesse the reuthe.

And few there ys but fyrst or last
  A tyme in loue ons shall they haue;
And glad I am my tyme ys past,
  Henceforthe my fredome to withsaue.   20
    Now in my hart there shall I grave
The groundyd grace that now I tast;
  Thankyd be fortune that me gave
So fayre a gyfft, so sure and fast.

Now suche as haue me sene or thys,   25
  When youthe in me sett forthe hys kynd,
And foly framd my thought amys,
  The faute wherof now well I ffynd,
    Loo, syns that so yt ys assynd
That vnto eche a tyme there ys,   30
  Then blame the lott that led my mynd
Sometyme to lyue in loves blys.

But frome henceforthe I do protest
   By presse of that that I haue past,
Shall neuer ceace within my brest   35
    The power of loue so late owt cast;
    The knott therof ys knytt ffull fast,
And I therto so sure proffest,
   Ffor euermore with me to last
The power wherin I am possest.   40

25 or] *ere*

126

Lo! how I seke and sew to haue
   That no man hathe and maye be had!
There ys no more but synk or saue,
   And bryng thys doute to good or bad.
   To lyue in sorows, allways sad,   5
I lyke not so to lynger fforthe;
   Hap evyll or good I shallbe glad
To take that comes as well in worthe.

Shold I sustayn thys gret dystres,
   Styll wandryng forthe thus to and froo, 10
In dredfull hope to hold my pese,
   And fede my sellf with secret woo?
   Nay, nay, certayne I wyll not soo;
But sure I shall my self aply
   To put in profe thys doute to knoo 15
And Rydd thys daunger Redely.

I shall assay by secret sute
   To show the mynd of myn entent,
And my desertes shall gyue suche frute
   As with my hart my wordes be ment. 20

118

So by the profe of thys consent
Sone, owt of doute, I shall be sure;
For to rejoyce or to Repent,
In joye or payn for to endure.

1 *sew] sue*

127

My loue ys lyke vnto th'eternall fyre,
And I as those whyche therin do remayn,
Whose grevous paynes ys but theyre gret desyre
To se the syght whyche they may not attayn.
So in helles heate my self I fele to be,   5
That am restraynd by gret extremyte
The syght of her whyche ys so dere to me.
O puissant loue and power of gret avayle,
By whome hell may be fellt or dethe assayle!

9 *or] ere*

128

Syns so ye please to here me playn,
And that ye do rejoyce my smart,
Me lyst no lenger to remayn
To suche as be so overthwart.

But cursyd be that cruell hart   5
Whyche hathe procuryd a careles mynd
Ffor me and myn vnfaynyd smart,
And forcythe me suche fautes to fynd.

More than to muche I am assuryd
Of thyn entent, wherto to trust;   10
A spedles proffe I haue enduryd,
And now I leve yt to them that lust.

119

129

Now must I lerne to lyue at rest
   And weyne me of my wyll,
Ffor I repent where I was prest
   My fansy to ffullfyll.

I may no lenger more endure   5
   My wontyd lyf to lede,
But I must lerne to put in vre
   The change of womanhede.

I may not see my seruys long
   Rewardyd in suche wyse,   10
Nor may I not sustayn suche wrong
   That ye my loue dyspyce.

I may not syghe in sorows depe,
   Nor wayle the wante of loue,
Nor I may nother cruche nor crepe   15
   Where hyt dothe not behoue.

But I of force must nedes forsake
   My faythe so fondly sett,
And frome henceforthe must vndertake
   Suche foly to fforgett.   20

Now must I seke some otherways
   My self for to withsaue,
And as I trust by myn assays
   Some Remedy to haue.

I aske none other Remedy   25
   To recompence my wronge
But ons to haue the lyberty
   That I haue lakt so long.

2 *weyne]* *ween* 15 *cruche]* *crouch*

130

FFORGET not yet the tryde entent
Of suche a truthe as I haue ment,
My gret travayle so gladly spent
    Fforget not yet.

Fforget not yet when fyrst began   **5**
The wery lyffe ye know syns whan,
The sute, the seruys none tell can.
    Fforgett not yett.

Fforget not yet the gret assays,
The cruell wrong, the skornfull ways,   **10**
The paynfull pacyence in denays,
    Fforgett not yet.

Fforget not yet, forget not thys,
How long ago hathe ben and ys
The mynd that neuer ment amys,   **15**
    Fforget not yet.

Fforget not then thyn owne aprovyd,
The whyche so long hathe the so lovyd,
Whose stedfast faythe yet neuer movyd,
    Fforget not thys.   **20**

131

O MYSERABLE sorow withowten cure
  Yf it plese the, lo, to haue me thus suffir,
At lest yet let her know what I endure,
    And this my last voyse cary thou thether
    Wher lyved my hope now ded for ever;   **5**
For as ill grevus is my banyshement
As was my plesur whan she was present.

132

BLAME not my lute for he must sownde
   Of thes or that as liketh me;
For lake of wytt the lutte is bownde
   To gyve suche tunes as plesithe me:
Tho my songes be sume what strange,   5
And spekes suche wordes as toche thy change,
     Blame not my lutte.

My lutte, alas, doth not ofende,
   Tho that perforus he must agre
To sownde suche teunes as I entende   10
   To sing to them that hereth me;
Then tho my songes be some what plain,
And tochethe some that vse to fayn,
     Blame not my lutte.

My lute and strynges may not deny,   15
   But as I strike they must obay;
Brake not them than soo wrongfully,
   But wryeke thy selff some wyser way:
And tho the songes whiche I endight
Do qwytt thy chainge with rightfull spight,   20
     Blame not my lute.

Spyght askyth spight and changing change,
   And falsyd faith must nedes be knowne;
The faute so grett, the case so strainge,
   Of right it must abrode be blown: 25
Then sins that by thyn own desartt
My soinges do tell how trew thou artt,
     Blame not my lute.

Blame but the selffe that hast mysdown
   And well desaruid to haue blame;   30
Change thou thy way, so evyll bygown,
   And then my lute shall sownde that same:

But if tyll then my fyngeres play
By thy desartt their wontyd way,
      Blame not my lutte.   35

Farwell, vnknowne, for tho thow brake
   My strynges in spight with grett desdayn,
Yet haue I fownde owtt for thy sake
   Stringes for to strynge my lute agayne;
And yf perchance this folysh Rymyme   40
Do make the blushe at any tyme,
      Blame nott my lutte.

9 *perforus*] *perforce* 29 *mysdown*] *misdone* 31 *bygown*]
 begone

133

ALL yn thi sight my lif doth hole depende;
   Thou hidist thyself and I must dye therefore;
But sins thou maiste so easilye saue thy frende,
   Why doste thou styk to heale that thou madist sore?
Whye doo I dye, sins thou maist me deffende?   5
   For if I dye, then maiste thou lyve no more:
Sins ton bye tother dothe lyve and fede thy herte,
I with thye sight, thou also with my smerte.

7 *ton*] *the one*

134

PERDYE I saide yt not
   Nor never thought to do,
As well as I ye wott
   I have no powre thereto;
And if I ded, the lott   5
   That first ded me enchaine
Do never slake the knott
   But strayt it to my payne.
           123

And if I ded, eche thing
   That maye do harme or woo   10
Contynuallye maye wring
   My herte whereso I goo;
Reporte maye always ring
   Of shame of me for aye,
Yf yn my herte ded spring   15
   The worde that ye doo saye.

Yf I saide so, eche sterre
   That is yn heven above
Maye frowne on me to marre
   The hope I have yn love;   20
And if I ded, suche warre
   As they brought vnto Troye
Bring all my lyf afarre
   From all this luste and joye.

And if I ded so saye,   25
   The bewtye that me bounde
Encresse from daye to daye
   More cruell to my wounde,
With all the mone that maye
   To playnte maye torne my song;   30
My lif maye sone dekaye
   Without redresse bye wrong.

Yf I be clere fro thought,
   Whye do ye then complaine?
Then ys this thing but sought   35
   To torne me to more payne.
Then that that ye haue wrought
   Ye must yt now redresse;
Of right therefore ye ought
   Suche Rigor to represse.   40

And as I haue deseruid,
   So graunte me nowe my hire;
Ye kno I never swervid,
   Ye never fownd me lyre.
For Rachell have I seruid,   45
   (For Lya carid I never)
And her I have Reseruid
   Within my herte for ever.

44 *lyre*] *liar* 46 *Lya*] *Leah*

135

THE fructe of all the seruise that I serue
   Dispaire doth repe, such haples hap have I;
But tho he have no powre to make me swarve,
   Yet bye the fire for colde I fele I dye.
In paradis for hunger still I sterve,   5
   And in the flowde for thurste to deth I drye;
So Tantalus ame I and yn worse payne,
Amyds my helpe and helples doth remayne.

136

YF with complaint the paine might be exprest
   That inwardelye dothe cause me sigh and grone,
Your harde herte and your cruell brest
Shulde sighe and playne for my vnreste;
   And tho yt ware of stone   5
Yet shulde Remorse cause yt relent and mone.

But sins yt ys so farre out of mesure
   That with my wordes I can yt not contayne,
My ouerlye truste, my hertes tresure,
Alas whye doo I still indure   10
   This resteles smerte and payne,
Sins yf ye list ye maye my woo restraine?

137

Sins you will nedes that I shall sing,
  Take yt in worth siche as I have,
Plentye of plaint, mone and morning,
    Yn depe dispaire and dedlye payne,
  Boteles for boote, crying to crave,   5
      To crave yn vayne.

Suche hammers worke within my hed
  That sounde nought els vnto my eris
But faste at borde and wake abed:
    Suche tune the tempre to my song   10
  To waile my wrong, that I wante teris
      To waile my wrong.

Dethe and dispaire afore my face,
  My dayes dekaes, my grefe doth gro;
The cause thereof is in this place,   15
    Whom crueltye dothe still constraine
  For to reioise, tho yt be wo
      To here me plaine.

A brokin lute, vntunid stringes
  With such a song maye well bere parte,   20
That nether pleasith him that singes
    Nor theim that here, but her alone
  That with her herte wold straine my herte
      To here yt grone.

Yf it greve you to here this same   25
  That you do fele but in my voyse,
Considre then what plesaunt game
    I do sustaine in everye parte
  To cause me sing or to reioyse
      Within my herte.   30

138

Me list no more to sing
Of love nor of suche thing,
Howe sore that yt me wring;
  For what I song or spake
  Men dede my songis mistake.   5

My songes ware to defuse,
Theye made folke to muse;
Therefor, me to excuse,
  Theye shall be song more plaine,
  Nothr of joye nor payne.   10

What vaileth then to skippe
At fructe over the lippe?
  For frute withouten taste
  Dothe noght but rott and waste.

What vailith vndre kaye   15
To kepe treasure alwaye,
That never shall se daye?
  Yf yt be not vsid,
  Yt ys but abusid.

What vayleth the flowre   20
To stond still and whither?
Yf no man yt savour,
  Yt servis onlye for sight
  And fadith towardes night.

Therefore fere not t'assaye   25
To gadre ye that maye
The flower that this daye
  Is fresher than the next:
  Marke well, I saye, this text.

Let not the frute be lost   30
That is desired moste;
Delight shall quite the coste.
　　Yf hit be tane in tyme,
　　Small labour is to clyme.

And as for siche treasure   35
That makithe the the richer,
And no dele the porer,
　　When it is gyven or lente
　　Me thinkes yt ware well spente.

Yf this be undre miste,   40
And not well playnlye wyste,
Vndrestonde me who lyste;
　　For I reke not a bene,
　　I wott what I doo meane.

139

To Rayle or geste ye kno I vse yt not,
　　Though that such cause some tyme in folkes I
　　finde:
　　And tho to chaung ye list to sett your minde,
　　Love yt who liste, in faithe I like yt not.
And if ye ware to me as ye are not,   5
　　I wolde be lothe to se you so unkinde;
　　But sins your faithe muste nedes be so, be kinde:
　　Tho I hate yt, I praye you leve yt not.
Thinges of grete waight I neuer thought to crave:
　　This is but small—of right denye yt not.   10
　　Your fayning wayis as yet forget them not,
But like rewarde let other lovers have:
　　That is to saye, for seruis true and faste,
　　To long delaies and changing at the laste.

3 *chaung*] *change* 14 *To*] *Too*

140

THE Joye so short, alas, the paine so nere,
 The waye so long, the departure so smarte,
The furst sight, alas, I bought to dere,
 That so sodainelye now from hens must parte;
 The bodye gone, yet remaine shall the herte 5
With her, the which for me salte teris ded raine,
And shall not chaunge till that we mete againe.

The tyme doth passe, yet shall not my love;
 Tho I be farre, always my hert is nere;
Tho other chaunge, yet will not I remove; 10
 Tho other care not, yet love I will and fere;
 Tho other hate, yet will I love my dere;
Tho other woll of lightnes saye adewe,
Yet woll I be founde stedefast and trewe.

When other laughe, alas then do I wepe; 15
 When other sing, then do I waile and crye;
When other runne, perforcyd I am to crepe;
 When other daunce, in sorro I do lye;
 When other joye, for paine welnere I dye;
Thus brought from welthe, alas, to endles paine,
That undeseruid, causeles to remayne. 21

141

Payne of all payne, the most grevous paine
Ys to loue hartelye and cannot be loued againe.

Love with vnkindenesse is cause of hevenis,
 Of inwarde sorro and sighis painefull.
Whereas I love is no redresse 5
 To no manner of pastime, the sprites so dull
 With prive morninges and lookes Rufull;
The boddye all wrislye, the collor pale and wan,
More like a gost then lyk a lyving man.

Whan Cupido hath inflamid the hertes desires   10
   To love there as ys disdayne,
Of good or ill the minde oblivyous,
   Nothing regarding but love t'attaine;
   Alwais imagining by what meane or traine
Yt may be at rest; thus in a momente   15
Now here, now there, being never contente.

Tossing and torning, whan the body wold rest,
   With dreamis opprest and visions fantastycall,
Sleping or waking love is ever preste,
   Some tyme to wepe, some tyme to crye and call,
   Bewayling his fortune and lif bestiall;   21
Nowe in hope of recure and now in dispaire,
This ys a sorye lyf to lyve alwaye in care!

Recorde of Therence in his commedis poeticall:
   Yn love ys jelosye and inimis mannye oon,   25
Angre and debate, with mynde sensuall,
   Nowe warre, nowe peace, musing all alone;
   Some tyme all morte and colde as enye stone.
This causith unkindenesse of suche as cannot skill
Of trewe love assurde with herte and good will. 30

Lucrese the Romaine for love of her lorde
   And bye cause perforce she had commit advow-
     trye
With Tarquinus (as the storye doth recorde)
   Her self ded slee with a knif most pituoslye
   Among her nigh frendes; bye cause that she   35
So falslye was betrayed, lo this was the guardon!
Where as true love hathe no domynyon.

To make rehersall of old antiquitye
   What nedeth yt? We see by experience
Among lovers yt chaunsith daylye   40

Displeasor and variaunce for none offens:
But if true love might gyve sentens,
That vnkindenes and disdayne shuld have no place,
But true harte for true love, yt ware a grete grace.

O Venus, ladye, of love the goddesse   45
  Help all true lovers to have love againe!
Bannishe from thye presens disdayne and vnkind-
    nesse,
  Kyndnesse and pytie to thy seruice Retayne;
  For true love, ons fixed in the cordiall vayne
Can never be revoulsid bye no manner of arte, 50
Vnto the sowle from the boddye departe.

24 *Therence*] *Terence*

142 [1]

LAMENT my losse, my labor, and my payne,
  All ye that here mye wofull playnte and crye;
Yf ever man might ons your herte constrayne
  To pytie wordes of right, yt shulde bee I,
That sins the tyme that youthe yn me ded rayne   5
  My pleasaunte yeris to bondage ded aplye,
Wiche as yt was I pourpose to declare,
Wherebye my frendes hereafter maye be ware.

And if perchaunce some redres list to muse
  What menith me so playnlye for to wright,   10
My good entente the fawte of yt shall skuse,
  Wiche meane nothing, but trulye to endyght
The crafte and care, the greef and long abuse
  Of lovers lawe and eke her puissaunte mighte,
Wiche though that man oft tymes bye paynis doth
    kno,   15
Lyttle theye wot wiche wayes the gylis doth growe.

[1] Chambers suggests that this poem is an envoi to a projected volume.

131

Yet well ye kno yt will renewe my smerte
   Thus to rehearse the paynes that I have past;
My hand doth shake, my pen skant dothe his parte,
   My boddye quakes, my wyttis begynne to waste:
Twixt heate and colde, in fere I fele my herte   21
   Panting for paine, and thus, as all agaste
I do remayne, skant wotting what I wright,
Perdon me then, rudelye tho I indyte.

And patiently, O Redre, I the praye,   25
   Take in good parte this worke as yt ys mente,
And greve the not with ought that I shall saye,
   Sins with good will this boke abrode ys sente,
To tell men howe in youthe I ded assaye
   What love ded mene and nowe I yt repente: 30
That musing me my frendes might well be ware,
And kepe them fre from all soche payne and care.

9 redres] readers

143

WHAT shulde I saye
   Sins faithe is dede,
And truthe awaye
   From you ys fled?
   Shulde I be led   5
With doblenesse?
Naye, naye, mistresse!

I promiside you
   And you promisid me
To be as true   10
   As I wolde bee;
   But sins I se
Your doble herte,
Farewell my perte!

Though for to take   15
  Yt ys not my minde
But to forsake—
  I am not blind—
  And as I finde
So will I truste.   20
Farewell, vniuste!

Can ye saye naye?
  But you saide
That I allwaye
  Shulde be obeide;   25
  And thus betraide
Or that I wiste—
Fare well, vnkiste!

27 *or*] *ere*

144

GYVE place all ye that doth reioise
  And loves panges doth clene forgett;
Let them drawe nere and here my voyse,
  Whom love dothe force in paynes to frett:
  For all of playnte my song is sett,   5
  Wiche long hath serued and nought can gett.

A faithefull herte so trulye mente
  Rewarded is full slenderelye;
A stedfaste faithe with good entente
  Ys recompensid craftelye: 10
  Such hap dothe hap vnhappelye
  To them that mene but honestlye.

With humble sute I have assayde
  To tourne her cruell-hertid minde;
But for rewarde I am delaide,   15

And to mye welthe here eris be blinde:
Lo! thus bye chaunse I am assignid
With stedfast love to serue the vnkinde.

What vaylithe trothe or stedfastenesse
    Or still to serue without repreffe?   20
What vaylith faithe or gentilnesse,
    Where crueltie dothe raine as chefe?
    Alas, there is no greter greeff
    Then for to love and lake releffe!

Care dothe constraine me to complaine   25
    Of love and her vncertaintye,
Wich grauntith nought but grete disdayne,
    For losse of all my libretye.
    Alas, this is extremytye,
    For love to finde suche crueltye!   30

For hertye love to finde suche stroke,
    Alas, it is a carefull lott;
And for to voide so fowle a moke,
    There is no waye but slip the knott.
    The gayne so colde, the payne so hott,   35
    Prayse yt who list, I like yt not.

16 *here*] *her*

145

DYVERS dothe vse as I have hard and kno,
    When that to chaunge ther ladies do beginne,
    To morne and waile, and neuer for to lynne,
Hoping therbye to pease ther painefull woo.
And some ther be, that when it chanseth soo   5
    That women change and hate where love hath bene,
    Thei call them fals, and think with woordes to wynne
The hartes of them wich otherwhere dothe gro.

But as for me, though that by chaunse indede
  Change hath outworne the favor that I had,   10
I will not wayle, lament, nor yet be sad;
Nor call her fals that falsley ded me fede:
  But let it passe and think it is of kinde,
  That often chaunge doth plese a womans minde.

146

  THE losse is small to lese such one,
    That shrynckith for a slendr naye;
  And wyt thei lak that wolde mak mone,
    Tho all such peakes ware wipid awaye

147

  SPIGHT hathe no powre to make me sadde
    Nor scornefulnesse to make me playne;
  Yt doth suffise that ons I had,
    And so to leve yt is no payne.

  Let theim frowne on that leste dothe gaine,   5
Who ded reioise must nedes be gladd;
  And tho with wordis thou wenist to rayne,
Yt doth suffise that ons I had.

Sins that in chekes thus overthwarte
  And coylye lookis thou doste delight,   10
Yt doth suffise that myne thou warte,
  Tho change hathe put thye faithe to flight.

  Alas, it is a pevishe spight
To yelde thiself and then to parte,
  But sins thou setst thie faithe so light,   15
Yt doth suffise that myne thou warte.

And sins thye love dothe thus declyne
  And in thye herte suche hate dothe grow,
Yt dothe suffise that thou warte myne,
  And with good will I quite yt soo.   20

  Some tyme my frende, fare well my foo,
Sins thou change I am not thyne,
  But for relef of all my woo
Yt dothe suffise that thou warte myne.

Prayeng you all that heris this song   25
  To iudge no wight, nor none to blame;
Yt dothe suffise she dothe me wrong
  And that herself doth kno the same.

And tho she chaing, it is no shame;
Theire kinde it is and hathe bene long;   30
  Yet I proteste she hath no name:
Yt dothe suffise she dothe me wrong.

29 *chaing*] *change*

148

Grudge on who liste, this ys my lott,
No thing to want if it ware not.

My yeris be yong even as ye see,
All thinges thereto doth well agre,
Yn faithe, in face, in eche degre   5
No thing doth wante, as semith me,
    If yt ware not.

Some men dothe saye that frendes be skarce,
But I have founde as in this cace
A frende wiche gyvith to no man place,   10
But makis me happiest that euer was,
    Yf it were not.

Grudge on who list, this is my lot,
No thing to want if yt ware not.

A hart I have besidis all this,   15
That hathe my herte and I have his;
If he dothe well yt is my blis,
And when we mete no lak there is
    Yf it ware not.

Yf he can finde that can me please,   20
A thinckes he dois his owne hertes ease;
And likewise I coulde well apease
The chefest cause of his misease,
    Yf it ware not.

Grudge on who list, this is my lot,   25
No thing to want if it ware not.

A master eke god hath me sente,
To hom my will is hollye bente,
To serue and love for the intente
That bothe we might be well contente,   30
    Yf it ware not.

And here an ende: yt dothe suffise
To speke fewe wordes among the wise.
Yet take this note before your eyes:
My mirthe shulde doble ons or twise,   35
    Yf it ware not.

Grudge on who list, this is my lot,
No thing to want if it ware not.

21 *A = he*
28 *hom] whom hollye] wholly*

149[1]

FFORTUNE dothe frowne:
  What remedye?
I am downe
  Bye destenye.

150

A! MY herte, a! what aileth the
To sett so light my libretye,
Making me bonde when I was fre?
  A! my herte, a! what aileth thee?

When thou ware rid from all distresse,   5
Voyde of all paine and pensifnesse,
To chose againe a new mistresse,
  A! my herte, a! what aileth thee?

When thou ware well, thou could not hold;
To tourne agayne that ware to bold: 10
Thus to renue my sorrowes olde,
  A! my herte, a! what aileth thee?

Tho knoist full well that but of late
I was tournid out of loves gate,
And now to guide me to this mate,   15
  A! my herte, a! what aileth thee?

I hopte full well all had ben done,
But nowe my hope is tane and won,
To my tourment to yelde so sone,
  A! my herte, a! what aileth thee?   20

---

[1] This quatrain is copied in the same hand as the surrounding
poems, which are all assumed to be Wyatt's.

151

HATE whome ye list, for I kare not;
Love whom ye list and spare not;
Do what ye list and drede not;
Think what ye liste, I fere not:
For as for me I am not,   5
But even as one that reckes not
Whyther ye hate or hate not;
For yn your love I dote not;
Wherefore I praye you, forget not,
But love whom ye liste, ffor I care not.   10

152

GRETING to you bothe yn hertye wyse
   As vnknowen I sende, and this mye entente
As I do here, you to aduertyse,
   Lest that perchaunce your deades you do repente.
    The vnknowen man dredes not to be shente,   5
But sayes as he thinkes: so fares yt bye me,
That nother ffere nor hope in no degree.

The bodye and the sowle to holde togiddre,
   Yt is but right and reason woll the same,
And ffryndelie the oon to love the other   10
   Yt incresith your brute and also your fame;
    But marke well my wordes, for I fere no blame:
Truste well your selves, but ware ye trust no mo,
For suche as ye think your frende maye fortune be your
    ffo.

Beware hardelye ere ye have enye nede,   15
   And to frendes reconsilide trust not greatelye;
Ffor theye that ons with hastie spede
   Exiled them selves out of your companye,
    Though theye tourne againe and speke farelye,

Fayning them selves to be your frendes faste,   20
Beware of them, for theye will disseyeve you at laste.

Fayre wordes makis ffoolys fayne,
   And bering in hande causith moche woo,
For tyme tryeth trothe, therefore refrayne:
   And from suche as be redye to doo—   25
   None doo I name but this I kno,
That bye this faute cause causith moche,
Therefore beware if yo do know anye suche.

To wise folkes fewe wordes is an old sayeng;
   Therefore at this tyme I will write nomore,   30
But this short lesson take fore a warninge:
   Bye soche light frendes sett littill store;
   Yf ye do othere wise ye will repent yt sore.
And thus of this lettre making an ende,
To the boddye and the sowle I me commend.   35

Wryting lyfles at the manner place
   Of him that hathe no chave nore no were dothe dwell,
But wandering in the wilde worlde, wanting that he hase,
   And nother hopis nor ffearis heven nor hell;
   But lyvith at adventure, ye kno him full well,   40
The twentie daye of marche he wrote yt yn his house,
And hathe him recommendyd to the kat and the mowse.

36 *manner place = some place or other*

153

MYE love toke skorne my servise to retaine
   Wherein me thought she vsid crueltie:
   Sins with good will I lost my libretye
To followe her wiche causith all my payne.

Might never care cause me for to refrayne,   **5**
  But onlye this wiche is extremytie:
  Gyving me nought, alas, not to agree
That as I was her man I might remayne.
But sins that thus ye list to ordre me,
  That wolde have bene your seruaunte true and
    faste,   **10**
  Displese the not, my doting dayes bee paste:
And with my losse to leve I must agre;
  For as there is a certeyne tyme to rage,
  So ys there tyme suche madnes to asswage.

154

Tanglid I was yn loves snare,
Opprest with payne, tormente with care,
Of grefe right sure, of Joye full bare,
  Clene in dispaire bye crueltye;
  But ha, ha, ha, full well is me,   **5**
  For I am now at libretye.

The wofull dayes so full of paine,
The werye night all spent in vayne,
The labor lost for so small gayne,
  To wryt them all yt will not bee;   **10**
  But ha, ha, ha, full well is me,
  For I am now at libretye.

Everye thing that faire doth sho,
When prof is made yt provithe not soo,
But tournith mirthe to bittre woo,   **15**
  Wiche in this case full well I see;
  But ha, ha, ha, full well is me,
  For I am now at libretye.

To grete desire was my guide,
And wanton will went bye my syde;   20
Hope rulid still and made me byde
    Of loves craft th'extremitye.
    But ha, ha, ha, full well is me,
    For I am now at libretye.

With faynid wordes wich ware but winde   25
To long delayes I was assind;
Her wylye lokes my wyttes ded blinde;
    Thus as she wolde I ded agree.
    But ha, ha, ha, full well is me,
    For I am now at libretye.   30

Was never birde tanglid yn lyme
That brake awaye yn bettre tyme,
Then I that rotten bowes ded clyme,
    And had no hurte but scaped fre.
    Now ha, ha, ha, full well is me,   35
    For I am nowe at libretye.

19 *to*] *too*

155

    LONGRE to muse
    On this refuse
    I will not vse,
        But studye to forget;
    Lett my all goo,   5
    Sins well I kno
    To be my foo
        Her herte is fermely sett.

    Sins my entent
    So trulye mente   10
    Cannot contente
        Her minde as I doo see,

To tell you playne
Yt ware yn vayne
For so small gaine   15
 To lese my libretie.

For if he thryve
That will goo stryve
A shippe to dryve
 Againste the streme and winde,   20
Vndoutedlye
Then thryve shuld I
To love trulye
 A cruell-hertid mynde.

But sithe that so   25
The worlde dothe goo
That everye woo
 Bye yelding doth incresse,
As I have tolde
I wilbe bolde   30
 Therebye my paynis to cese.

Prayeng you all
That after shall
Bye fortune fall
 Ynto this folishe trade,   35
Have yn your minde,
As I do finde,
That oft bekinde
 All womens love do fade.

Wherefore apace,   40
Come, take my place,
Some man that hase
 A lust to berne the fete;
For sins that she
Refusith me,   45
I must agre
 And perdye to forgett.

156

Love doth againe
Put me to payne
   And yet all is but lost,
I serve yn vayne
And am certeyne   5
   Of all mislikid most.

Bothe heate and colde
Dothe so me holde
   And combred so my minde,
That when I shulde   10
Speke and beholde
   Yt dryvith me still behinde.

My wittis be paste,
My lif doth waste,
   My comforte is exild,   15
And I in haste
Am like to taste
   How love hathe me begilde.

Onles that right
Maye yn her sight   20
   Obtaine pitye and grace,
Whye shulde a wight
Have bewtye bright
   Yf mercye have no place?

Yett I, alas,   25
Am in soche cace
   That bak I cannot goo,
But still forth trace
A patiente pace
   And suffre secret woo: 30

Ffor with the winde
My fyred mynde
   Dothe still inflame;
And she vnkinde
That ded me binde   35
   Dothe turne yt all to game.

Yet can no payne
Make me refraine
   Nor here and there to range;
I shall retaine   40
Hope to obtayne
   Her hert that is so straunge.

But I require
The paynefull fire
   That oft doth make me swete,   45
For all my yre,
Withe lyke desire
   To gyve her herte a hete.

Then shall she prove
Howe I her love   50
   And what I have offerde,
Wiche shulde her move
For to remove
   The paynes that I have sufferd.

And bettre ffe   55
Then she gave me
   She shall of me attayne,
For whereas she
Showde crueltye,
   She shall my hert obtayne.   60

swete] *sweat* 55 *ffe*] *fee*
45 -

157

WYTH seruing still
  This have I wone,
For my godwill
  To be vndone;

And for redresse   5
  Of all my payne,
Disdaynefulnes
  I have againe.

And for reward
  Of all my smarte   10
Lo, thus vnharde,
  I must departe!

Wherefore all ye
  That after shall
Bye ffortune be,   15
  As I am, thrall,

Example take
  What I have won,
Thus for her sake
  To be vndone!   20

158

Now all of chaunge
  Must be my songe
And from mye bonde nowe must I breke,
  Sins she so strange
  Vnto my wrong
Doth stopp her eris to here me speke.   5

FROM THE DEVONSHIRE MS. ADD. 17492

Yet none doth kno
    So well as she
My greefe wiche can have no restrainte;
    That faine wolde follo   10
    Nowe nedes must fle
For faute of ere vnto my playnte.

I am not he
    Bye fals assayes
Nor faynid faith can bere in hande,   15
    Tho most I see
    That such alwaes
Are best for to be vnderstonde.

But I that truth
    Hath alwaies ment   20
Dothe still procede to serue in vayne;
    Desire pursuith
    My tyme mispent,
And doth not passe vppon my payne.

O fortunes might   25
    That eche compellis,
And me the most, yt dothe suffise
    Now for my right
    To aske nought ells
But to withdrawe this entreprise.   30

And for the gaine
    Of that good howre,
Wiche of my woo shalbe relefe,
    I shall refrayne
    Bye paynefull powre   35
The thing that most hathe bene my grefe.

147

POEMS

I shall not misse
        To exersyse
The helpe therof wich doth me teche,
        That after this   40
        In any wise
To kepe right within my reche.

        And she vniuste,
            Wich ferithe not,
Yn this her fame to be defilyd,   45
        Yett ons I truste
            Shalbe my lott,
To quite the crafte that me begild.[1]

48 *quite*] *quit*

159

DRYVEN bye desire I dede this dede,
    To daunger my self without cause whye,
To truste the vntrue, not like to spede,
    To speke and promise faithefullie;
    But now the proof dothe verifie   5
That who so trustithe or he kno
Dothe hurte himself and please his ffoo.

6 *or*] *ere*

160

I ABIDE and abide and better abide,
    And after the olde prouerbe, the happie daye;
    And ever my ladye to me dothe saye:
    'Let me alone and I will prouyde.'
I abide and abide and tarrye the tyde,   5
    And with abiding spede well ye maye:

[1] There is a version of stanzas 1, 2, 5, 6, and 8 in A; at the foot of the poem is written 'To Smithe of Camden', but as Miss Hughey suggests, this may refer to the tune.

148

Thus do I abide I wott allwaye,
Nother obtayning nor yet denied.
Aye me! this long abidyng
   Semithe to me as who sayethe   10
   A prolonging of a dieng dethe
Or a refusing of a desyred thing.
   Moche ware it bettre for to be playne
   Then to saye 'abide' and yet shall not obtayne.

161

ABSENS absenting causithe me to complaine;
   My sorofull complayntes abiding in distresse
And departing most pryvie increasithe my paine:
   Thus lyve I vncomfortid, wrappid all in hevines.

In hevenes I am wrapid, devoyde of all solace,   5
   Nother pastyme nor pleasure can revyve my dull
      wytt;
My sprites be all taken, and dethe dothe me manace,
   With his fatall knif the thrid for to kitt.

Ffor to kit the thred of this wretchid lif
   And shortelye bring me owt of this cace;   10
I se yt avaylith not, yet must I be pensif,
   Sins fortune from me hathe turnid her face.

Her face she hathe turnid with cowntenance contra-
      rious,
   And clene from her presens she hath exilid me,
Yn sorrowe remayning as a man most dolorous,   15
   Exempte from all pleasure and worldelye felicitie.

All worldelie felicitye nowe am I pryvate,
   And left in deserte moste solitarilye,
Wandring all about, as on withowt mate:
   My dethe aprochithe—what remedye?   20

What remedye, alas, to reioise my wofull herte,
  With sighis suspiring most rufullie?
Nowe wellcome! I am redye to deperte.
Fare well all plesure, welcome paine and smerte!

8 *kitt*] *cut*

162

PATIENS, for I have wrong,
  And dare not shew whereyn,
Patiens shalbe my song,
  Sins truthe can no thing wynne;
Patiens then for this fytt,   5
Hereafter commis not yett.

163

WHAN that I call vnto my mynde
  The tyme of hope that ons I hade,
The grete abuse that ded me blinde
  Dothe force me allwaies to be sad.
  Yet of my greef I fayne me glad;   5
But am assurid I was to bolde
To truste to such a slipper holde.

I thought yt well that I had wrought,
  Willing forthwith so to ensue;
But he that sekis as I have sought   10
  Shall finde most trust oft tymes vntrue:
  For lest I reckte that most I rue,
Of that I thought my self most sure
Ys nowe the wante of all my cure.

Amiddes my welthe I dede not reke,   15
  But sone, alas, or that I wiste,
The tyme was come that, all to weake,
                  150

    I had no powre for to resiste;
      Nowe am I prof to theim that liste
To flee such woo and wrongfull paine,   20
As in my hart I doo sustayne.

    For faynid faithe is alwaies free,
      And dothe inclyne to bee vniuste,
That sure I thinck there can none bee
      To muche assurid without mistruste;   25
      But hap what maye to theim that muste
Sustaine suche cruell destenye,
Wythe patiens for remedye.

    As I am on wich bye restrainte
      Abides the tyme of my retorne,   30
Yn hope that fortune bye my playnte
      Wyll slake the fire wherewith I burne;
      Sins no waies els maye serue my torne:
Yet for the dowt of this distresse,
I aske but right for my redresse.   35

16 *or*] ere 29 *on*] one

164

    To make an ende of all this strif,
      No lenger tyme for to sustaine,
But now withe dethe to chaung the lif
      Of him that lyves alwaies in payne;
Dispaire suche powre hathe yn his hande,   5
      That helpith most I kno certeyne
        Maye not withstonde.

    May not withstande that is electe
      Bye fortunis most extremytie;
But all in worthe to be excepte   10
      Withouten lawe or libretye;

POEMS

What vaylithe then vnto my thought?
    Yf right can have no remedie,
        There vaylith nought.

There vaylithe nought, but all in vaine;   15
    The fawte thereof maye none amende
But onlie dethe, for to constraine
    This spightfull happe to have an ende:
So grete disdaine dothe me provoke
    That drede of deth cannot deffende   20
        This dedelye stroke.

This dedelie stroke, wherebye shall seace
    The harborid sighis within my herte,
And for the gifte of this relese
    My hand in haste shall playe his parte,   25
To doo this cure againste his kinde,
    For chaunge of lif from long deserte
        To place assignid.

To place assignid for ever more,
    Nowe bye constrainte I do agre   30
To loose the bonde of my restore,
    Wherein is bounde my liberte;
Dethe and dispaire doth vndretake
    From all mishappe now hardelye
        This ende to make.   35

165

WYLL ye se what wonderous love hathe wrought?
    Then come and loke at me;
There nede no where els to be sought,
    Yn me ye maye theim see,

Ffor vnto that that men maye see   5
  Most monstruous thing of kinde,
My self maye beste compared bee,
  Love hathe me soo assignid.

There is a Rok in the salte floode,
  A Rok of suche nature   10
That drawithe the yron from the woode
  And levithe the shippe vnsure.

She is the Rok, the shippe ame I,
  That Rok my dedelie ffoo,
That drawithe me there, where I muste die, 15
  And robbithe my harte me ffroo.

A burde there fliethe and that but one,
  Of her this thing enswethe,
That when her dayes be spent and gone,
  With fyre she renewithe.   20

And I with fire maye well compare
  My love that is alone,
The flame whereof doth aye repare
  My lif when yt is gone.

18 *enswethe*] *ensueth*

166

DEME as ye list vppon goode cause
  I maye and think of this or that,
But what or whye my self best knowes,
  Wherebye I thinck and fere not;
But there vnto I maye well think   5
  The doubtefull sentence of this clause:
I wolde yt ware not as I think,
  I wolde I thought yt ware not.
153

Ffor if I thought yt ware not soo,
  Though yt ware so yt greved me not;   10
Vnto my thought yt ware as tho
  I harkenid tho I here not.
At that I see I cannot wynk,
  Nor from mye thought so let it goo:
I wolde yt ware not as I think,   15
  I wolde I thought yt ware not.

Lo how my thought might make me free
  Of that perchaunce yt nedeth nott;
Perchaunce no doubte the drede I see,
  I shrink at that I bere not;   20
But in my harte this worde shall sink
  Vnto the proffe maye better be:
I wolde yt ware not as I think,
  I wolde I thought yt ware not.

Yf yt be not, shewe no cause whye   25
  I shoulde so think, then care I not;
For I shall soo my self applie
  To bee that I apere not;
That is as one that shall not shrink
  To be your owne vntill I dye: 30
And if yt be not as I think,
  Lyke wyse to think yt is not.

167

I AM as I am and so wil I be,
But how that I am none knoith trulie,
Be yt evill, be yt well, be I bonde, be I fre,
I am as I am and so will I be.

I lede my lif indifferentelye,   5
I meane no thing but honestelie,
And thoughe folkis judge full dyverslye,
I am as I am and so will I dye.

I do not reioyse nor yet complaine,
Bothe mirthe and sadnes I doo refraine,   10
Ande vse the meane sins folkes woll fayne,
Yet I am as I am be it plesure or payne.

Dyvers do judge as theye doo troo,
Some of plesure and some of woo,
Yet for all that no thing theye knoo,   15
But I am as I am where so ever I goo.

But sins judgers do thus dekaye,
Let everye man his judgement saye;
I will yt take yn sporte and playe,
For I am as I am who so ever saye naye.   20

Who judgith well, well god him sende;
Who judgith evill, god theim amende;
To judge the best therefore intende,
For I am as I am and so will I ende.

Yet some there be that take delight   25
To judge folkes thought for envye and spight,
But whyther theye judge me wrong or right,
I am as I am and so do I wright.

Prayeng you all that this doo rede
To truste yt as you doo your crede,   30
And not to think I change my wede,
For I am as I am howe ever I spede.

But how that is I leve to you;
Judge as ye list false or true;
Ye kno no more then afore ye knewe;   35
Yet I am as I am whatever ensue.

And from this minde I will not flee;
But to you all that misiuge me
I do proteste as ye maye see
That I am as I am and so will I bee.   40

11 *woll*] *will* **13** *troo*] *trow* **27** *whyther*] *whether*

POEMS
from Minor Manuscripts

POEMS

from Minor Manuscripts

168

Syghes ar my foode, drynke are my teares;
   Clynkinge of fetters suche musycke wolde crave;
Stynke and close ayer away my lyf wears:
   Innocencie is all the hope I have.
Rayne, wynde, or wether I iudge by myne eares.   5
   Mallice assaulted that rightiousnes should have:
Sure I am, Brian, this wounde shall heale agayne,
But yet, alas, the scarre shall styll remayne.

169

Of Love [1]

Lyke as the wynde with raginge blaste
   Dothe cawse eche tree to bowe and bende,
Even so do I spende my tyme in wast,
   My lyff consumynge vnto an ende.

Ffor as the flame by force dothe quenche the fier, 5
   And runnynge streames consume the rayne,
Even so do I my self desyer
   To augment my greff and deadly payne.

Whear as I fynde that whot is whott,
   And colde is colde, by course of kynde,   10
So shall I knet an endeles knott:
   Suche fruite in love, alas, I fynde.

[1] Tottell prints a poem of six stanzas, three of which are similar
to the above, and ascribes it to Surrey. A version in P contains
nine stanzas of which five are like Wyatt's.

When I forsaw those christall streames,
   Whose bewtie dothe cawse my mortall wounde,
I lyttyll thought within those beames   15
   So swete a venim for to have founde.

I fele and se my owne decaye,
   As on that bearethe flame in his brest,
Forgetfull thought to put away,
   The thynge that breadethe my vnrest.   20

Lyke as the flye dothe seke the flame
   And afterwarde playethe in the fyer,
Who fyndethe her woe and sekethe her game,
   Whose greffe dothe growe of her owne desyer:

Lyke as the spider dothe drawe her lyne,   25
   As labor lost so is my sute;
The gayne is hers, the lose is myne,
   Of euell sowne seade suche is the frute.

170

Luckes, my faire falcon, and your fellowes all,
   How well plesaunt yt were your libertie!
Ye not forsake me that faire might ye befall.
   But they that somtyme lykt my companye,
Like lyse awaye from ded bodies thei crall: 5
   Loe, what a profe in light adversytie!
But ye, my birdes, I swear by all your belles,
Ye be my fryndes, and so be but few elles.

171

A face that shuld content me wonders well
   Shuld not be faire but louelie to behold,
With gladsome cheare all grief for to expell;
   With sober lookes so wold I that it should

Speake without wordes, such woordes as non can tell;
   The tresse also should be of crysped gold;   **6**
With witt: and thus might chaunce I might be tyde,
And knyt agayne the knott that should not slide.

172

LIKE as the byrde in the cage enclosed,
   The dore vnsparred and the hawke without,
Twixte deth and prison piteously oppressed,
    Whether for to chose standith in dowt:
     Certes! so do I, wyche do syeke to bring about   **5**
Wyche shuld be best by determination—
By losse off liefe libertye, or liefe by preson.

Oh! myscheffe by myscheffe to be redressed!
   Wher payne is the best ther lieth litell pleasure:
By schort deth out off daunger yet to be delyuered, **10**
    Rather then with paynfull lieffe, thraldome and dol-
     oure;
    Ffor small plesure moche payne to suffer;
Soner therfore to chuse, me thincketh it wysdome,
By losse off life lybertye then liefe by preson.

By leynght off liefe yet shulde I suffer,   **15**
   Adwayting time and fortunes chaunce:
Manye thinges happen within an hower;
    That wyche me oppressed may be avaunce.
    In time is trust, wyche by deathes greuaunce
Is vtterlye lost: then were it not reson   **20**
By deathe to chuse libertye, and not lieffe by preson?

But deathe were deliueraunce and liefe lengthe off
    payne;
   Off two ylles, let see nowe, chuse the best:
This birde to deliuer, youe that here her playne,
    Your aduise, yowe louers! wyche shalbe best?   **25**

In cage in thraldome, or by the hauke to be opprest?
And which for to chuse, make playne conclusyon:
By losse off liefe libertye, or liefe by prison?

173

THE piller pearisht is whearto I lent,
 The strongest staye of myne vnquyet mynde;
 The lyke of it no man agayne can fynde,
 Ffrom East to West, still seking thoughe he went.
To myne vnhappe! for happe away hath rent   5
 Of all my ioye the vearye bark and rynde;
 And I (alas) by chaunce am thus assynde
 Dearlye to moorne till death do it relent.
But syns that thus it is by destenye,
 What can I more but have a wofull hart,   10
 My penne in playnt, my voyce in carefull crye,
My mynde in woe, my bodye full of smart,
 And I my self, my self alwayes to hate,
 Till dreadfull death do ease my dolefull state?

174

A LADYE gave me a gyfte she had not;
And I receyvid her guifte I toke not:
She gave it me willinglye and yet she wold not;
And I receyvid it, albeit I coulde not.
If she geve it me, I force not;   5
And yf she take it agayne, she cares not:
Conster what this is, and tell not,
Ffor I am fast sworne—I maye not.

175

THE flamyng sighes that boile within my brest
   Somtyme breake forth, and they can well declare
   The hartes vnrest and how that it doth fare,
   The payne thearof, the greef, and all the rest.
The watrid eyes from whence the teares do fall   5
   Do feele some force or ells they wolde be drye:
   The wasted flesshe of cowlour dead can trye,
   And Something tell what Sweetnes is in gall.
And he that list to see and to discerne
   How care can force within a weried mynd,   10
   Come hee to me! I am that place assynd.
But for all this no force, it dothe no harme;
   The wound, alas, happ in some other place,
   Ffrom whence no toole away the skarr can race.

But you that of suche like have had your part   15
   Can best be iudge; whearfore, my frend so deare,
   I thought it good my state shuld now appeare
   To you, and that there is no great desert.
And whear as you in weightie matters great
   Of ffortune saw the shadow that you know,   20
   Ffor trifling thinges I now am stryken soo
   That though I feele my hart doth wound and beat,
I sitt alone, save on the second day
   My ffeaver comes with whome I spend the tyme
   In burning heat whyle that she list assigne: 25
And whoe hath health and libertie alwaye,
   Lett hym thanck god and lett hym not provoke
   To have the lyke of this my paynefull stroke.

176

Stond who so list vpon the Slipper toppe
  Of courtes estates, and lett me heare reioyce;
And vse me quyet without lett or stoppe,
    Vnknowen in courte, that hath suche brackishe ioyes:
      In hidden place, so lett my dayes forthe passe, 5
    That when my yeares be done, withouten noyse,
      I may dye aged after the common trace.
For hym death greep'the right hard by the croppe
      That is moche knowen of other; and of him self
        alas,
        Doth dye vnknowen, dazed with dreadfull face. 10

The Courte of Venus

Songes and Sonettes

POEMS FROM BOOKS

The Courte of Venus

Songes and Sonettes

177

DYSDAINE me not without desert
  Nor leaue me not so sodeynly,
Sence wel ye wot that in my hart
  I meane nothing but honesty,
    Dysdayne me not.   5

Refuse me not without cause why
  Nor thynke me not to be vniust,
Synce that by lot of fantasye
  The careful knot nedes knyt I must,
    Refuse me not.   10

Mystrust me not, though some therbe
  That fayne would spot my stedfastnes.
Beleue them not, seyng that ye se
  The profe is not as they expresse.
    Mystrust me not.   15

Forsake me not til I deserue,
  Nor hate me not til I offend,
Destroy me not tyll that I swerue,
  For syth you know what I entend,
    Forsake me not.   20

Dysdaine me not, being your owne;
  Refuse me not that am so true;
Mystrust me not til al be knowen;
  Forsake me neuer for no new:
    Disdayne me not.   25

178 [1]

ACCUSED though I be without desert,
   Sith none can proue, beleue it not for true;
For neuer yet, since that you had my hert,
   Intended I to false, or be vntrue.
Sooner I would of death sustayn the smart   5
   Than breake one word of that I promised you.
Accept therfore my seruice in good part:
   None is alyue that can yll tonges eschew.
Hold them as false; and let not vs depart
   Our frendship olde, in hope of any new.   10
Put not thy trust in such as vse to fayn,
Except thou mynde to put thy frend to payn.

179 [2]

WITHIN my brest I neuer thought it gain
Of gentle mynde the fredom for to lose;
Nor in my hart sanck neuer such disdain
To be a forger, faultes for to disclose;
Nor I can not endure the truth to glose,   5
To set a glosse vpon an earnest pain;
Nor I am not in nomber one of those
That list to blow retrete to euery train.

180 [3]

PASSE forth, my wonted cryes,
   Those cruell eares to pearce,
Which in most hatefull wyse
   Doe styll my plaintes reuerse.

[1] Title in T: *The louer suspected of change praieth that it be not beleued against him.*
[2] Title in T: *The louer professeth himself constant.*
[3] Title in T: *The louer sendeth his complaintes and teares to sue or grace.*

Doe you, my teares, also   **5**
   So wet her barrein hart,
That pitye there may grow
   And crueltie depart.

For though hard rockes among
   She semes to haue bene bred,   **10**
And of the Tigre long
   Bene nourished and fed:
Yet shall that nature change,
   If pitie once win place,
Whom as vnknowen and strange   **15**
   She now away doth chase.

And as the water soft,
   Without forcyng or strength,
Where that it falleth oft,
   Hard stones doth perse at length: **20**
So in her stony hart
   My plaintes at last shall graue,
And, rygour set apart,
   Winne grant of that I craue.

Wherfore, my plaintes, present   **25**
   Styll so to her my sute,
As ye, through her assent,
   May bring to me some frute;
And as she shall me proue,
   So bid her me regarde,   **30**
And render loue for loue:
   Which is a iust reward.

181 [1]

Your lokes so often cast,
  Your eyes so frendly rolde,
Your sight fixed so fast,
  Always one to behold:
   Though hyde it fayn ye would,   5
It plainly doth declare
  Who hath your hart in hold,
And where good will ye bare.

Fayn would ye finde a cloke
  Your brennyng fire to hyde: 10
Yet both the flame and smoke
  Breakes out on euery syde.
   Yee can not loue so guide
That it no issue winne;
  Abrode nedes must it glide,   15
That brens so hote within.

For cause your self do wink,
  Ye iudge all other blinde;
And secret it you think,
  Which euery man doth finde.   20
   In wast oft spend ye winde,
Your self in loue to quit:
  For agues of that kinde
Will show who hath the fit.

Your sighes yow fet from farre,   25
  And all to wry your wo:
Yet are ye nere the narre,
  Men ar not blinded so.
   Depely oft swere ye no,
But all those othes ar vaine: 30
  So well your eye doth showe
Who puttes your hert to paine.

[1] Title in T: *The louers case can not be hidden how euer he dissemble.*

170

Thinke not therfore to hide,
  That still it selfe betrayes;
Nor seke meanes to prouide   35
  To darke the sunny daies.
    Forget those wonted waies;
Leaue of such frowning chere;
  There will be found no stayes
To stoppe a thing so clere.   40

182 [1]

FOR want of will, in wo I playne
  Vnder colour of sobernesse,
Renewyng with my sute my payne,
  My wanhope with your stedfastnesse.
    Awake, therfore, of gentlenesse.   5
Regard at length, I you require
The swelting paynes of my desire.

Betimes who geueth willingly,
  Redoubled thankes aye doth deserue;
And I that sue vnfaynedly   10
  In frutelesse hope (alas) do sterue.
    How great my cause is for to swerue!
And yet how stedfast is my sute
Lo here ye see: where is the frute?

As hounde that hath his keper lost,   15
  Seke I your presence to obtayne,
In which my hart deliteth most,
  And shall delight though I be slayne.
    You may release my band of payne.
Lose then the care that makes me crye   20
For want of helpe, or els I dye.

[1] Title in T: *The louer lamenteth his estate with sute for grace.*

171

I dye, though not incontinent,
　　By processe yet consumingly
As waste of fire, which doth relent,
　　If you as wilfull wyll denye.　　　　25
　　Wherfore cease of such crueltye,
And take me wholy in your grace,
Which lacketh will to change his place.

183 [1]

If euer man might him auaunt
　　Of fortunes frendly chere,
It was my selfe I must it graunt,
　　For I haue bought it dere;
And derely haue I helde also　　　　5
　　The glory of her name,
In yelding her such tribute, lo!
　　As did set forth her fame.

Sometyme I stode so in her grace
　　That, as I would require,　　　　10
Ech ioy I thought did me imbrace,
　　That furdered my desire;
And all those pleasures lo! had I,
　　That fansy might support,
And nothing she did me denye　　　　15
　　That was to my comfort.

I had (what would you more perdee?)
　　Ech grace that I did craue:
Thus fortunes will was vnto me
　　All thing that I would haue.　　　　20
But all to rathe, alas the while,
　　She built on such a ground:
In little space, to great a guyle
　　In her now haue I found.

[1] Title in T: *The louer waileth his changed ioyes.*
172

For she hath turned so her whele,   25
    That I, vnhappy man,
May waile the time that I did fele
    Wherwith she fedde me than;
For broken now are her behestes
    And pleasant lokes she gaue;   30
And therfore now all my requestes
    From perill can not saue.

Yet would I well it might appere
    To her my chiefe regard,
Though my desertes haue ben to dere   35
    To merite such reward.
Sith fortunes will is now so bent
    To plage me thus, pore man,
I must my selfe therwith content
    And beare it as I can.   40

184 [1]

SUCH is the course that natures kinde hath wrought,
That snakes haue time to cast away their stynges.
Ainst chainde prisoners what nede defence be sought?
The fierce lyon will hurt no yelden thinges.
Why shoulde such spite be nursed then in thy thought,
Sith all these powers are prest vnder thy winges   6
And eke thou seest, and reason thee hath taught,
What mischief malice many waies it bringes.
Consider eke that spight auaileth naught:
Therfore this song thy fault to thee it singes.   10
Displease thee not for saiyng thus my thought,
Nor hate thou him from whom no hate forth springes;
    For furies that in hell be execrable,
    For that they hate, are made most miserable.

[1] Title in T: *To his ladie cruel ouer her yelden louer.*

185 [1]

SUFFISED not, madame, that you did teare
My wofull hart, but thus also to rent
The weping paper that to you I sent,
Wherof eche letter was written with a teare.
Could not my present paines, alas, suffise   5
Your gredy hart, and that my hart doth fele
Tormentes that prick more sharper then the stele
But new and new must to my lot arise?
Vse then my death. So shall your cruelty,
Spite of your spite, rid me from all my smart, 10
And I no more such tormentes of the hart
Fele as I do: this shalt thou gain thereby.

186 [2]

WHEN first mine eyes did view and marke,
      Thy faire beawtie to beholde;
And when mine eares listned to hark
      The pleasant wordes that thou me tolde:
I would as then I had been free   5
From eares to heare, and eyes to see.

And when my lips gan first to moue,
      Wherby my hart to thee was knowne;
And when my tong did talk of loue
      To thee that hast true loue down throwne:
I would my lips and tong also   11
Had then bene dum, no deale to go.

¹ Title in T: *The louer blameth his loue for renting of the letter he sent her.*
² Title in T: *The louer curseth the tyme when first he fell in loue.*
In T the poem is not divided into stanzas.

And when my handes haue handled ought
   That thee hath kept in memorie;
And when my fete haue gone, and sought 15
   To finde and geat thy company:
I would eche hand a foote had bene,
And I eche foote a hand had sene.

And when in mynde I did consent
   To folow this my fansies will; 20
And when my hart did first relent
   To tast such bayt, my life to spyll:
I would my hart had bene as thyne,
Or els thy hart had bene as mine.

16 *geat*] *get*

187 [1]

SYNCE loue wyll nedes that I shall loue,
   Of very force I must agree;
And since no chance may it remoue,
   In welth and in aduersitie,
I shall alway my self apply 5
To serue, and suffer paciently.

Though for good will I finde but hate,
   And cruelty my life to wast;
And though that still a wretched state
   Should pine my dayes vnto the last: 10
Yet I professe it willingly,
To serue, and suffer paciently.

For since my hart is bound to serue,
   And I not ruler of mine owne,
What so befall, tyll that I sterue, 15
   By proofe full well it shall be knowne:
That I shall still my selfe apply
To serue, and suffer paciently.

[1] Title in T: *The louer determineth to serue faithfully.*
175

Yea, though my grief finde no redresse,
  But still increase before mine eyes;   20
Though my reward be cruelnesse,
  With all the harme happe can deuise:
Yet I professe it willingly
To serue, and suffer paciently.

Yea, though fortune her pleasant face   25
  Should shew, to set me vp a loft,
And streight, my wealth for to deface,
  Should writhe away, as she doth oft:
Yet would I styll my self apply
To serue and suffer paciently.   30

There is no grief, no smart, no wo,
  That yet I fele or after shall,
That from this mynde may make me go;
  And whatsoeuer me befall,
I do professe it willingly,   35
To serue and suffer paciently.

15 *sterue = die*

MYSTRUSTFULL mindes be moued
  To haue me in suspect:
The troth it shalbe proued,
  Which time shall once detect.

Though falshed go about   5
  Of crime me to accuse,
At length I do not doute
  But truth shall me excuse.

Such sawce as they haue serued
  To me without desart,   10
Euen as they haue deserued,
  Therof god send them part.

¹ Title in T: *The louer suspected blameth yll tonges.* It is probably
misleading.

189 [1]

Louer. It burneth yet, alas, my hartes desire.

  Lady.   What is the thing that hath inflamde thy hert?

Louer. A certain point, as feruent as the fyre.

  Lady.   The heate shall cease, if that thou wilt con-
       uert.

Louer. I cannot stoppe the feruent raging yre.   5

  Lady.   What may I do, if thy self cause thy smart?

Louer. Heare my request and rew my weping chere.

  Lady. With right good wyll. Say on: lo! I thee here.

Louer. That thing would I, that maketh two content.

  Lady.   Thou sekest perchance of me, that I may not.

Louer. Would god thou wouldst, as thou maist, well
       assent.   11

  Lady.   That I may not, thy grief is mine, God wot.

Louer. But I it fele what so thy wordes haue ment.

  Lady.   Suspect me not: my wordes be not forgot.

Louer. Then say, alas, shall I haue help, or no?   15

  Lady. I see no time to answer yea, but no.

Louer. Say ye, dere hart, and stand no more in dout.

  Lady.   I may not grant a thing that is so dere.

Louer. Lo! with delayes thou drieues me still about.

  Lady.   Thou wouldest my death: it plainly doth ap-
       pere.   20

Louer. First may my hart his bloode and life blede out

  Lady.   Then for my sake, alas, thy will forbere.

Louer. From day to day thus wastes my life away.

  Lady. Yet, for the best, suffer some small delay.

Louer. Now, good, say yea: do once so good a dede.

  Lady.   If I sayd yea, what should therof ensue?   26

Louer. An hart in pain of succour so should spede.

       Twixt yea and nay my doute shall styll re-
       new.

       My swete, say yea and do away this drede.

[1] Title in T: *The louer complaineth and his lady comforteth.*

Lady.   Thou wilt nedes so; be it so: but then be
            trew.   30
Louer. Nought would I els, nor other treasure none.

          Thus hartes be wonne by loue, request, and
            mone.

190 [1]

I SEE that chance hath chosen me
    Thus secretely to liue in paine,
And to an other geuen the fee
    Of all my losse, to haue the gayn.
By chance assinde, thus do I serue: 5
And other haue, that I deserue.

Vnto my self sometime alone
    I do lament my wofull case:
But what auaileth me to mone,
    Since troth and pitie hath no place   10
In them, to whom I sue and serue,
And other haue, that I deserue?

To seke by meane to change this minde,
    Alas, I proue it will not be;
For in my hart I cannot finde   15
    Once to refrain, but still agree,
As bounde by force, alway to serue:
And other haue, that I deserue.

Such is the fortune that I haue,
    To loue them most that loue me lest;   20
And to my pain to seke and craue
    The thing that other haue possest:
So thus in vain alway I serue,
And other haue, that I deserue.

[1] Title in T: *The Louer complayneth his estate.*

And till I may apease the heate,   25
   If that my happe will happe so well,
To waile my wo my hart shall freate,
   Whose pensif pain my tong can tell.
Yet thus vnhappy must I serue:
And other haue, that I deserue.   30

20 *lest*] *least* 27 *freate*] *fret*

191 [1]

FOR shamefast harm of great and hatefull nede,
In depe despayre, as did a wretch go
With ready corde out of his life to spede.
His stumbling foote did finde an hoorde, lo!
Of golde, I say, where he preparde this dede: 5
And, in eschange, he left the corde tho.
   He that had hidde the golde and founde it not,
   Of that he founde he shapte his neck a knot.

6 *tho* = *then*

192 [2]

THROUGH out the world, if it wer sought,
Faire wordes ynough a man shall finde:
They be good chepe, they cost right nought.
Their substance is but onely winde:
   But well to say and so to mene,   5
   That swete acord is seldom sene.

[1] Title in T: *Against hourders of money.*
[2] Title in T: *Of dissembling wordes.*

179

193 [1]

IN court to serue decked with freshe aray,
Of sugred meates felyng the swete repast,
The life in bankets, and sundry kindes of play
Amid the presse of lordly lokes to waste
Hath with it ioynde oft times such bitter taste,   5
    That who so ioyes such kinde of life to holde,
    In prison ioyes, fettred with cheines of gold.

194 [2]

SPEAKE thou and spede, where will or power ought
    helpthe;
Where power dothe want, will must be wonne by welth.
For nede will spede, where will workes not his kinde,
And gayne, thy foes, thy frendes, shall cause thee finde.
For sute and golde, what do not they obtaine?   5
Of good and bad the triers are these twaine.

195 [3]

IF thou wilt mighty be, flee from the rage
    Of cruell wyll, and see thou kepe thee free
From the foule yoke of sensuall bondage;
    For though thy empyre stretche to Indian sea,
    And for thy feare trembleth the fardest Thylee,   5
If thy desire haue ouer thee the power,
Subiect then art thou and no gouernour.

[1] Title in T: *The courtiers life.*
[2] Title in T: *That speaking or profering bringes alway speding.*
[3] Title in T: *He ruleth not though he raigne ouer realmes that is
subiect to his owne lustes.*

If to be noble and high thy minde be meued,
   Consider well thy grounde and thy beginnyng;
For he that hath eche starre in heauen fixed,   10
   And geues the Moone her hornes and her eclipsyng,
   Alike hath made the noble in his workyng,
So that wretched no way thou may bee,
Except foule lust and vice do conquere thee.

All were it so thou had a flood of golde   15
   Vnto thy thirst, yet should it not suffice;
And though with Indian stones, a thousande folde
   More precious then can thy selfe deuise,
   Ycharged were thy backe, thy couitise
And busye bytyng yet should neuer let   20
Thy wretchid life ne do thy death profet. [1]

5 *Thylee*]   *Thule*

[1] The poem is an adaptation of three passages in Boethius, probably in Chaucer's translation. Tillyard explains the last lines: 'Your greed of gain and busy consuming of wealth would still never leave your wretched life in peace, nor profit you after death at all.'

SATIRES

SATIRES

Myne owne John Poynz, sins ye delight to know
   The cause why that homeward I me drawe,
   And fle the presse of courtes wher soo they goo,
Rather then to lyve thrall, vnder the awe
   Of lordly lokes, wrappid within my cloke,   5
   To will and lust lerning to set a lawe;
It is not for becawse I skorne or moke
   The powar of them, to whome fortune hath lent
   Charge over vs, of Right, to strike the stroke:
But true it is that I have allwais ment   10
   Lesse to estime them then the common sort,
   Of owtward thinges that juge in their intent,
Withowt regarde what dothe inwarde resort.
   I grawnt sumtime that of glorye the fyar
   Dothe touche my hart: me lyst not to report   15
Blame by honowr and honour to desyar.
   But how may I this honour now atayne
   That cannot dy the coloure blak a lyer?
My Poynz, I cannot frame me tune to fayne,
   To cloke the trothe for praisse withowt desart,   20
   Of them that lyst all vice for to retayne.
I cannot honour them that settes their part
   With Venus and Baccus all theire lyf long;
   Nor holld my pece of them allthoo I smart.
I cannot crowche nor knelle to do so grete a wrong,
   To worship them, lyke gode on erthe alone,   26
   That ar as wollffes thes sely lambes among.
I cannot with my wordes complayne and mone,
   And suffer nought; nor smart wythout complaynt,
   Nor torne the worde that from my mouthe is gone.
I cannot speke and loke lyke a saynct,   31
   Vse wiles for witt and make deceyt a pleasure,

And call crafft counsell, for proffet styll to paint.
I cannot wrest the law to fill the coffer
    With innocent blode to fede my sellff fat,   35
    And doo most hurt where most hellp I offer.
I am not he that can alow the state
    Off highe Cesar and dam Cato to dye,
    That with his dethe dyd skape owt off the gate
From Cesares handes (if Lyve do not lye)   40
    And wolld not lyve whar lyberty was lost:
    So did his hert the commonn wele aplye.
I am not he suche eloquence to boste,
    To make the crow singing as the swane,
    Nor call the lyon of cowarde bestes the moste   45
That cannot take a mows as the cat can:
    And he that dithe for hungar of the golld
    Call him Alessaundre; and say that Pan
Passithe Apollo in musike manyfolld;
    Praysse Syr Thopas for a nobyll talle,   50
    And skorne the story that the knyght tolld.
Praise him for counceill that is droncke of ale;
    Grynne when he laugheth that bereth all the swaye,
    Frowne when he frowneth and grone when he is
        pale;
On othres lust to hang boeth nyght and daye: 55
    None of these poyntes would ever frame in me;
    My wit is nought—I cannot lerne the waye.
And much the lesse of thinges that greater be,
    That asken helpe of colours of devise
    To joyne the mene with eche extremitie,   60
With the neryst vertue to cloke alway the vise:
    And as to pourpose like wise it shall fall,[1]
    To presse the vertue that it may not rise;
As dronkenes good felloweshippe to call;
    The frendly ffoo with his dowble face   65
    Say he is gentill and courtois therewithall;

---

[1] Nott explains the line: 'As it may suit the occasion'.

And say that Favell hath a goodly grace
   In eloquence; and crueltie to name
   Zele of justice and chaunge in tyme and place;
And he that sufferth offence withoute blame   70
   Call him pitefull; and him true and playn
   That raileth rekles to every mans shame.
Say he is rude that cannot lye and fayn;
   The letcher a lover; and tirannye
   To be the right of a prynces reigne.   75
I cannot, I. No, no, it will not be.
   This is the cause that I could never yet
   Hang on their slevis that way as thou maist se
A chippe of chaunce more then a pownde of witt.
   This maketh me at home to hounte and to hawke
   And in fowle weder at my booke to sitt.   81
In frost and snowe then with my bow to stawke,
   No man doeth marke where so I ride or goo;
   In lusty lees at libertie I walke,
And of these newes I fele nor wele nor woo,   85
   Sauf that a clogg doeth hang yet at my hele:
   No force for that for it is ordered so,
That I may lepe boeth hedge and dike full well.
   I ame not now in Ffraunce to judge the wyne,
   With saffry sauce the delicates to fele;   90
Nor yet in Spaigne where oon must him inclyne
   Rather then to be, owtewerdly to seme.
   I meddill not with wittes that be so fyne,
Nor Fflaunders chiere letteth not my sight to deme
   Of black and white, nor taketh my wit awaye   95
   With bestlynes, they beeste do so esteme;
Nor I ame not where Christe is geven in pray
   For mony, poison and traison at Rome,
   A commune practise vsed nyght and daie:
But here I ame in Kent and Christendome   100
   Emong the muses where I rede and ryme;
   Where if thou list, my Poynz, for to come,
Thou shalt be judge how I do spend my tyme.

197

Mʏ mothers maydes when they did sowe and spynne,
 They sang sometyme a song of the feld mowse,
 That forbicause her lyvelood was but thynne,
Would nedes goo seke her townysshe systers howse.
 She thought her self endured to much pain,   5
 The stormy blastes her cave so sore did sowse,
That when the forowse swymmed with the rain
 She must lye cold and whete in sorry plight;
 And wours then that, bare meet there did remain
To comfort her when she her howse had dight,   10
 Sometyme a barly corne, sometyme a bene,
 For which she laboured hard boeth daye and nyght,
In harvest tyme whilest she myght goo and glyne;
 And when her stoore was stroyed with the flodd,
 Then wellawaye! for she vndone was clene.   15
Then was she fayne to take in stede of fode
 Slepe if she myght her hounger to begile.
 'My syster' (quoth she) 'hath a lyving good,
And hens from me she dwelleth not a myle.
 In cold and storme she lieth warme and dry   20
 In bed of downe; the dyrt doeth not defile
Her tender fote. She laboureth not as I.
 Richely she fedeth and at the richemans cost,
 And for her meet she nydes not crave nor cry.
By se, by land, of delicates the moost   25
 Her Cater sekes and spareth for no perell;
 She fedeth on boyled, bacon meet, and roost,
And hath therof neither charge nor travaill;
 And when she list the licor of the grape
 Doeth glad her hert, till that her belly swell.'   30
And at this jorney she maketh but a jape;
 So fourth she goeth trusting of all this welth
 With her syster her part so for to shape
That if she myght kepe her self in helth
 To lyve a Lady while her liff doeth last.   35

And to the dore now is she come by stelth,
And with her foote anon she scrapeth full fast.
　　Th'othre for fere durst not well scarse appere,
　　Of every noyse so was the wretche agast.
At last she asked softly who was there, 40
　　And in her langage as well as she cowd,
　　'Pepe,' quoth the othre syster, 'I ame here.'
'Peace,' quoth the towny mowse, 'Why spekest thou so
　　lowde?'
　　And by the hand she toke her fayer and well.
　　'Welcome,' quoth she, 'my sister by the Roode!' 45
She fested her, that joy it was to tell
　　The faere they had: they drancke the wyne so clere.
　　And as to pourpose now and then it fell
She chered her with 'How, syster, what chiere?'
　　Amyddes this joye befell a sorry chaunce 50
　　That well awaye! the straunger bought full dere
The fare she had; for as she loked ascaunce,
　　Vnder a stole she spied two stemyng Ise
　　In a rownde hed with sherp erys. In Fraunce
Was never mowse so ferd for tho the vnwise 55
　　Had not Isene suche a beest before,
　　Yet had nature taught her after her gyse
To knowe her ffoo and dred him evermore.
　　The towney mowse fled: she knewe whether to goo.
　　Th'othre had no shift but wonders sore, 60
Fferd of her liff: at home she wyshed her tho,
　　And to the dore, alas, as she did skippe—
　　Thevyn it would, lo, and eke her chaunce was so—
At the threshold her sely fote did trippe,
　　And ere she myght recover it again 65
　　The traytor Catt had caught her by the hippe
And made her there against her will remain,
　　That had forgotten her poure suretie and rest
　　For semyng welth wherin she thought to rayne.
Alas, my Poynz, how men do seke the best, 70
　　And fynde the wourst by error as they stray!

And no marvaill: when sight is so opprest,
And blynde the gyde, anon owte of the way
   Goeth gyde and all in seking quyete liff.
   O wretched myndes, there is no gold that may   75
Graunt that ye seke! No warr, no peace, no stryff,
   No, no, all tho thy hed were howpt with gold,
   Sergeaunt with mace, hawbert, sword nor knyff
Cannot repulse the care that folowe should.
   Eche kynd of lyff hath with hym his disease.   80
   Lyve in delight evyn as thy lust would,
And thou shalt fynde when lust doeth moost the please
   It irketh straite and by it self doth fade.
   A small thing it is that may thy mynde apese.
Non of ye all there is that is so madde   85
   To seke grapes vpon brambles or breers,
   Nor none, I trow, that hath his wit so badd
To set his hay for Conys over Ryvers,
   Ne ye set not a dragg net for an hare,
   And yet the thing that moost is your desire   90
Ye do mysseke with more travaill and care.
   Make playn thyn hert that it be not knotted
   With hope or dred, and se thy will be bare
Ffrom all affectes whome vice hath ever spotted;
   Thy self content with that is the assigned,   95
   And vse it well that is to the allotted.
Then seke no more owte of thy self to fynde
   The thing that thou haist sought so long before,
   For thou shalt fele it sitting in thy mynde.
Madde, if ye list to continue your sore,   100
   Let present passe and gape on tyme to come
   And diepe your self in travaill more and more.
Hens fourth, my Poynz, this shalbe all and some:
   These wretched fooles shall have nought els of me
   But to the great god and to his high dome   105
None othre pain pray I for theim to be
   But when the rage doeth led them from the right

That lowking backwards vertue they may se
Evyn as she is so goodly fayre and bright;
 And whilst they claspe their lustes in armes a crosse,
 Graunt theim, goode lorde, as thou maist of thy
  myght,   111
 To frete inwards for losing suche a losse.

63 *thevyn*] *the heaven* 105 *dome*] *doom*

198

A SPENDING hand that alway powreth owte
 Had nede to have a bringer in as fast,
 And on the stone that still doeth tourne abowte
There groweth no mosse: these proverbes yet do last.
 Reason hath set theim in so sure a place   5
 That lenght of yeres their force can never wast.
When I remembre this and eke the case
 Where in thou stondes, I thowght forthwith to write,
 Brian, to the, who knowes how great a grace
In writing is to cownsell man the right.   10
 To the, therefore, that trottes still vp and downe,
 And never restes, but runnyng day and nyght
Ffrom Reaulme to Reaulme, from cite, strete and
  towne.
 Why doest thou were thy body to the bones,
 And myghtst at home slepe in thy bed of downe 15
And drynck goode ale so noppy for the noyns,
 Fede thy self fat and hepe vp pownd by pownd?
 Lykist thou not this? *No.* Why? *For swyne so groyns
In stye and chaw the tordes molded on the grownd,
 And dryvell on perilles, the hed still in the maunger,* 20
 Then of the harp the Asse to here the sownd.
*So sackes of durt be filled vp in the cloyster
 That servis for lesse then do thes fatted swyne.
 Tho I seme lene and dry withoute moyster,*

191

Yet woll I serve my prynce, my lord and thyn, 25
  And let theim lyve to fede the panche that list,
  So I may fede to lyve both me and myn.
By god, well sayde! But what and if thou wist
  How to bryng in as fast as thou doest spend?
  That would I lerne, And it shall not be myst 30
To tell the how. Now hark what I intend.
  Thou knowst well first who so can seke to plese
  Shall pourchase frendes where trowght shall but offend.
Ffle therefore trueth: it is boeth welth and ese.
  For tho that trouth of every man hath prayse, 35
  Full nere that wynd goeth trouth in great misese.
Vse vertu as it goeth now a dayes:
  In word alone to make thy langage swete,
  And of the dede yet do not as thou sayse;
Elles be thou sure thou shalt be farr vnmyt 40
  To get thy bred, eche thing is now so skant.
  Seke still thy proffet vpon thy bare fete.
Lend in no wise, for fere that thou do want,
  Onles it be as to a dogge a chese;
  By which retorne be sure to wyn a kant 45
Of half at lest: it is not goode to lese.
  Lerne at Kittson that in a long white cote
  From vnder the stall withoute landes or feise
Hath lept into the shopp; who knoweth by rote
  This rule that I have told the here before. 50
  Sumtyme also riche age begynneth to dote:
Se thou when there thy gain may be the more.
  Stay him by the arme, where so he walke or goo;
  Be nere alway: and if he koggh to sore,
When he hath spit tred owte and please him so. 55
  A diligent knave that pikes his maisters purse
  May please him so that he withouten mo
Executor is: and what is he the wourse?
  But if so chaunce you get nought of the man,
  The wedow may for all thy charge deburse. 60

192

A ryveld skyn, a stynking breth, what than?
　A tothles mowth shall do thy lips no harme:
　The gold is good and tho she curse or ban,
Yet where the list thou maist ly good and warme;
　Let the old mule byte vpon the bridill,　　　　65
　Whilst there do ly a swetter in thyn arme.
In this also se you be not Idell:
　Thy nece, thy cosyn, thy sister or thy doghter,
　If she be faire, if handsom be her myddell,
Yf thy better hath her love besoght her,　　　　70
　Avaunce his cause and he shall help thy nede.
　It is but love: turne it to a lawghter.
But ware, I say, so gold the helpe and spede.
　That in this case thow be not so vnwise
　As Pandare was in suche a like dede;　　　　75
Ffor he, the ffooll, of conscience was so nyse
　That he no gayn would have for all his payne.
　Be next thy self, for frendshipp beres no prise.
Laughst thou at me? Why, do I speke in vayne?
　No, not at the, but at thy thrifty gest.　　　　80
　Wouldest thou I should for any losse or gayne
Chaunge that for gold that I have tan for best
　Next godly thinges, to have an honest name?
　Should I leve that, then take me for a best !
Nay then, farewell! And if thou care for shame,　　85
　Content the then with honest pouertie,
　With fre tong what the myslikes to blame,
And for thy trouth sumtyme aduersitie:
　And therewithall this thing I shall the gyve—
　In this worould now litle prosperite,　　　　90
And coyne to kepe as water in a syve.

PSALMS

Psalm 37. Noli emulari

ALTHO thow se th'owtragius clime aloft,
    Envie not thowe his blinde prosperitye;
    The welth of wretches, tho it semith soft,
Move not thy hert by theyre felicity.
    They shalbe found like grasse turnd into hay,   5
    And as the herbes that wither sodenlye.
Stablisshe thy trust in god, seke right allway,
    And on the yerth thowe shalte inhabite longe;
    Ffede and encreace such hope from day to day,
And if with god thow tune thy hartie songe   10
    He shal the giue what soo thy hart can lust.
    Cast vppon god thy will that right thy wrong;
Gyve him the charge, for he vpright and iust
    Hath cure of the and of thy cares all,
    And he shall make thy trowgh to be discust   15
Bright as the sone, and thy rightwisnes shall
    (The cursids welth tho now do it deface)
    Shine like the daylight that we the none call.
Paciently abide the Lordes assured grace;
    Bere with even minde the trouble that he sendes;
    Dismay the not tho thou se the purchace   21
Encresse of some, for such like lucke god sendes
    To wicked folke [—so prosper the untrue.]
    Refrayne thy mind from wrath that ay offendes;
Do way all rage, and see thou do eschewe   25
    By theire like dede suche dedes for to committ:
    Ffor wikked folke their overthrow shal rewe.
Who pacientlie abid and do not flitt,
    They shall possede the world from heire to hayre:
    The wikked shall of all his welth be quitt   30

So sodainly and that without repaire
 That all his pomp and his scaring aray
 Shall from thyn Iye departe as blast of ayre.
The sobre thenne the world shall weld, I say,
 And live in welth and pes soo plentifull. 35
 Him to distroy the wikked shall assay
And gnasshe his teethe eke with girninge yrefull.
 The Lorde shall scorne the threatninges of the wretche,
 Ffor he doth know the tyde is nighe at full
When he shall syncke and no hand shall hym seeche.
 They have vnsheathed eke their blouddye bronds
 And bent theire bowe to prove if they might reache 42
To overthrowe the [just; stretched forth their honds,]
 Bare of relief the harmelesse to devoure.
 The sworde shall pearce the hart of suche that fonds;
Theire bow shall breake in their moste endevoure. 46
 A little livinge gotten rightfullie
 Passithe the ritchesse and eke the highe powre
Of that that wretches have gatherd wickedlye.
 Pearishe shall the wickedes posteritie, 50
 And god shall stablishe the iuste assuredlye.
The iust mans dayes the Lorde doth know and see,
 Their heritage shall laste for evermore,
 And of their hope beguylde they shall not be.
When dismolde dayes shall wrappe the t'other sore, 55
 They shall be full when other faynte for foode;
 Thearwhyl'ste shall faile theise wicked men thearfore.
To godes ennemyes suche end shall be allowdd
 As hath Lambs greace wastinge in the fyre,
 That is consumde into a smokye clowde. 60
Borow'th th'vniust without will or desyre
 To yelde agayne; the iuste freelye dothe geve,
 Wheare he seethe neede as marcye dothe requyre

Who will'the hym well for right thearfore shall leve;
   Who bannyshe hym shall be rooted awaye;   65
   His steppes shall god directe still and relieve,
And please hym shall what lyf hym lust assaye;
   And thoughe he fall vnder foote lye shall not he;
   Catchinge his hand for god shall streight hym staye.
[The righteous yet, though age has stolen on me,   70
   Forsaken by the Lord I ne'er have seen,]
   Nor yet his seede foodelesse seeme for to be.
The iuste to all men mercyfull hathe bene,
   Busye to do well: thearfore his seede, I saye,
   Shall have habundaunce all waye fresshe and grene.
Fflee yll, do good, that thow may'ste last allwaye,   76
   Ffor god dothe love for evermore th'vpright:
   Never his Chosen dothe he cast awaye;
Ffor ever he them myndeth daye and night,
   And wicked seede alwaye shall waste to nought: 80
   The iuste shall welde the worlde as their owne rights
And longe thearon shall dwell as theye have wrought.
   Withe wisdome shall the wyse mans mowthe hym
      able;
   His tongue shall speake alwaye even as it ought;
With godes learninge he hathe his harte stable;   85
   His foote thearfore from slydinge shall be sure.
   The wicked watchethe the iust for to disable,
And for to se hym dothe his busye cure;
   But god will not suffer hym for to quaile
   By tyrannye, nor yet bye faulte vnpure   90
To be condemn'd in iudgement without faile.
   Awayte thearfore the commynge of the Lorde;
   Live withe his Lawes in pacience to prevayle,
And he shall raise the of thyne owne accorde
   Above the earth, in suretye to beholde   95
   The wickedes deathe, that thow maye it recorde.
I have well seene the wycked sheene lyke goolde,
   Lustie and grene as Lawrell lasting aye;
   But even anon and scantt his seate was colde:

When I have paste agayne the self same waye,   100
  Wheare he did raigne, he was not to be fownde;
  Vanyshte he was for all his fresshe arraye.
Let vprightnes be still thie stedfast grownde.
  Ffollowe the right: suche one shall alwaye fynde
  Hym self in peace and plentie to habounde.   105
All wicked folke reversyd shall vntwynde,
  And wretchidnes shall be the wickedes ende:
  Healthe to the iuste from god shall be assignde.
He shall them strengthe, whome troble shoulde offend:
  The Lord shall helpp, I saye, and them delyver 110
  Ffrom curssed handes, and healthe vnto them send,
For that in Hym they sett their truste for ever.

15 *trowgh*] *truth* 18 *none*] *noon* 34 *weld*] *wield*

Th' Argument [1]

SOMTYME the pryde of mye assured trothe
  Contemned all helpp of god and eke of man:
But when I saw man blyndlye how he goi'the
  In demyng hartes, whiche none but god there can,
And his domes hyd, wheareby mans Malyce grow'th;
  Myne Earle, this doute my hart did humble than,
Ffor errour so might murder Innocence.
Then sang I thus in god my Confydence.

[1] The psalm is followed in A by these eight lines, possibly addressed to Surrey, and probably belonging to a psalm in which is no longer extant, as some leaves are lacking in the manuscript at this point.

PENITENTIAL PSALMS

PENITENTIAL PSALMS

200 [1]

Love to gyve law vnto his subiect hertes
   Stode in the Iyes of Barsabe the bryght;
And in a look annone hymsellff convertes,
   Cruelly plesant byfore kyng David syght;
First dasd his Iyes, and forder forth he stertes,   5
   With venemd breth as sofftly as he myght
Towcht his sensis and ouerronnis his bonis
With creping fyre, sparplid for the nonis.

And when he saw that kendlid was the flame,
   The moyst poyson in his hert he launcyd,   10
So that the sowle did tremble with the same;
   And in this brawle as he stode and trauncyd,
Yelding vnto the figure and the frame
   That those fayre Iyes had in his presens glauncid,
The forme that love had printyd in his brest   15
He honorth it as thing off thinges best.

So that forgott the wisdome and fore-cast
   (Wych wo to Remes when that thes kynges
      doth lakk)
Forgettyng eke goddes maiestie as fast
   Ye, and his own, forthwith he doth to mak   20
Vrye to go into the feld in hast,
   Vrye, I say, that was his Idolles mak,
Vnder pretence off certen victorye,
For enmy's swordes a redy pray to dye.

Wherby he may enjoy her owt of dowt,   25
   Whom more then god or hymsellff he myndyth;
And after he had browght this thing abowt
   And off that lust posest hym sellff, he fyndyth

[1] The Penitential Psalms are in Wyatt's handwriting, apart from the lines missing in E from Psalm 6.

That hath and doth reuerse and clene torn owt   29
   Kynges from kyndomes and cytes vndermyndyth:
He blyndyd thinkes this trayne so blynd and closse
To blynd all thing that nowght may it disclosse.

But Nathan hath spyd owt this trecherye
   With rufull chere, and settes afore his face
The gret offence, outrage and Iniurye,   35
   That he hath done to god as in this Case,
By murder for to clok Adulterye;
   He shewth hym ek from hevyn the thretes, alas;
So sternly sore this prophet, this Nathan,
That all amasid this agid woofull man: 40

Lyke hym that metes with horrour and with fere,
   The hete doth strayt forsake the lymms cold,
The colour eke drowpith down from his chere,
   So doth he fele his fyer maynifold.
His hete, his lust and plesur all in fere   45
   Consume and wast; and strayt his crown of gold,
His purpirll pall, his sceptre he lettes fall,
And to the ground he throwth hymsellff withall.

The pompous pryd of state and dygnite
   Forthwith rabates repentant humblenes;   50
Thynner vyle cloth then clothyth pouerte
   Doth skantly hyde and clad his nakednes;
His faire, hore berd of reverent gravite
   With ruffeld here knowyng his wykednes:
More lyke was he the sellff same repentance   55
Then statly prynce off worldly governance.

His harpe he taketh in hand to be his guyde,
   Wherwith he offerth his plaintes his sowle to save,
That from his hert distilles on euery syde,
   Withdrawyng hym into a dark Cave   60

Within the grownd wherin he myght hym hyde,
　Fleing the lyght, as in pryson or grave:
In wych as sone as David enterd had,
The dark horrour did mak his fawte a drad.

But he withowt prolonging or delay　　　　　　　　65
　Rof that that myght his lord, his god, apese,
Fallth on his knees and with his harp, I say,
　Afore his brest, frawtyd with disese
Off stormy syghes, his chere colourd lyk clay,
　Dressyd vpryght, seking to conterpese　　　　　70
His song with syghes, and towching of the strynges
With tendre hert, Lo thus to god he synges.

18 *Remes*] *Realms*　30 *vndermyndyth*] *undermineth*

201

Psalm 6. Domine ne in furore

O LORD, sins in my mowght thy myghty name
　Sufferth it sellff my Lord to name and call,
　Here hath my hert hope taken by the same;
That the repentance wych I have and shall
　May at thi hand seke marcy as the thing,　　　5
　Only confort of wrechid synners all;
Wherby I dare with humble bymonyng
　By thy goodnes off the this thing require:
　Chastyse me not for my deserving,
Acordyng to thy just conceyvid Ire.　　　　　　10
　O Lord, I dred; and that I did not dred
　I me repent, and euermore desyre
The, the to dred. I open here and spred
　My fawte to the; but thou, for thi goodnes,
　Mesure it not in Largenes nor in bred.　　　15
Punish it not, as askyth the grettnes
　Off thi furour, provokt by my offence.
　Tempre, O Lord, the harme of my excesse

With mendyng will, that I for recompense
    Prepare agayne; and rather pite me,   20
    For I ame wek and clene withowt defence:
More is the nede I have of remede,
    For off the hole the Leche takyth no cure.
    The shepe that strayth the sheperd sekes to se:
I, lord, ame stray'd; I, sek withowt recure,   25
    Fele al my lymms, that have rebelld for fere,
    Shake in dispayre onles thou me assure.
Mye flesshe is troubled, my hart doth feare the
       speare;
    That dread of death, of death that ever lastes,   29
    Threateth of right and draweth neare and neare.
Moche more my sowle is trowbled by the blastes
    Of theise assawltes that come as thick as hayle
    Of worldlye vanytie, that temptacion castes
Agaynst the weyke bulwarke of the flesshe frayle:
    Wheare in the sowle in great perplexitie   35
    Ffeelethe the sensis, with them that assayle,
Conspyre, corrupte by vse and vanytie ;
    Whearby the wretche dothe to the shade resorte
    Of hope in the, in this extreamytie.
But thow, O Lord, how longe after this sorte   40
    Fforbearest thow to see my myserye?
    Suffer me yet, in hope of some comforte,
Ffeare and not feele that thow forgettest me.
    Returne, O Lorde, O Lorde, I the beseche,
    Vnto thie olde wonted benignitie.   45
Reduce, revyve my sowle: be thow the Leche,
    And reconcyle the great hatred and stryfe
    That it hath tane agaynste the flesshe, the wretche
That stirred hathe thie wrathe bye filthie life.
    Se how mye sowle doth freat it to the bones,   50
    Inwarde remorce so sharp'the it like a knife;
That but thow helpp the caitife, that bemones
    His great offence, it turnes anon to dust.
    Heare hath thie mercye matter for the nones;

Ffor if thie rightwise hand that is so iuste   55
  Suffer no Synne or stryke with dampnacion,
  Thie infinyte marcye want nedes it must
Subjecte matter for his operacion:
  For that in deth there is no memorie
  Amonge the Dampnyd, nor yet no mencion   60
Of thie great name, grownd of all glorye.
  Then if I dye and goe wheare as I feare
  To thinck thearon, how shall thie great mercye
Sownde in my mowth vnto the worldes eare?   64
  Ffor theare is none that can thee lawde and love,
  Ffor that thow nilt no love among them theare.
Suffer my Cryes thie marcye for to move,
  That wonted is a hundred yeares offence
  In momente of repentaunce to remove.
How ofte have I calde vpp with diligence   70
  This slowthful flesshe longe afore the daye
  Ffor to confesse his faulte and negligence;
That to the done for ought that I coold say
  Hath still returnd to shrowde it self from colde;
  Whearbye it suffers nowe for suche delaye.   75
By nightlye playntes in stede of pleasures olde
  I wasshe my bed with teares contynuall,
  To dull my sight that it be never bolde
To stirr mye hart agayne to suche a fall.
  Thus drye I vpp among my foes in woe,   80
  That with my fall do rise and grow with all,
And me bysett evin now, where I am so,
  With secrett trapps to troble my penaunce.
  Sum do present to my weping yes, lo,
The chere, the manere, bealte and countenaunce   85
  Off her whose loke, alas, did mak me blynd.
  Sum other offer to my remembrans
Those plesant wordes now bitter to my mynd;
  And sum shew me the powre of my armor,
  Tryumph and conquest, and to my hed assind   90
Dowble diademe. Sum shew the favor

Of peple frayle, palais, pompe, and ryches,
   To thes marmaydes and theyre baytes off error.
I stopp myn eris with help of thy goodnes;
   And for I fele it comith alone of the   95
   That to my hert thes foes have non acces,
I dare them bid: *Avoyd wreches and fle!*
   The lord hath hard the voyce off my complaint;
   Your engins take no more effect in me.
The lord hath herd, I say, and sen me faynt   100
   Vnder your hand and pitith my distres.
   He shall do mak my sensis by constraint
Obbey the rule that reson shall expres,
   Wher the deceyte of yowr glosing baite
   Made them vsurpe a powre in all exces.   105
Shamid be thei all that so ly in whaite
   To compas me, by missing of theire pray!
   Shame and rebuke redound to suche decayte!
Sodayne confusion's strok withowt delay
   Shall so defface theire craffty sugestion   110
   That they to hurt my helthe no more assay,
Sins I, O lord, remayne in thi protection.

1 *mowght*] mouth   15 *bred*] breadth   84 *yes*] eyes
85 *bealte*] beauty

202

WHO so hathe sene the sikk in his fevour,
   Affter treux taken with the hete or cold
And that the fitt is past off his faruour,
   Draw faynting syghes, let hym, I say, behold
Sorowfull David affter his langour,   5
   That with the terys that from his iyes down rold,
Pausid his plaint and layd adown his harp,
Faythfull record of all his sorows sharp.

It semid now that of his fawt the horrour
   Did mak aferd no more his hope of grace,   10
The thretes whereoff in horrible errour
   Did hold his hert as in dispaire a space,
Till he had willd to seke for his socour
   Hym selff accusing, beknowyng his cace,
Thinking so best his Lord for to apese,   15
Eesd, not yet heled, he felith his disese.

Semyth horrible no more the dark Cave
   That erst did make his fault for to tremble,
A place devout or refuge for to save;
   The socourles it rather doth resemble: 20
For who had sene so knele within the grave
   The chieff pastor of thebrews assemble
Wold juge it made by terys of penitence
A sacrid place worthi off reuerence.

With vapord iyes he lokyth here and there,   25
   And when he hath a while hymsellff bethowght,
Gadryng his sprites that were dismayd for fere;
   His harp agayne into his hand he rowght,
Tunyng accord by jugement of his ere:
   His hertes botum for a sigh he sowght,   30
And there withall apon the holow tre
With straynid voyce agayne thus cryth he.

2 *treux*] *truce* 22 *assemble*] *assembly*

203

Psalm 32. Beati quorum remisse sunt

OH happy ar they that have forgiffnes gott
   Off theire offence (not by theire penitence
   As by meryt wych recompensyth not

T.W.—I   209

Altho that yet pardone hath non offence
  Withowte the same) but by the goodnes   5
  Off hym that hath perfect intelligens
Off hert contrite, and coverth the grettnes
  Off syn within a marcifull discharge.
  And happy ar they that have the willfullnes
Off lust restraynd, afore it went at large,   10
  Provokyd by the dred of goddes furour
  Wherby thei have not on theyre bakes the charge
Of othrs fawte to suffer the dolour;
  For that thire fawte was neuer execute
  In opyn syght example of errour.   15
And happi is he to whom god doth impute
  No more his faut by knoleging his syn,
  But clensid now the lord doth hym repute
As adder freshe new stryppid from his skin;
  Nor in his sprite is owght vndiscoverd.   20
  I for by cawse I hidd it still within,
Thynking by state in fawte to be preferd,
  Do fynd by hyding of my fawte my harme,
  As he that feles his helth to be hinderd
By secret wound concelid from the charme   25
  Of lechis cure, that elles had had redresse,
  And fele my bonis consume and wax vnfarme
By dayly rage roryng in excesse.
  Thy hevy hand on me was so encrest
  Both day and nyght, and held my hert in presse 30
With priking thowghtes byreving me my rest,
  That wytherd is my lustyness away
  As somer hettes that hath the grene oprest;
Wherfore I did an othr way assay,
  And sowght forthwith to opin in thi syght   35
  My fawt, my fere, my filthines, I say,
And not to hide from the my gret vnryght.
    I shall (quod I) *agaynst my sellff confesse*
    Vnto the lord all my synfull plyght;
And thou forthwith didst washe the wikkednes   40

Off myne offence, of trowght ryght thus it is.
Wherfor they that have tastid thi goodnes
At me shall take example as of this,
    And pray and seke in tyme for tyme of grace.
    Then shall the stormes and fluddes of harme him
        mis,   45
And hym to rech shall neuer have the space.
    Thow art my refuge and only savegard
    From the trobles that compasse me the place.
Such joy as he that skapis his enmis ward
    With losid bondes hath in his libertie,   50
    Such joy, my joy, thow hast to me prepard;
That as the seman in his jeopretie
    By soden lyght perceyvid hath the port,
    So by thy gret marcifull propertie
Within thi loke thus rede I my confort.   55
    I shall the tech and gyve vnderstondyng,
    And poynt to the what way thou shalt resort;
For thi adresse to kepe the from wandryng,
    Myn iye shall take the charge to be thy guyde.
    I aske therto of the alone this thing: 60
Be not like horse or mule that man doth ryde,
    That not alone doth not his master know,
    But for the good thou dost hym must be tyde
And brydeld, lest his guyd he bite or throw.
    Oh dyuerse ar the chastysinges off syn!   65
    In mete, in drynk, in breth that man doth blow,
In slepe, in wach, in fretyng styll within,
    That neuer soffer rest vnto the mynd;
    Filld with offence, that new and new begyn
With thowsand feris the hert to strayne and bynd. 70
    But for all this he that in god doth trust
    With mercy shall hymsellff defendid fynd.
Joy and reioyse, I say, ye that be just,
    In hym that makth and holdyth yow so still;
    In hym your glory alwey set yow must,   75
All ye that be off vpryght hart and will.

204

THIS song endid David did stint his voyce,
    And in that while abowt he with his iye
Did seke the Cave with wiche withowten noyce
    His sylence semid to argew and replye
Apon this pees; this pees that did reioyce   5
    The sowle with mercy, that mercy so did crye,
And fownd mercy at mercyes plentifull hand,
Neuer denid but where it was withstand.

As the servant that in his masters face
    Fyndyng pardon of his passid offence,   10
Consyderyng his gret goodnes and his grace,
    Glad teris distills, as gladsome recompense;
Ryght so David that semid in that place
    A marble ymage off singuler reuerence
Carffd in the rokk, with iyes and handes on hygh,
Made as by crafft to plaine, to sobbe, to sygh.   16

This while a beme that bryght sonne forth sendes,
    That sonne the wych was neuer clowd cowd hide,
Percyth the cave and on the harpe discendes,
    Whose glauncyng light the cordes did ouerglyde;
And such luyster apon the harpe extendes   21
    As lyght off lampe apon the gold clene tryde:
The torne wheroff in to his iyes did stert,
Surprisd with joye, by penance off the hert.

He then inflamd with farr more hote affecte   25
    Of god then he was erst off Bersabe,
His lifft fote did on the yerth erecte,
    And just therby remaynth the tothr kne;
To his lifft syde his wayght he doth directe.
    Sure hope of helth, and harpe agayne takth he;
His hand his tune, his mynd sowght his lay,   31
Wych to the Lord with sobre voyce did say.

205

Psalm 38. *Domine ne in furore tuo arguas me*

O LORD as I the have both prayd and pray,
  (Altho in the be no alteration
  But that we men like as our sellffes we say,
Mesuryng thy Justice by our mutation)
    Chastice me not, O lord, in thi furour,   5
    Nor me correct in wrathfull castigation.
Ffor that thi arrows off fere, off terrour,
  Of sword, of sekenes, off famine and fyre
  Stikke diepe in me, I, lo, from myn errour
Ame plongid up, as horse owt of the myre   10
  With strok off spurr: such is thi hand on me
  That in my fleshe for terrour of thy yre
Is not on poynt of ferme stabilite,
  Nor in my bonis there is no stedfastnes:
  Such is my drede of mutabilite,   15
Ffor that I know my frailefull wykednes.
  For why? My sinns above my hed ar bownd,
  Like hevi wheyght that doth my force oppresse
Vnder the wych I stopp and bowe to grownd,
  As whilow plant haled by vyolence;   20
  And off my fleshe ech not well curyd wound,
That festred is by foly and neclegens,
  By secret lust hath ranklyd vnder skyn,
  Not duly curyd by my penitens.
Perceyving thus the tyranny off sin,   25
  That with his wheit hath humblid and deprest
  My pryde; by gruging off the worme within
That neuer dyth, I lyve withowten rest.
  So ar myn entrayles infect with fervent sore,
  Fedyng the harme that hath my welth oprest,   30
That in my fleshe is lefft no helth therfore.

So wondrus gret hath bene my vexation
   That it hath forst my hart to crye and rore.
O lord, thow knowst the inward contemplation
   Off my desire; thou knowst my syghes and plaintes;
   Thou knowst the teres of my lamentation   36
Can not expresse my hertes inward restraintes.
   My hart pantyth; my force I fele it quaile;
   My syght, myne iyes, my loke dekays and fayntes:
And when myn enmyes did me most assayle,   40
   My frendes most sure, wherein I sett most trust,
   Myn own vertus sonest then did ffaile,
And stond apart, reson and witt vniust,
   As kyn vnkynd were fardest gone at nede.
   So had thei place theire venim owt to thrust   45
That sowght my deth by nowghty word and dede:
   Their tonges reproche, theire wittes did fraude
      aplye,
   And I like deffh and domme forth my way yede,
Lyk one that heris not, nor hath to replye
   One word agayne, knowyng that from thi hand   50
   Thes thinges procede and thow O lord shalt sup-
      plye
My trust in the wherein I stikk and stand.
   Yet have I had gret cawse to dred and fere
   That thou woldst gyve my ffoos the ouerhand;
Ffor in my ffall they shewd suche plesant chere,   55
   And therwithall I alway in the lashe
   Abyd the stroke: and with me euery where
I bere my fawte, that gretly doth abashe
   My dowlfull chere; ffor I my fawt confesse,
   And my desert doth all my comffort dashe.   60
In the mene while myn Enmys saffe encresse
   And my provokars herby do augment,
   That withowt cawse to hurt me do not cesse;
In evill for good agaynst me they be bent,
   And hinder shall my good persuyt off grace.   65
   Lo now, my god, that seist my hole intent,

My lord, I ame, thow knowst well, in what case.
  Fforsak me not; be not farr from me gone:
  Hast to my help, hast, lord, and hast apace,
O Lord, the lord off all my helth alone.   70

61 *saffe*] *safe*

206

LIK as the pilgryme that in a long way
  Fayntyng for hete, provokyd by some wind
In some fresh shaade lith downe at mydes off day,
  So doth off David the weryd voyce and mynd
Tak breth off syghes when he had song this lay,   5
  Vnder such shaad as sorow hath assynd;
And as the tone still myndes his viage end,
So doth the tother to mercy still pretend.

On sonour cordes his fingers he extendes,
  Withowt heryng or jugement off the sownd;   10
Down from his iyes a streme off terys discendes
  Withowt feling that trykill on the grownd,
As he that bledes in baigne ryght so intendes
  Th'altryd sensis to that that they ar bownd;
But syght and wepe he can non othr thing,   15
And lok vp still vnto the hevins kyng.

But who had bene withowt the Cavis mowth,
  And herd the terys and syghes that he did strayne,
He wold have sworne there had owt off the sowth
  A lewk warme wynd browght forth a smoky rayne;
But that so close the Cave was and vnkowth   21
  That none but god was record off his payne:
Elles had the wynd blowne in all Israells erys
The woffull plaint and off theire kyng the terys.

Off wych some part, when he vpp suppyd hade,   25
   Lik as he whom his owne thowght affrays,
He torns his look. Hym semith that the shade
   Off his offence agayne his force assays
By violence dispaire on hym to lade:
   Stertyng like hym whom sodeyne fere dismays,   30
His voyce he strains, and from his hert owt brynges
This song that I not wyther he crys or singes.

32 not = *do not know*

207

Psalm 51. *Miserere mei, Domine*

REW on me, lord, for thy goodnes and grace,
   That off thy nature art so bountefull,
   Ffor that goodnes that in the world doth brace
Repugnant natures in quiete wonderfull;
   And for thi mercys nomber withowt end   5
   In hevin and yerth perceyvid so plentefull
That ouer all they do them sellffes extend:
   Ffor those marcys much more then man can synn
   Do way my synns that so thy grace offend.
Agayne washe me, but washe me well within,   10
   And from my synn that thus makth me affrayd
   Make thou me clene, as ay thy wont hath byn.
Ffor vnto the no nombre can be layd
   For to prescrybe remissions off offence
   In hertes retornd, as thow thy sellff hast sayd.   15
And I beknow my ffawt, my neclegence,
   And in my syght my synn is fixid fast,
   Theroff to have more perfett penitence.
To the alone, to the have I trespast,
   Ffor none can mesure my fawte but thou alone;   20
   For in thy syght I have not bene agast

For to offend, juging thi syght as none,
   So that my fawt were hid from syght of man,
   Thy maiestye so from my mynd was gone:
This know I and repent. Pardon thow than,   25
   Wherby thow shalt kepe still thi word stable,
   Thy justice pure and clene; by cawse that whan
I pardond ame, then forthwith justly able,
   Just I ame jugd by justice off thy grace.
   Ffor I my sellff, lo thing most vnstable,   30
Fformd in offence, conceyvid in like case,
   Ame nowght but synn from my natyvite.
   Be not this sayd for my excuse, alase,
But off thy help to shew necessite:
   Ffor lo thou loves the trowgh off inward hert,   35
   Wich yet doth lyve in my fydelite;
Tho I have fallen by fraylte ouerthwart,
   Ffor willfull malice led me not the way,
   So much as hath the fleshe drawne me apart.
Wherfore, O lord, as thow hast done alway,   40
   Tech me the hydden wisdome off thy lore,
   Sins that my fayth doth not yet dekay;
And as the juyz do hele the liepre sore
   With hysope clense, clense me, and I ame clene.
   Thow shalt me washe, and more then snow
      therfore
I shall be whight. How fowle my fawt hath bene!   46
   Thow off my helth shalt gladsome tydynges bryng,
   When from above remission shall be sene
Descend on yerth: then shall for joye vpspryng
   The bonis that were afore consumd to dust.   50
   Looke not, O lord, apon myn offendyng,
But do away my dedes that ar vnjust.
   Make a clene hert in the myddes off my brest
   With spryte vpryght, voydyd from fylthye lust.
Ffrom thyn iys cure cast me not in vnrest,   55
   Nor take from me thy spryte of holynesse.
   Rendre to me joye off thy help and rest;

My will conferme with spryte off stedfastnesse:
   And by this shall thes goodly thinges ensue.
   Sinners I shall in to thy ways adresse: 60
They shall retorne to the and thy grace sue.
   My tong shall prayse thy justification
   My mowgh shall spred thy gloryus praysis true.
But off thi sellff, O god, this operation
   It must proced by purging me from blood, 65
   Among the just that I may have relation;
And off thy lawdes for to let owt the flood,
   Thow must, O lord, my lypps furst vnlose:
   Ffor if thou hadst estemid plesant good
The owtward dedes that owtward men disclose, 70
   I wold have offerd vnto the sacryfice.
   But thou delyghtes not in no such glose
Off owtward dede, as men dreme and devyse.
   The sacryfice that the lord lykyth most
   Is spryte contrite. Low hert in humble wyse 75
Thow dost accept, O god, for plesant host.
   Make Syon, Lord, accordyng to thy will,
   Inward Syon, the Syon of the ghost:
Off hertes Hierusalem strengh the walles still.
   Then shalt thou take for good thes vttward dedes,
   As sacryfice thy plesure to fullfyll. 81
Off the alone thus all our good procedes.

208

Off diepe secretes that David here did sing,
   Off mercy, off fayth, off frailte, off grace,
Off goddes goodnes and off justyfying,
   The grettnes dyd so astonne hymselff a space,
As who myght say: who hath exprest this thing?
   I synner, I, what have I sayd, alas?
That goddes goodnes wold within my song entrete,
Let me agayne considre and repete.

And so he dothe; but not exprest by word:
   But in his hert he tornith and paysithe   10
Eche word that erst his lypps myght forth aford.
   He poyntes, he pawsith, he wonders, he praysythe
The marcy that hydes off justice the swourd,
   The justice that so his promesse complysythe,
For his wordes sake, to worthilesse desert,   15
That gratis his graces to men doth depert.

Here hath he comfort when he doth mesure
   Mesureles marcys to mesureles fawte,
To prodigall sinners Infinite tresure,
   Tresure termeles that neuer shall defawte.   20
Ye, when that sinn shall fayle and may not dure,
   Mercy shall reygne; gaine whome shall no assaute
Off hell prevaile; by whome, lo, at this day,
Off hevin gattes Remission is the kay.

And when David hath ponderd well and tryd,   25
   And seith hym sellff not vtterly deprivid
From lyght of grace that derk of sinn dyd hyde,
   He fyndes hys hope so much therwith revivid
He dare importune the lord on euery syde;
   (For he knowth well to mercy is ascrybid   30
Respectles labour) Importune crye and call:
And thus begynth his song therwithall.

209

Psalm 102. *Domine exaudi orationem meam*

LORD, here my prayre, and let my crye passe
   Vnto the lord withowt impediment.
   Do not from me torne thy mercyfull fase,
Vnto my sellff leving my government.
   In tyme off troble and aduersitye   5
   Inclyne to me thyn ere and thyn Intent;
And when I call, help my necessitye:

Redely graunt th'effect off my desyre.
Thes bold demaundes do plese thy maiestye,
And ek my Case such hast doth well require.   10
  Ffor like as smok my days bene past awaye,
  My bonis dryd vp as forneis with the fyre,
My hert, my mynd is wytherd vp like haye,
  By cawse I have forgot to take my brede,
  My brede off lyff, the word of trowth, I saye: 15
And ffor my plaintfull syghes, and my drede,
  My bonis, my strenght, my very force off mynde
  Cleved to the flesh and from the spryte were flede,
As dispairate thy mercy for to fynd.
  So made I me the solaine pelycane,   20
  And lyke the owle that fleith by propre kynd
Lyght of the day and hath her sellff betane
  To ruyne lyff owt off all companye.
  With waker care that with this wo bygane,
Lik the sparow was I solytarye,   25
  That sittes alone vnder the howsis effes.
  This while my foes conspird continually,
And did provoke the harme off my dises.
  Wherfor lik ashes my bred did me savour,
  Of thi just word the tast myght not me ples.   30
Wherfore my drynk I temperd with lycour
  Off weping teris that from myn iyes do rayne:
  By cawse I know the wrath off thy furour
Provokt by ryght had off my pride disdayne;
  For thou didst lyfft me vp to throw me downe,   35
  To tech me how to know my sellff agayne.
Wherby I knew that helples I shold drowne,
  My days lik shadow declyne and I do drye;
  And the for euer eternite doth crowne;
World withowt end doth last thy memorye.   40
  Ffor this frailte that yokyth all manekynd,
  Thou shallt awake and rue this misery,
Rue on Syon, Syon that as I ffynd
  Is the peple that lyve vnder thy law;
                    220

For now is tyme, the tyme at hand assynd,   **45**
The tyme so long that doth thy servantes draw
  In gret desyre to se that plesant day,
  Day off redeming Syon ffrom sins Aw:
Ffor they have ruth to se in such dekay
  In dust and stones this wrechid Syon lowr.   **50**
  Then the gentilles shall dred thy name alway;
All erthly kinges thy glory shall honour,
  Then when that grace thi Syon thus redemith,
  When thus thou hast declard thy myghty powre.
The iord his servauntes wishis so estemith   **55**
  That he hym tornth vnto the poores request.
  To our discent thys to be written semith,
Off all comfortes as consolation best;
  And thei that then shalbe regenerate   **59**
  Shall praise the lord therfore both most and lest.
Ffor he hath lokt from the heyght off his astate,
  The lord from hevyn in yerth hath lokt on vs,
  To here the mone off them that ar algate
In fowle bondage; to lose and to discus
  The sonns off deth owt from theire dedly bond,   **65**
  To gyve therby occasion gracius,
In this Syon hys holy name to stond
  And in Hierusalem hys laudes lastyng ay:
  When in one chirche the peple off the lond
And remes bene gaderd to serve, to lawd, to pray   **70**
  The lord alone so just and mercyfull.
  But to this samble runyng in the way
My strenght faylith to reche it at the full.
  He hath abrigd my days; they may not dure,
  To se that terme, that terme so wonderfull.   **75**
Altho I have with herty will and Cure
  Prayd to the lord, take me not, lord, away
  In myddes off my yeres, tho thyn euer sure
Remayne eterne, whom tyme can not dekay.
  Thow wrowghtst the yerth, thy handes thevyns did
    mak;   **80**

Thei shall peryshe and thou shalt last alway,
And althinges age shall were and ouertake
   Like cloth; and thou shalt chainge them lik aparell,
   Tourne and translate and thei in worth it tak.
But thou thy sellff the sellff remaynist well   85
   That thou wast erst, and shalt thi yeres extend.
   Then sins to this there may nothing rebell,
The gretest comfort that I can pretend
   Is that the childerne off thy servantes dere
   That in thy word ar gott shall withowt end   90
Byfore thy face be stablisht all in fere.

210

WHEN David had perceyvid in his brest
   The sprite off god retournd that was exild,
By cause he knew he hath alone exprest
   Thes grete thinges that greter spryte compilde,
As shalme or pype letes owt the sownd imprest   5
   By musikes art forgid tofore and fyld,
I say when David had perceyvid this
The sprite of confort in hym revivid is.

Ffor therapon he makyth argument
   Off reconsiling vnto the lordes grace,   10
Altho sometyme to prophecy have lent
   Both brut bestes and wikkyd hertes a place;
But our David jugith in his intent
   Hym sellff by penance clene owt off this cace,
Wherby he hath remission off offence,   15
And gynnyth to alow his payne and penitence.

But when he weyth the fawt and recompense
   He damth his dede and fyndyth playne
A twene them to no whitt equivalence,
   Wherby he takes all owtward dede in vayne   20
222

To bere the name off ryghtfull penitence;
  Wich is alone the hert retornd agayne
And sore contryt that doth his fawt bymone,
And owtward dede the sygne or fruyt alone.

With this he doth deffend the slye assault   25
  Off vayne alowance off his voyde desert,
And all the glory off his forgyven fault
  To good alone he doth it hole convertt.
His owne merytt he fyndyth in deffault;   29
  And whilst he ponderd thes thinges in his hert
His knee, his arme, his hand susteind his chyn,
When he his song agayne thus did begyn.

19 *to*] *two*

211

Psalm 130. *De profundis Clamavi*

FFROM depth off sin and from a diepe dispaire,
  From depth off deth, from depth off hertes sorow,
  From this diepe Cave off darknes diepe repayre,
The have I cald, O lord, to be my borow;
  Thow in my voice, O lord, perceyve and here   5
  My hert, my hope, my plaint, my ouerthrow,
My will to ryse: and let by graunt apere
  That to my voyce thin eres do well entend.
  No place so farr that to the is not nere;
No depth so diepe that thou ne maist extend   10
  Thin ere therto: here then my wofull plaint.
  Ffor, lord, if thou do observe what men offend
And putt thy natyff mercy in restraint,
  If just exaction demaund recompense,
  Who may endure, O lord? Who shall not faynt
At such acompt? Dred, and not reuerence   16
  Shold so raine large. But thou sekes rathr love,
  Ffor in thi hand is mercys resedence,

223

By hope wheroff thou dost our hertes move.
  I in the, Lord, have set my confydence;   20
  My sowle such trust doth euermore aprove.
Thi holly word off eterne excellence,
  Thi mercys promesse that is alway just,
  Have bene my stay, my piller and pretence.
My sowle in god hath more desyrus trust   25
  Then hath the wachman lokyng for the day,
  By the releffe to quenche of slepe the thrust.
Let Israell trust vnto the lord alway,
  Ffor grace and favour arn his propertie;
  Plenteous rannzome shall com with hym, I say,
And shall redeme all our iniquitie.   31

27 *thrust*] *thirst*

212

THIS word redeme, that in his mowght did sownd,
  Did put David, it semyth vnto me,
As in a traunce to starre apon the grownd,
  And with his thowght the heyght of hevin to se;
Where he beholdes the word that shold confownd
  The sword off deth: by humble ere to be   6
In mortall mayd, in mortall habitt made,
Eternall lyff in mortall vaile to shade.

He seith that word, when full rype tyme shold come,
  Do way that vayle, by fervent affectione   10
Torne off with deth, for deth shold have her dome:
  And leppeth lyghter from such coruptione
The glint of lyght that in the Ayre doth lome.
  Manne redemid, deth hath her distructione,
That mortall vaile hath immortalite,   15
David assurance off his iniquite.

Wherby he frames this reson in his hert:
> *That goodnes wych doth not forbere his sonne*
From deth for me and can therby convert
> *My deth to lyff, my synn to salvation,* 20
Both can and woll a smaller grace depert
> *To hym that suyth by humble supplication;*
And sins I have his larger grace assayd,
To aske this thing whi ame I then affrayd?

He grauntyth most to them that most do crave, 25
> *And he delyghtes in suyte withowt respect;*
Alas, my sonne persuys me to the grave,
> *Sufferd by god my sinne for to correct:*
But of my sinne sins I may pardonne have,
> *My sonnis persuyt shall shortly be reiect;* 30
Then woll I crave with suryd confidence.
And thus begynns the suyt off his pretence.

1 *mowght*] mouth

213

Psalm 143. *Domine exaudi orationem meam*

HERE my prayer, O Lord, here my request;
> Complyshe my bone; answere to my desire,
> Not by desert but for thyn own byhest,
In whose ferme trowgh thou promest myn empyre
> To stond stable: And, after thy Justyse, 5
> Performe, O lord, the thing that I require.
But not off law after the forme and guyse,
> To entre Jugement with thy thrall bond slave,
> To plede his ryght; for in such maner wyse
By fore thy syght no man his ryght shall save. 10
> Ffor off my sellff lo this my ryght wisenes,
> By skourge and whipp and prykyng spurrs I have

225

Skante rysen vp: such is my bestlynes.
  Ffor that my enmy hath pursuyd my lyff.
  And in the dust hath foyld my lustynes;   15
Ffor that in heins to fle his rage so ryff,
  He hath me forst as ded to hyd my hed;
  And for by cawse within my sellff at stryffe
My hert and spryte with all my force were fled.
  I had recourse to tyms that have ben past,   20
  And did remembre thy dedes in all my dred;
And did peruse thi workes tha' euer last,
  Wherby I knew above those wondres all
  Thy mercys were. Then lyfft I vp in hast
My handes to the. My sowle to the did call,   25
  Like bareyne soyle for moystre off thy grace.
  Hast to my help, O lord, afore I fall:
Ffor sure I fele my spryte doth faynt apace.
  Torne not thi face from me that I be layd
  In compt off them that hedlyng down do pase
In to the pitt. Shew me by tyms thyn Ayde: 31
  Ffor on thy grace I holly do depend;
  And in thi hand sins all my helth is stayde
Do me to know what way thou wolt I bend,
  Ffor vnto the I have reysd vp my mynd.   35
  Rydd me, O lord, from that that do entend
My foos to me: ffor I have me assind
  Allway within thi secrette protection.
  Tech me thy will, that I by the may fynd
The way to work the same in affection: 40
  Ffor thou my god, thy blyssyd spryte vpryght,
  In lond of trowght shalbe my dyrection.
Thow for thy name, lord, shalt revive my spryte
  Within the ryght that I receyve by the,
  Wherby my lyff off danger shalbe quyte.   45
Thow hast fordon theire grete Iniquite
  That vext my sowle: thou shalt also confownd
  My foos, O lord, for thy benignite,
Ffor thyn ame I, thy servant ay most bownd.

DOUBTFUL POEMS

DOUBTFUL POEMS

214

THYE promese was to loue me best,
And that thy hart with myn shold rest,
And not to brek thys thy behest,
   Thy promese was, thy promese was.

Thy promese was not to aquyt   5
My ffathffulnes with sech desyt,
But recompense yt as thou myght,
   Thy promese was, thy promese was.

Thy promese was I tel the pleyn
My ffayth shold not be spent in wene,   10
But to have mor shold be my gayne,
   Thy promese was, thy promese was.

Thy promes was to have obsarwed
My ffayth lyke as yt hath deserwed,
And not casles thus to ha' swaru'd,   15
   Thy promese was, thy promese was.

Thy promes was, I dar avow,
But yt ys changyt I wot well how,
Tho then wer then and now ys now
   Thy promese was, thy promese was.   20

But sens to change thou doos delyt,
And that thy ffayth hath tayn hes fflyghte,
As thow desarwes I shall the quyt,
   I promese the, I promese the.

10 *wene*] *vain*

229

215

I se the change ffrom that that was,
    And how thy ffayth hath tayn hes fflyght;
But I with pacyence let yt pase
    And with my pene thys do I wryt
        To show the playn be prowff off syght: 5
            I se the change.

I se the change off weryd mynd,
    And sleper hold hath quet my hyer;
Lo! how by prowff in the I ffynd
    A bowrnyng ffath in changyng ffyer.   10
        Ffarwell my part, prowff ys no lyer!
            I se the change.

I se the change off chance in loue;
    Delyt no lenger may abyd.
What shold I sek ffurther to proue?   15
    No, no, my trust, ffor I haue tryd
        The ffollowyng of a ffallse gyd:
            I se the change.

I se the change as in thys case
    Has mayd me ffre ffrom myn avoo;   20
Ffor now another has my plase,
    And or I wist, I wot ner how,
        Yt haf net thys as ye here now:
            I se the change.

I se the change, seche ys my chance   25
    To sarue in dowt and hope in weyn;
But sens my surty so doth glance,
    Repentans now shall quyt thy payn,
        Neuer to trust the lyke agayne:
            I se the change.   30

8 *sleper*] *slipper* 10 *bowrnyng*] *burning*

230

216 [1]

To my meshap alas I ffynd
   That happy hap ys dangerus;
And ffortun worketh but her kynd
   To make the joyffull dolorus.
But all to lat yt comes in mynd   5
To waile the want wych made me blynd,
     So offten warnd.

Ameds my merth and pleasantnesse
   Such chaunce ys chaunced sudenly,
That in despayr to haue redresse   10
   I finde my chiefest remedy.
No new kynd of vnhappinesse
Shold thus haue lefft me comffortlesse.
     So offten warnd.

Who cold haue thought that my request   15
   Should haue broght forth such bitter frute?
But now ys hapt that I fferd lest,
   And all thys greff comes by my sute:
For wher I thought me happiest,
Euen then I ffownd my chiefe vnrest,   20
     So offten warnd.

In better case was never non,
   And yet vnwares thus am I trapt;
My chiefe desyer doth cause me mone,
   And to my payn my welth is hapt: 25

[1] It has been suggested that the initial letters of each stanza form an anagram—TAWIT (cf. M.L.N. 1922). Two of Surrey's poems in T have similar anagrams of Wyatt's name. Some of Wyatt's own poems have anagrams also (e.g. 121 IAWTI; 150 AWWTI; 50 WTIA; 224 TWWITA; 107 SHELTUN). The last of these has Mary Shelton's name at the foot of the page. The anagrams on Wyatt's name may be accidental, for many lines naturally begin with Who, Which, What, When, If, It, In, I, And, As, A, To, The, Thus, Thou.

Was never man but I alone
That had suche hap to wayll and grown,
   So offten warnd.

Thus am I tawght ffor to beware
   And not to trust such pleasant chance;   30
My happy hap has bred this care,
   And turned my merth to gret meschance.
There ys no man that hap wyll spare
But when she list our welth ys bare,
   Thus am I warnd.   35

217 [1]

HARTTE aprest with dessperott thoughte
   Ys fforsyd euere to laymentte,
Wyche nowe yn me so sore hathe wrought
   That nedes to ytt I mought consentte:
Whereffor all ioye I do reffusse,   5
And cruell wyll thereoff acusse.

Yff cruell wyll had nott byne gyde,
   Dysspare in me had had no plasse,
Ffor my true menynge she well asspyde,
   But yett ffor all thatt wold geve no grase:
Whereffor all ioye I do reffusse,   11
And cruell wyll thereoff acusse.

She mowt well see and yett wold nott,
   And maye daylly yff that she wyll,
Howe paynffull ys my happelesse lotte,   15
   Ioynd with dysspeare me ffor to spyll:
Whereffor all ioy I do reffueys,
And cruell wyll thereoff acuys.

[1] Ascribed to Wyatt by Nott. It is followed in D, in a different handwriting, by nine of Wyatt's poems. In A, it follows Nos. 175–6.

218 [1]

A Balad of Will

I WILL and yet I may not,
    The more yt is my payne;
What thynge I will I shall not,
    Wherfore my will is vayne.

Will willinge is in vayne—   5
    This may I right well see,
Althoughe my will wolde fayne,
    My will yt may not be.

By cawse I will and may not,
    My will is not my owne;   10
For lacke of will I cane not
    The cawse wherof I mone.

Say that I will and cannot,
    Yet styll I do sustayne
Betwene I will and shall not,   15
    My love cane not optayne.

Thus wyshers wantes ther willes,
    And theie that will do crave;
But they that will not will,
    Ther will the sonest have.   20

Syns that I will and shall not,
    My will I will refrayne,
Thus forto will and will not,
    Will willinge is but vayne.

[1] In H, on the same page as No. 86.

219 [1]

An Epitaphe of Sir Thomas Gravener, knyght

VNDER this stone ther lyethe at rest
    A frendly man, a worthie knyght,
Whose hert and mynde was euer prest
    To favor truthe, to farther ryght.

The poores defence, his neighbors ayde,   5
    Most kynde always vnto his kyne,
That stint all stryf that myght be stayed,
    Whose gentell grace great love dyd wyne.

A man that was full ernest sett
    To serve his prince at all assayes: 10
No sycknes cowlde hym from that lett,
    Which was the shortnynge of his dayes.

His lyf was good, he dyed full well;
    The bodie here, the sowle in blys.
With lenght of wordes whie shoulde I tell, 15
    Or farther shewe that well knowne is.

Sins that the tears of more and lesse
Rightwell declare his worthynes.

      Vivit post funera virtus.

6 *kyne*] *kin* 8 *wyne*] *win*

220

PLAYN ye, myn eyes, accompany my hart,
For, by your fault, Loe! here is death at hand.
Ye brought him first into this bytter band,
And of his harme as yet ye felt no part;

---

[1] This poem is signed W in H, but the only known Sir Thomas
Gravener died after Wyatt.

But now ye shall: Loe! here begyns your smart.　　5
Wet shall ye be—ye shall yt not withstand—
With weeping teares that shall make dymm your sight,
And mistie clowdes shall hang still in your light.
Blame but your selves that kyndyld have this brand,
Withe such desire to straine that past your might.　　10
　　But synce by yow the part hathe cawght his harme,
　　His flamed heate shall sometyme make ye warme.

221

　　　I SEE my plaint with open eares
　　　　　Ys hard, alas, and lawghing eyes;
　　　I see that scorne beholds my teares,
　　　　　And all the harme hap can devyse;
　　　I se my lyfe away so weares　　　　　5
　　　　　That I my self my self dispyse;
　　　And most of all wherewith I stryve
　　　　　Ys that I see my self alyve.

2 *hard*] *heard*

222 [1]

　　WHEN ffortune gave good wynde vnto my saile,
　　　　Lo! then of frendes I had no lytle nomber:
　　But a pirrye rose and fortune gan to faile;
　　　　Adversytie blew my frendes and me a sonder;
　　Amydes the Sea, my Shypp was all to shaken,　　5
　　And I of frendes and fortune cleane forsaken.

　　[1] If this is Wyatt's it was probably written in the period of his
disgrace, following Cromwell's execution. Cf. Nos. 168, 170, 172–
3. The poem, however, as Miss Hughey points out, is a version of
Ovid's *Ex Ponto*, II. 3; and it appears also earlier in the manuscript, 'possibly in Sir John Harington's hand'.

223 [1]

WHAT thing is that, that I both have and lack,
   With good will grawnted and yet is denyde?
How may I be receav'd and putt aback,
   Alway doing and yet vnoccupy'de,
   Moste slow in that I have moste applyde?   5
Thus may I say I leese all that I wynne,
And that was readye is new to begynne.

In wilfull Riches I have found povertie,
   And in great pleasure I lyved in heavynes;
In too moche freedome I lacked libertie;   10
   Nothing but plentie caused my scarcenes:
   Thus was I both in ioye and in distresse;
And in few woordes if I shuld be playne,
In a Paradyse I suffred all this payne.

224 [2]

To whom should I sue to ease my payne?
To my mystres? Nay, nay, certayne.
For feare she should me then disdayne
I dare not sue, I dare not sue.

When I should speake to my mystres,   5
In hope for to get redres
(. . . . . .)
When I should speake, when I should speake.

[1] In A, on the same page as No. 217. In H there is a version of
the first stanza, entitled 'A Ridle', and followed by this answer:

     Love thou hast which thou dost lacke,
       With goodwill graunted of her treuly;
     But yet to graunt her frendes be slacke,
       So ye be doinge and yet schasely:
     Ffor slothe and fere you cane not wyne,
     So you ar readie newe to begyne.

[2] F claims this as Wyatt's.

What hap had I that suffereth payne,
And if I myght her grace attayne,   10
Or els she would here me complayne,
What hap had I, what hap had I!

I fly for feare to be espyed,
Or of euil wil to be destroyed,
The place wher I would faynest abyde   15
I fly for feare, I fly for feare.

Though I were bold who should me blame?
Loue caused me to do the same.
Wyth honesty it were no shame
Though I were bold, though I were bold.   20

And here an end, wyth ful glad wyl
In purpose for to serue her styl;
And for to part I thinke none yl,
And here an end, and here an end.

225 [1]

DURING of payne and greuous smart
    Hath brought me lowe and wonderous weake,
That I cannot comfort my hart:
    Why sighest thou, hart, and wil not breake?

The sighes and plaintes are al in vaine,   5
    The teares that from thyne eyes doth leake;
This life is death, this ioy is payne:
    Why syghest thou, hart, and wil not breake?

Thou clymest to catche wher is no hold;
    Thou pullest the stringes that be to weake; 10
Thy careful lyfe cannot be told:
    Why syghest thou, hart, and wyl not breake?

    [1] V. Wyatt uses a similar refrain in No. 74.

The faythfuller thou dost endure,
   Lesse she regarded to heare the speke;
Askyng pytye wyl the not cure: 15
   Why sighest thou, hart, and wil not breake?

As good thou were a sunder to ryue
   As thus in thought thy selfe to breake;
Better to dy then thus to lyue:
   Why syghest thou, hart, and wil not breake?

I pray the, pytye, shew redresse   21
   Or els come, death, thy selfe awreake;
And if thou fynd no gentlenesse,
   Syth no more but, hart, thou breake!

226 [1]

LOUE whom you lyst and spare not,
   Therwyth I am content.
Hate whom you lyst and spare not
   For I am indyfferent.

Do what you lyst and dread not   5
   After your owne fantasye;
Thynke what you lyst and feare not,
   For al is one to me.

For, as for me, I am not
   Wauering as the wind,   10
But euen as one that reketh not
   Whych way you turne your mind.

For in your loue I doubt not,
   But as one that reketh not;
Whether you hate or hate not   15
   Is least charge of my thought.

[1]V. Variations on the theme of No. 151 by Wyatt or another.

Wherfore I pray you forget not
    But that I am wel content
To loue whom you list and spare not
    For I am indyfferent.   20

227

SHAL she neuer out of my mynd,
    Nor shal I neuer out of this payne?
Alas her loue doth me so blinde,
    Except her helpe I am now slayne.

I neuer told her of my mynd: 5
    What payne I suffer for her sake.
Alas! what meanes myght I now find
    That no displeasure with me she take.

Yf I speake fayre she sayth I flatter,
    And if I dare not, I shal not spede;   10
If I to her do wryte a letter
    Then will she say she cannot rede.

Shal I dyspayre yet for al this?
    Nay, nay, my hart wil not do so.
I wold ones my swete hart kys,   15
    A thousand tymes to bynd more wo.

I am abashed when I shuld speake:
    Alas! I can not my mind expresse.
Yt maketh my hart in peces breake
    To se her louing gentelnes.   20

228

DRYUEN by dissyr to set affection
    A great way, alas, aboue my degre,
Chosen I am, I thinke by election,
    To couet that thing that will not be.

239

I serue in loue, not lyke to sped;   5
   I loke, alas, a lytell to hie.
Agaynst my will I do in ded
   Couet that thing that will not be.

My fanzy, alas, doth me so bynd
   That I can se no remedy   10
But styll to folow my folych mind
   And couet that thing that wyll not be.

I hopyd well whan I began;
   And sens the proue is contrary,
Why shold I any longer than   15
   Couet that thing that wyll not be?

But rather to leaue now at the last
   Then styll to folowe fanzy;
Content with the payn that is past
   And not couet that thing that will not be. 20

229

Fragment

But Lorde how straunge is this   that to the iust befall,
To end with shame lyke synfull folke   and lyve to
    slaunder thrall!
Theise Impps lyke wyse of death   as maskers weare for
    synne,
Disguysed walke in vertues Cloke   and hyde their
    measlid skynne.
Such fruteles travayles then   vnto my thought com-
    mend   5
Their nature mylde and harmles hart   that gladsome
    life entend;
That myngle drincke with sporte,   and sawce their food
    with myrth,

Convert theire sower into sweete, what wold they
    more on earthe?
Thus whyle I sweate in searche   of wisdomes vncowthe
    leere,
And to discipher the vnrest   whearein man walketh
    heare;   10
Then with suche hongrie thrust   as greedynes forbadd,
The head to seace, the eye to wynck,   in sifting good
    from badd.
When in that shoreles floode   long tyme my shipp had
    ronne,
I fownde by state of mortall spryte soche secreasye
    not wonne;
Suche mysteries to revaile   what witt doth moste
    endevour   15
Shall waste his tyme, as I have done, and deeper doutes
    discever.

11 *thrust*] *thirst*

TWO LETTERS

TWO LETTERS (1537)

1

IN as mitch as now ye ar come to sume yeres of vnder-
standing, and that you should gather within your self
sume frame of honestye, I thought that I should not
lese my labour holy if now I did something advertise
you to take the suer fondations and stablisht opinions,
that leadeth to honestye. And here I call not honestye
that men comenly cal honestye, as reputation for
riches, for authorite, or some like thing, but that
honestye that I dare well say your Granfather (whos
soule god pardon) had rather left to me then all the
lands he did leaue me—that was wisdome, gentlenes,
sobrenes, disire to do good, frendlines to get the love
of manye, and trougth above all the rest. A great part
to haue al thes things is to desire to haue them: and
altho Glorye and honest name are not the verye endes
wherfor thes thinges are to be folowed, yet surly they
must nedes folowe them, as light folowth fire, though
it wer kindled for warmth. Out of these things the
chiefest and infallible grond is the dread and Reuerens
of God, wherapon shall ensue the eschewing of the
contraries of thes sayd vertues,—that is to say, Ignor-
ans, unkindnes, Raschnes, desire of harme, unquiet
enmytie, hatred, manye and crafty falshed, the verie
Rote of al shame and dishonestye.

I say the only dred and reuerens of god that seeth al
things is the defens of the creping in of al thes mischiefs
into you. And for my part, altho I do not say ther is no
man that wold his son better then I, yet on my faith I
had rathir haue you liueles then subiect to these vices.
Think and ymagine alwais that you are in presens of
some honist man that you know, as Sir Jhon Russel,

your father-in-law, your vnkle, parson, or some other such, and ye shal, if at ony time ye find a plesur in naughtye touchis, remember what shame it wer afore thes men to doo naughtily. And sure this imagination shal cause you remember that the pleasure of a naughty dead is sone past, and that rebuke, shame, and the note therof shal remayne euer. Then if thes things ye take for vayne imaginations, yet remember that it is certayn and no imagination that ye are alwaye in the presens and sight of god: and tho you see him not, so mitch is the reuerens the more to be had, for that he seeth and is not seen. Men punish with shame as greatist punischment on erth, ye greater then death, but his punischment is first the withdrawing of his fauour and grace, and in leuing his hand to rule the sterne, to let the ship runne without guyde to your owne distruction, and suffreth so the man that he forsaketh to runne hedlong, as subiect to al mishaps, and at last with shameful end to euirlasting shame and deth. Ye may see continual examples both of the one sort and th'othir, and the bettir if ye mark them wel that your self are come of. And consider wel your good grandfathir what things ther wer in him, and his end; and they that knew him notid him thus: first and chiefly to haue a great reuerens of god and good opinion of godly things, next that ther was no man more piteful, no man more trew of his word, no man faster to his frend, no man diligenter nor more circumspect, which thing both the kings his masters notid in him greatly. And if thes things, and specially the grace of god that the feare of god alway kept with him, had not ben, the chansis of thes troblesome worlde that he was in had long ago ouirwhelmid him. This preseruid him in prison from the handes of the tirant that could find in his hart to see him rakkid, from two yeres and more prisonment in Scotland, in Irons and Stoks, from the danger of sodeyn changes and commotions diuers,

till that welbelouid of many, hatid of none, in his fair
age and good reputation godly and Christenly he went
to him that louid him for that he always had him in
reuerens. And of my self I may be a nere example unto
you of my foly and unthriftnes that hath as I wel deseruid broght me into a thousand dangers and hazardes, enmyties, hatrids, prisonments, despits and
indignations: but that god hath of his goodnes chas-
tized me and not cast me cleane out of his fauour,
which thing I can impute to no thing but to the goodnes of my good fathir, that I dare wel say purchasid
with continual request of god his grase towards me
more then I regardid or considred my self, and a litel
part to the smal fear that I had of god in the most of
my rage and the litel delite that I had in mischiefe. You
therefor, if ye be sure and haue god in your sleue, to
cal you to his grase at last, ventur not hardily by myne
example apon naughty unthriftines in trust of his goodnes; and besides the shame I dare lay ten to one ye shal
perisch in the aduentur: for trust not that my wisch or
desire of god for you shall stand you in as mitch effect
as I think my fathirs did for me, we ar not all acceptid
of him. Beginne therfore betimes, make god and goodnes your fundations. Make your examples of wise and
honist men; shote at the mark; be no mokker—mokkes
folow them that delite therin. He shal be suer of shame
that felith no grefe in othir mens shames. Haue your
frends in a reuerens and think vnkindnes to be the
greatist offens, and lest punishid amongst men, but so
mitch the more to be dread, for god is Iustiser apon
that alone. Loue wel and agre with your wife, for where
is noyse and debate in the hous, ther is unquiet dwell-
ing. And mitch more wher it is in one bed. Frame wel
your self to loue, and rule wel and honestly your wife
as your felow, and she shal loue and reuerens you as
her hed. Such as you are unto her such shal she be
unto you. Obey and reuerens your father-in-law as you

wold me; and remember that long life foloweth them that reuerens theyr fathirs and eldirs. And the blissing of god for good agrement between the wife and husband is fruyt of many children, which I for the like thinge doe lack, and the faulte is both in your mother and me, but chieflie in her.

Rede oft this my lettre and it shal be as tho I had oftin writtin unto you. And think that I haue herin printid a fatherly affection to you. If I may see that I haue not lost my payne, myne shal be the contentation and yours the profit. And apon condition that you folow my aduertisement I send you gods blessing and myne, and as wel to come to honestye as to encreas of yeres.

At Paris, the 15th of Aprill, your lovinge father,

THOMAS WYAT [1]

II [1]

I DOUBT not but long ere this time my lettres are come to you. I remember I wrate to you in them that if you read them oftin it should be as tho I had written oftin to you: for al that I can not so content me but stil to cal apon you with my lettres. I wold not for al that that if any thing be wel warnid in the othir, that you shold leaue to remember it bicaus of this new, for it is not like with aduertisments as it is with apparel that with long wering a man castith away when he hath new. Honest teching neuir were onles they were out of his remembrans that shold kepe and folow them to the shame and hurt of him self.

Think not also that I haue any new or chang of aduertisments to send you, but stil it is one that I wold: I haue nothing to crye and cal apon you for but honestye, honestye. It may be diuersly namid, but

[1] From E, with some corrections and additions from Add. MS. 33271 (as given in *Modern Language Notes*, 1934).

248

alway it tendith to one end. And as I wrate to you last,
I meane not that honestye that the comen sort callith
an honist man: Trust me that honist man is as comen a
name as the name of a good felow, that is to say, a
dronkerd, a tauerne hanter, a riotter, a gamer, a
waster: so are among the comen sort al men honist
men that are not knowin for manifest naughtye knaues.
Seke not, I pray the, my son, that honesty which
aperith and is not in dead. Be wel assured it is no
comen thing nor no comen mans iugement to iuge wel
of honestye, nor it is no comen thing to come by: but
so mitch it is the more goodlye for that it is so rare and
strang. Folow not therfor the comen reputation of
honestye: if you wil seme honist, be honist, or els
seame as you are. Seke not the name without the thing,
nor let not the name be the only mark you shote at:
that wil folow tho you regard it not, ye and the more
you regard it the lesse. I meane not by regard it not,
esteme it not; for wel I wot honist name is goodly, but
he that huntith only for that is like him that had rathir
seame warme then be warme, and edgith a single cote
about with a furre. Honist name is to be kept preseruid and defendid; and not to employ al a mans wit
about the studye of that for it smellith of a glorious
and ambitious fole. I say as I wrote unto you in my
last lettirs, get the thing and the othir must of necessite
folow as the shadow foloweth the thing that it is of.
And euin so mitch is the verye honeste bettir then the
name as the thing is bettir then the shadow.

The coming to this pointe that I wold so fayne haue
you haue is to consider a mans awne self, what he is
and wherfor he is. And herin let him think verilye that
so goodly a work as man is, for whom al othir things
wer wroght, was not wroght but for goodly things.
Aftir a man hath gottin a wil and desire to them is first
to auoyd euil and lerne that poynt alone neuir to doo
that that within your self you find a certain grudging

against. No doubt in any thing you doo, if you axe your self or examine the thing for your self afore you do it, you shal find, if it be euil, a repining against it. My son, for our lords love, kepe wel that repining: suffer it not to be darkid and corruptid by noughtye example, as tho any thing were to you excusable bicaus othir men doo the same. That same repining, if it did punisch as he doth iuge, ther wer no such iusticer. And, of truth, so doth it punisch, but not so apparantly. Here how we think it is no smal grefe of a consciens that condemnith it self, but be wel asurid aftir this life it is a continual gnawing.

When ther is a custome gottin of auoyding to do euil, then cannot a gentle courage be contented to be Idle and to rest without doing enything. Then loo had ye nede to gathir an hepe of good opinions and to get them perfectly as it wer on your fingers ends: Reason not greatly apon the approuing of them, take them as alreadye approuid bicaus they wer of honist mens leauings, of them of god ther is no question. And it is no smal help to them the good opinion of moral philosophers, among whom I wold Senek were your studye and Epictetus, bicaus it is litel to be euir in your bosome.

Thes things shall lead you to know goodly thinges, which when a man knoweth and takith plesure in them, he is a best that foloweth not them, no nor he can not but folow them. But take this for conclusion and sume of al, that if god and his grase be not the fundation, nother can ye auoyd euil nor iuge wel, nor doo any goodly thing. Let him be fundation of al, wil thes things, desire them ernestly, and seke them at his hands and knolege them to come of him, and questionles he wil both geve you the use and plesur in using them, and also reward you for them that come of him, so liberal and good is he. I wolde fayne se that my lettres myght worke to frame you honist: And think

that without that I esteme nothing of you, no not that you are my sone; for I reken it no small deshonistye to my self to haue an unhonist taught child. But the fault shal not be in me. I shal do the part of a fathir: And if you answer not to that I loke for at your hands, I shal aswel studye with that that I shal leaue to make sum honist man as you. I remitt you wholie to youre father-in-lawe. Recomend me to my daughter Jane and my daughter Besse; and write vnto me, at the least to exercise your hand. And farewell, with Gods blessinge.

TEXTUAL NOTES
GLOSSARY
INDEX

TEXTUAL NOTES

THIS edition is derived from the following sources:

I. Manuscripts in the British Museum.
    E. Egerton MS. 2711.
    D. Devonshire MS. Add. 17492.
    R. Royal MS. 17 A. xxii.
    P. Add. MS. 36529.
    H. Harleian MS. 78.

II.   A. Manuscript at Arundel Castle.

III. Manuscript at Corpus Christi College, Cambridge.
    C. Parker MS. 168.

IV. Printed Texts.
    T. Tottel's *Songes and Sonnettes* (ed. Rollins).
    V. *The Courte of Venus* (fragment reprinted in *Sir Thomas Wyatt and other studies* by E. K. Chambers, 1933).

V. Editions.
    N. Nott, 1815–16.
    F. Foxwell, 1913.
    Y. Tillyard, 1929.
    M = Muir.

Of these, E is by far the most important. It contains 101 of Wyatt's poems, as well as the satires and the psalms, some of them in his own hand and others corrected by him. There is a transcript of this manuscript in *Anglia*, vols. 18 and 19, by Flügel (Fl.). Miss Foxwell assumes that the poems in E are copied in chronological order; but the first part of the manuscript is an elegant fair copy with corrections by Wyatt and nothing can be deduced about the order of composition. The poems at the end, including those written in Spain and the Psalms, can be dated more accurately. The

poems are classified under five headings (shorter lyrics, sonnets, longer lyrics, psalms and satires); but as this classification is neither consistent nor the poet's own I have ignored it. The lyrics and sonnets are here printed in the order of the manuscript (1–101), but the satires and the psalms have been segregated (196–213).

Many of the poems, as Miss Hughey has shown, have corrections by Grimald and others: these have been ignored except where they make a necessary emendation. Deleted readings, superseded by Wyatt's own corrections, are recorded when they are legible. (Wyatt's corrections = W, deleted readings = OE).[1]

D is the other important manuscript. It contains many poems which appear in no other (102–67) and about 50 which appear also in E. Where poems appear in both manuscripts the text of D is nearly always earlier and corresponds to deleted versions in E. The D poems are also printed in the order of the manuscript. The earlier part of the manuscript is in various hands: some of the poems are ascribed to Wyatt, others are certainly his, but some may be by imitators. All the poems numbered 133–67 (except 162) are written in a single hand. As this group is interspersed with poems which appear also in E, it is reasonable to assume that they are all Wyatt's; but they are not signed with the initials T. V. as Miss Foxwell asserts, but with the less conclusive F. S. (=Finis). As the manuscript also contains some 50 poems by other writers, I have given in roman numerals the folio where each poem may be found.[2]

The other manuscripts are of minor importance. A, of which MS. Add. 28635 is a copy, contains four

---

[1] It is not always possible to distinguish between decorative flourishes and marks of omission. When in doubt I have printed the word which looks less odd (e.g. *remembre* rather than *remembr*). In no case is the sense of a passage affected.

[2] I have printed these 50 poems in the *Proceedings of the Leeds Literary and Philosophical Society*, 1947.

poems which appear in no other manuscript, and the missing lines of three poems defective in E; but it shows signs of 'unauthorized improvements' on what Wyatt wrote. R contains the Penitential Psalms. The other manuscripts (P, H, C) together provide the texts of six more poems; and C supplies missing lines in the first satire. The poems from these four manuscripts are here numbered 168–76, 218–23.[1]

The Courte of Venus contains the better text of a poem which appears also in Tottel, together with a number of poems which are definitely Wyatt's and some which I have printed as doubtful poems. Tottel

[1] There is a group of Wyatt's poems in H (XXIII–XXV), including Nos. 68, 76, 168, 59, 169, 86 and 100. Another poem in the same group (No. 219) is usually ascribed to him. There are several poems by Surrey in the same section of the manuscript, together with some anonymous riddles. The remaining poem, on the same page as No. 86, is here printed as a doubtful poem (No. 218).

P contains a group of nine poems (XXX–XXXIII), of which the first seven are known to be Wyatt's (i.e. Nos. 196, 26, 76, 60, 170, 171, and 46). The other two poems, in the same handwriting, may also be his (Nos. 220–1). One of these was printed as Wyatt's by Padelford (No. 220). All except the first (No. 196) of these nine poems were printed in *Nugae Antiquae* (1769, 1779), but Harington apparently did not have access to P. These poems may have been on missing folios of A, destroyed by the printer of *Nugae Antiquae*.

The majority of the Wyatt poems in A are to be found between LX and CXIX: Nos. 173–4, 16, 4, 7, 9–10, 44, 196, 12–13, 16, 24–5, 27–33, 47, 49–50, 56, 79, 92, 95, 42, 48, 54, 59, 61, 43, 39–40, 58, 62, 53, 57, 82–3, 96, 101, 198, 197, 8, 200–13, 199. These poems are preceded by three poems ascribed by Tottel to uncertain authors (LIX*v*, LX*r*): 'With Petrarke to compare there may no wight', 'It was the day on whiche the Sonne', and 'I ne can close in short and cunning vearse'. Between No. 197 and No. 8 on CI*v* is another poem Tottel ascribes to an uncertain author: 'In Grece somtyme theare dwelt a man of worthie fame'. Although these four poems are included in the Wyatt section of the manuscript they are unlikely to be his. One other poem in this section of the manuscript (CV*r*) seems to be a fragment of a genuine Wyatt poem (No. 229), It follows No. 8 in the manuscript.

Later in the manuscript (fol. CCXVI*v*) occur two poems ascribed by Tottel to Wyatt (Nos. 175–6). On the preceding page (CCXVI*r*) is a poem in Wyatt's style (No. 222); and on the page following (CCXVII*r*) there is one poem, often ascribed to Wyatt, which also appears in D (No. 217), and another poem which appears in another form amongst the Wyatt poems in H (No. 223).

has eighteen poems which are not to be found in any of the manuscripts. Unfortunately Tottel, or an editor employed by him, took great liberties with the texts of poems which appear also in E, and there is no reason to believe that the poems peculiar to T are as Wyatt wrote them. They are here numbered 178–95.

As this edition is intended for the general reader, it seemed superfluous to give exhaustive textual variants; but I have given all significant D variants. It is generally agreed that the other manuscripts are later and less reliable, and there seemed to be little point in recording all their deviations. For the same reason I have only given variants from T where the manuscripts appear to be unreliable.

The spelling of the manuscripts has been preserved; but punctuation has been supplied or emended where necessary, lines and proper names have been given initial capitals, abbreviations have been expanded, apostrophes have been added to separate elided words, and stanzas have been printed to display their form. I have not always followed the manuscripts in their use of capitals—some of the scribes have capitals in the middle of words. I have occasionally used italics for the sake of clarity. All other deviations from the manuscripts have been recorded. I have ventured to make a few emendations where I could not be satisfied that the original made sense.

As my text frequently differs from Miss Foxwell's, and as her edition has been the standard for twenty-five years, I have recorded her mistakes, though not the alterations she makes in the spelling. Her versions of some of the poems are less accurate than Nott's. It would be ungrateful, however, not to acknowledge my indebtedness to Miss Foxwell's edition.[1]

[1] Apart from a large number of spelling alterations, Miss Foxwell departed from the manuscripts in the following lines:
V, 5. VIII, 5, 40, 117. IX, 14. XVIII, 3. XXII, 13. XXVII, 13. XXVIII, 5 13. XXX, 14. XXXV, 5. LVI, 8. LVII, 12. LXXIII,

No.

1. D LXIX, T. *2* payne] greef–D. *3* The] thy–D. *4*+Behold love–D. *6* Thou haste weapon vnarmid she sytteth–D. *8* spitefull] dispitefull–D. *13* sorrowe] sorrowes–D.

2. T. *2* attayne–*corr.* E] be tayne–OE (i), F. obtayne–OE (ii). *13* a] à–E (*other examples of the use of the accent are not recorded*).

3. D LXX, T. *1* when that] when–D. *5* him shitt] did flitt–D. *6* from him and to Rome did her whele relente–D. *7* ded laugh among them whom tearis had besprent–D. *8* her cruell dispight inwardelye to shitt–D. *12* whereby if I laugh at eny season–D. *13* is for] is–D. nother] none othr–D.

4. A, T. *6* lustes] lust–OE (*the correction is in a later hand*).

5. D II (*last three stanzas only*). *5* ouer–*late corr.*] our–OE. *16–17* (Perdy . . . prouff)–E. *24* prevent] present–D. *30* lust] liste–D.

6. *Not in* F.

7. A. *6* Diere–OE] Dere–E. *8* Sins–W] Sithens–OE.

8. A, T. (*First three stanzas are lacking in E and are taken from A.*) *5* Charged] Changed–F. *40* robbeth] robbed–F. *117* gnawen] ynawen–F. *128*–T.] *line obliterated by later writing*. *140* worthy–Fl.] worth–E.

9. A, T. *14* ye] yow–*unauthorized correction*. you–F.

21, 31. LXXVIII, 10. LXXXV, 11, 17, 23. LXXXVII, 28, 33. LXXXVIII, 4. XCI, 29. XCIII, 25, 41. XCIV, 4. CI, 59, 71. CIV, 21, 30. CV, 11. CVI, 11, 23. CVII, 7, 12, 19, 28. CVIII, 30. CIX, 11. CX, 6. CXI, 4. CXIV, 29. CXVII, 1. CXVIII, 14. CXXIV 18. CXXXII, 2, 40. CXXXIII, 4. CXXXVI, 9. CXXXVII. 8, 16. CXL, 6, 10. CXLI, 12, 24, 38. CXLII, 7, 11, 14, 17, 22, 24, 31. CXLIV, 4, 16. CXLV, 3. CXLVI, 2, 4. CXLVIII, 19, 27, 28. CXLIX, 2. CLII, 8, 11, 15, 21. CLIV, 7, 25. CLVI, 54. CLVIII, 36, 39. CLIX, 6. CLXIII, 12, 13, 27, 29. CLXV, 23. CLXVII, 9, CLXIX, 4. CLXX, 8. CLXXII, 22, 26. CLXXV, 5, 9. CLXXX, 15. CLXXXI, 14. CLXXXIV, 5, 7. CLXXXIX, 4, 26, 27. CXCV, 4. CXCVI, 7, 29, 32, 41. CXCVIII, 22. CXCIX, 32, 37, 60, 67, 99, 106. CCI, 29, 45, 57, 75. CCII, 3. CCIV, 10. CCV, 4, 8. CCVI, 11. CCIX, 7, 19, 23, 63, 82. CCXI, 4. CCXII, 13. CCXIII, 15, 30. CCXIX, 7.

10. D LXXV, A, T. *1* me telleth] tells me–D. moost]
of–D. *3* like] even–D. *8–9* dyversnes–D] dyvernes–
E. *11* in the] the–D. *13* wordes–D] word–?E. not]
never–D. *14* oon] as–D.

11. T. *14* a part–T] apart–E.

12. A, T.

13. D LXXV, A, T. *1* Ffarewell] Nowe fare well–D. all
thy] thy–D. *3* Senec ... call] To sore a profe hath
called–D. *4* To surer welthe my wyttes to endevor–D.
5 when] whylist–D. *6* pricketh ay] prycketh–D.
8 And ... syns] But scape forth for–D. *12* theron]
therupon go–D. thy many] thy–D. *13* though I]
I–D. *14* lusteth] liste–D.

14. D III (*imperfect*), LXXV, T. *6* this] suche–D. *7* syns]
syns that–D. *8* refrain] restraine–D. *10* be] bye–D.
11 om.–D. *14* Plowithe ... soweth–D] *sheet torn*–E.
the sand–E] sande–D.

15. D LXXV. *3* trouth–D] trought–E. *6* reioyse] refuse–D. *7* to] so–D. *8* sesse] loosse–D. *11* thincke]
thinckes–D.

16. D XIX, A, T. *1* There was never] Was neuer yet–D.
2 every] any–D. *4* othres] other–D. *5* hath ...
follie] at my foly hathe–D. *7* of ... yeres] my lytyll
perseyvyng–D. *8* me lede] lede me–D. *9* Yet]
But–D. of full] by–D. *13–14* And gyls Reward is
small trust for euer | Gyle begyld shuld be blamyd
neuer–D.

18. *3* myn] my–F. *7* revoultid–W] revoulsed–OE.

19. D LXIX. *1* that] that eke–D. *2* by] by good–D.
3 saieth a proverbe] the proverb saith right–D.
4 Eche] every–D. *5* thy] thy owne–D. *6* on] vppon–
D. *7* Nor] Nother–D. is–W] of–OE. *8* thyn ... is]
the hert is thus–D. *10* thought] demed–D. *12* fas-
shion] fasten–D. mutable] so dobtable–D.

20. D LXI, T. *2* whiche pites] with pite–OE. with
piteus–D. *6* the] you–D.

21. **T.** *11* libertes] liberte–?E.
22. D LXXII, **T.** *2* vales causing] valeis causers of–D.
    6 pitie I fynde] I finde pitye–D. *7* seke] sought–D.
    10 a tere] atree–D. *13* howgy] howyy–F. *14* com-
    playning] moving–D. their] the–D. *17* Joye] joyes–
    D. *18* stony] tygres–D. thus joyned] this joyned–E.
    so clokid–D. *19* So . . . beaultie] That arte so cruell
    covered with bewtye–D. *20* No . . . the] There is no
    grace from the that–D. *21* rewarded] rewarde–D
    (*perhaps the better reading*).
23. **T.** *4* joy full dolourous–N] joyfull dolours–E.
    9 thy chaunge] by change–T, N. *13* have me–T]
    have–E.
24. A, T.
25. A, T. *2* I] *del.*–E, *not by W. 7* towerd] kowerd–
    late cor. E.
26. D LXXXII, P, **T.** *3* above the wynde] about the
    heavin–D. *4* seson] leson–D. *8* none–P] me–E, D.
    Petrarch: 'E non m'ancide Amor'. *13* dethe and
    lyf–D] lyffe and deth–E.
27. A. *13* my dere] my–F (*textual note in F is inaccu-
    rate*).
28. A, T. *5* owre] F *assumes this*=hour. *11* Wrethed]
    Wretched–OE. *13* consort–E, N] comfort–F, con-
    fort–Fl.
29. A, T. *10* thought] though–E.
30. A, T. *4* Tigre-like] Tigre like–E. *6* mountain]
    moyntain–E. *14* That] And–F.
31. A, T. *8* in–*corr.* E] and–OE.
32. A, T.
33. A, T. *9* boystrous–A, T] boyseus–E. *13* of the] of
    that–E.
34. **T.** *8, 9* Yea–T] &–E.
35. *5* apaire] apaise–F.
36. *This poem is partly obliterated. 13*–F] *illeg.*–E.
37. D LXIX, **T.** *3* gentill] boeth gentill–D. *7* seking
    with a] seking–D. *9* speciall] esspeciall–D. *13* There-

withall] But therwithall–D. did] she ded–D. *15* I]
for I–D. *18* goo] parte–D. *19* also] likewise–D.
20 kyndely] gentillye–D. *21* What think you bye
this that she hat deserued–D.

39. D xiii, A. *2* require] desyryd–D. *4* my moost
desire] that I requiryd–D. *7* they] she–D. *10* boeth
... nyte] that ons I myght–D. *15* they knowe] she
knows–D. *16* they] she–D. their] her–D. *18* that]
where–D. *22* hele] ease–D.

40. D lxxi, A. *3* contraries] contrarye–D. *4* Is ever
the] must nedes be–D. *8* you have] yours hathe–D.
9 you] your–E. Truste me that stondes awrye–D.
10 sometyme to] may some tyme–D. *11* then ...
vp] then saye and supp–D. *12* And dryncke] a
taste–D. *14* But] yet–D. *16* no man knowe] folkes
perceyve–D. *17* evyn at] at–D. *18* is owte of] hathe
no–D.

41. D lxxiii (*1–23 are missing from* E). *26* all right]
nature–D. *27* frowerdle] scornefullye–D. *31 om.*–D.
32 hard–F. *conj.*] *Space in* E. But if your herte doth
not relent–D. *33* Sins I do kno that this ye kno | Ye
shall sle me all wilfullye–D. *34* That I] For me–D.

42. D lxxiii, A, T. *1* crueltye–W] tyranny–OE, D.
2 remembred] remembre–D. *5* myn–W] my–OE, D.
8 herd] her–D.

43. D xxxiv, A. *12* faith] faith for–D. *13–16 om.*–D.
28 stedfast–D] stedfastnes–E, A. *34* As I] As–D.

44. A, T. *1* stelyng–W] robbing–OE. *5* Revenge you
then and sure you shall not mysse–OE. *6* To have
my liffe with an othre ended–OE. *7* first–W] ton–
OE. *8* next shall clene–W] othre shall–OE.

45. D xix. *6* trayed] tryed–E, trayde–D.

46. D xxxv, P, T. *1* gadlyng–W] galdyng–OE.

47. D xxxvi, A, T. *9* istricken] I stricken–E. *12* falt]
fall–*late corr.* E.

48. A, T. *1* thretning] threning–E, threatnyng–A, T.
49. A, T.

50. A, T. *3* aunswer] Anna–T, *late title in* E.
51. D XII. *38* Restrain my] Refrayn me–D. *39* my]
   me–D. *41* Thus–D] Ffor–E. *42-8 om.*–E.
52. D XVI, T. (*In* E *each stanza is divided into two.*)
   13 who that] who–D. *21* How shuld I do than–D.
   22 tasted] tast–D. *29* And yf suche chance do
   chawnce–D. souche–*late corr.*–E.
53. A, T. *4* to repete–OE] repete–*late corr. 34* Where]
   Where is–*late corr.*–E. *36* left] lest–E. *39* shall not
   releve] nought shall releve–A, T. *40* wery] very–E,
   wretched–T.
54. D LXXIII, A, T. *3* in–W] and–OE. *7* Made–W]
   With–OE, D. do–W] did make–OE, D. *8* in–W, D]
   a–OE.
55. D XXII (*fragment*), XXIV. *3* leman] lady–D. *6* alack]
   alas–D. *7* loveth] loves–D. me] I–D. *10* I] For I–D.
   13 while that] yf ytt–D. *16* like] as–D. *17-20 om.*–E
   causing erroneous headings for remaining stanzas).
   20 have] hau/han–D. *21* harme] hurt–D.
56. D XXXI, A, T. *7* do] doeth–D. *8* locking–E] lacking–OE, D, F. *9* disdaynfull] that skornefull–OE,
   the skornfull–D.
57. D XXXVII, A. *9* vouchesave] wytsave–D. *12* thus]
   this–F. *16* But–W] Ffor–OE, D. *20* Reioyse not
   at–W] to rew vpon–OE, D.
58. D LXXI, A. *5* howre] nyght–D. *6* with] of–F. *17*
   hereth] heris–D. *18* Pitieth] pitis–D. *27* relesse for
   to trete] relef for to intreate–D.
59. D XXXVIII, A, T, H. *2* By see, by land–W] by hilles
   and dales–OE, By hyllys by dales–D.
60. D LXXIV, P, T. *1* I ame not ded all though I had a
   fall–OE, D. *7* stowpeth] stoppeth–E, stowpith–D.
61. A, T. *1* The furyous gonne–W] Like as the canon–
   OE (i), bombard–OE (ii). *6* whose flame–W] Which
   daily–OE. *7* wych ... owt–W] Whose flame to
   open–OE.
62. D LXXIV, A. *12* wonderly] wonderuslye–D. *13*

thought–D] though–E. *19* from] for–D. *20* my–
D] me–E. *29* do] dothe–D.

63. D xxxix, lxxiv. *3* My wele, my joye, my–W] my
worldly joye and–OE, D. *19* goo–W] gro–OE, D.
23 alyve] a lyffe–D.

64. T.

65. D lxxi (1–8), lxxiii, **T.** *1* Ons as] Ons–D. *8* to
mone–D] mone–E. *10* had] hathe–D. *16* wonderly]
wondreslye–D.

66. D xiv, T. *3* and] the–Y. *4* sung] song–E. *11*
Rokkes do] Rokk dothe–D. *21* shall] may–D.
23 thinck] trow–D. *26* Perchaunce] May chawnce–
D. the lye–W] they lay–OE, they lye–D. *27* nyghtes–
D] nyght–E. *34* beaultie] beawte is–D. *38* we] I
haue now–D. *39* sung] song–E.

67. D lxx. *7* onlye–D] *om.*–E. *15, 19, 40* thone] ton–D.

68. D lxxi, H, **T.** *2* fynd–W] get–OE, D. *4* poyson]
poysons–D. *7* these–W] those–OE.

69. D lxxi. *12* regardeth] regardes–D. *17* please]
eese–D. *19* do] side–D. *21* rueleth] rulis–D.
23 None othre] no nothr–D.

70. D lxxiii. (*Leaf torn in E, and the second part of
each line is taken from D.*) *6* dedly] delye–D.
19 verye–D] wearye–N.

71. D lxxii. (*Leaf torn. First part of each line is taken
from D.*) *1* determed] determinid–D.

72. D lxxii. *19* slain] I stayne–D. *27* se me] se–D.
35 For] For for–D.

73. D xi (*last three stanzas*). *21* stay] save–F. *30* drery]
dere–D. *31* have] hathe–D. vnto] into–F.

74. D lxxiv. *3* length] lenght–E.

75. D lxxiii, **T.** *1* Desire alas] Cruell desire–D. *2* So
… selff] thy self so chainged for shame–D. *3–5*–W]
Whome I did seke now chasith me to and fro |
Whom thou didst reule now rewlyth the and
me | Tyrant it is to rewle thy subjectes so–OE.
3 That I have sought dothe chase me to and froo–D

4 D=OE. *5* What right is to rule thy subiectes
soo–D. *6* By . . . and] And to be ruled bye–D.
7 For] Lo–D. *8* hate] dred–D.

76. D LXXII, P, H, T. *3* oftyme] oftymes–D. *4* And to
his helthe dothe make the man renue–D. *5* Fyre
that allthing consumeth so clene–D. *6* thes bene]
this be–D.

77. D LXIX. *12* lyveth] lyve–D. *13* That he] that–D.
24 These] this–D.

78. *1* this the–N] this–E. *10* fleteth] floteth–F. *14, 21,
28* galere] galerie–E.

79. A, T.

80. T.

81. T. *8* thus–W] lo–OE.

82. A. *18* boote–N, F] *om.* E.

83. A. *10* her did–N] hid–E, A. *11* thought] though–E.

84. *38* playne–Y] payne–E.

85. *11* Leffer] Lesser–F. *17* Left] Lest–F. *23* lo] to–F.

86. H. *6* that] thou–H.

87. (I) *5* grownd of–M, Scott] grownd is–E, grounded–
N, growndles–Fl. *18* aduyse] admyse–F. *28* lofd]
losd–F. (II) *33* Love] Such–F. *41*] *om.*–E. (III)
Ambs–as] ambs as–E.

88. *3* vnrest–OE] re (?ye) vnrest–?W. *4* dyspyte]
dyspyse–F.

89. D LIII. *2* yn] now within–D. *5* Ffor–D] From–E.
10 highe] gret–D. *12* alas hathe] hathe–D. *13* My
poore trew] A symple–D.

90. T. *17* seithe] sleithe–M. That toucht your frend
so nere with pangs of paine–T. *20* will doth–T]
will–E.

91. *15* it–*conj.* Y] *om.*–E. worst] worse–F.

92. A, T. *9* Sephame] Sephances–A, Stephan–T.

93. *The first four stanzas, deleted, appear also before
No. 89. 1* Iye] Ie–E. *2* stryke–E (i), streke–E (ii).
25 is it] it is–F. Jelowsye–E (ii) of Jelowsye–E (i),
my jealousy–*conj.* N. *41* astart] ascart–F.

94. T. *2* still–W] small–OE. *3* ay–W] still–OE. *4* tyll] Iyll–F. *7* resistans ... none–W] then botyth no deny–OE. *8* remedy alone–W] only remedy–OE.

95. A, T. *6* Be–T] By–E, A. *8* Brunet ... rore–W] Her that ded set our country in a rore–OE.

96. D XLIX, A, T. *2* hevy–W] sory–OE. in dekay–W] with his sway–OE. *3* elles ... soccours–W] from elles where some aide or socours–OE. *5* Ffor sins] sins–D. that did] dyd–D. *6* staide–W] held–OE. *7* Wych–W] That–OE. suche–W] with such like–OE. sory–W] wofull–OE. *11* ons maist–W] maist ons–OE. *14* and I] and–D. *15* flete–W] passe–OE. *16* fast–W] fast alas–OE. *18* straite–W] sellff–OE. *19* as fast–W] agayne–OE. where he] where–D. *20* jornei–W] viage–OE. *28* fele] fle–D. *30* wich–W] that–OE. *32* where–W] that–OE. well embrace] embrace–D. *35* sins I] I–D. *41* also–W] also to know–OE. *44* wich–W] that–OE. *48* all ... still–W] to think on nowght and–OE. *50* bewray–W] declare–OE. *54* that–W] seke–OE. *55* most–W] all–OE. *60* Lyke as–W] sins that–OE. Loke as–D. *67* accompagnie] accopagnie–E. *68* were] wher–D. the smert] smart–D. *72* towch me] touch–D. *74* such–W] erst–OE. *75* Be–W] ar–OE. *76* that that] that I–D. *77* lingerd–W] all my–OE, linger–D. *78* in–W] with–OE. to vertu–W] in vertu–OE. *81* mone–W] playne–OE, morn–D. *83* sterne] streme–D. *84* lovely] louyth–D. *85* well–W] offt–OE. *86* rage] charge–D. *88*–W] my faintyng hope my brytill lyff welling dispaire fulfilles–OE. *90* excesse] express–D. *91* sort–W] fere–OE. *94* may ... repose–W] may sometyme take repose–OE. *W left a word undeleted.* *96* may ... grace–W] perchaunce she shew this grace–OE. *98* she the] se the–D. *99*–W] Then say I come for here I may not tary–OE, her I–D. *100* this–W] my–OE.

97. T. *7* alone ... lyve–W] for whome only alone–OE.

98. T. *2* For ... that–W] For yff he myght have sene–
OE. *4* His bow your hand–W] Your hand his
bow–OE. *6* he blind and–W] by cawse he–OE.

99. T. *1* what kynd–W] excesse–OE. *2* What plage
... mynd–W] what poyson doth my mynd opresse–
OE. *3* my–W] the–OE. is assind–W] doth not
cesse–OE. *4* What ... swete–W] the poysond
plesantnesse–OE. *5* myn eyes–W] my chekes–OE.
6 away slepless–W] sleples away–OE. *8* sustayne–W]
sustaine–OE (i), redresse–OE (ii). *9* In ... wound–
W] The stroke dothe stretche–OE. *10* To–W]
In–OE. *13* cure–W] ruthe–OE. *14* plaint–W] woos–
OE (i), deth–OE (ii). *16* rebell–W] vnkynd–OE.
17 ons ... love–W] Myghtst thou so love–OE.
18 Myghtst thou so love and neuer more attayne–
OE. *19* Myght wrathfull love so threte you with
disdayne–OE. *20* thy cruell hert to prove–OE (i),
thy cruellty reprove–OE (ii).

100. H, T. *3* strength–H] strengh–E. in naught]
naught–H. *4* Angre] slaughter–H. *5* and] or–H.
6 see ... of] land see or–H. *7* Know] Have–H.

101. (*The last letters of several lines have been cut
away.*) A, T. *2* lyght] lygh–E. *4* on–W] and–OE.
8 repugnant–W] the diverse–OE. alone] alo–E.
9 liuing–W] lyvely–OE. *12.* The sterry skye vnder
the wich thre movith othr sevyn–OE. *13* that same–
W] this skye–OE. *15* the first–W] this hevyn–OE.
his restles sours–W] restles recours–OE. *16* eight–
W] seven with–OE. *18* pointes–W] sings–OE.
19 obiect–W] direct–OE. *20* deviding] devididng–E.
22 towchith–W] passith–OE. for] *del.*–E. *23* discribd ... bryght–W] as axell is this lytt–OE. *24*
northward we–W] that we do–OE. *26* thevins–W]
the hole–OE. *27* have–W] hath–OE. *28* those–W]
the–OE. *29* but thei ben–W] ffor it is–OE. symple–
W] vnmixt symple–OE. *30* all those–W] those–OE.
31 erryng–W] wandryng–OE, F. *32* that first–W]
267

the hevin–OE. *40* sli ... not–W] so slow to preve I will it passe–OE. *41* next ... sterry–W] that moveth vnder that–OE (i), vnder the firmament–OE (ii). *44* yeres complete–W] yeres–OE. *46* of all–W] of–OE. with–W] eke with–OE. *48* viage–W] jorney–OE. *50* frendly ... signe–W] defence and frendly signe–OE. *51* berth–W] hath cruell–OE. in three hundred days–W] mevith all this warre–OE. *53* A–W] the–OE. houres therto–W] therto houres–OE. *58* so–W] and so–OE. *59* sterr] stern–F. *61* next ... gone–W] and next thee hath–OE. *64* now bent] no bent–E. owt] ow–E. *65* thire owne–W] them sellffes–OE. *67* where ... bodies–W] his body–OE (i), alyve his body–OE (ii). *71* movinges] movinge–F. *72* alofft–W] thevin–OE. *76* about] bout–W. ap–OE a *del. by mistake*).

DEVONSHIRE POEMS

102. II. *7* Iyes] Ies–D. *11* they] thye–D. *15* lengthe they] leynthe thye–D. *18* yt] yot–D.

103. III.

104. IV. *5* alive] aleve–D. *11* thought] though–D. *21* heate] hart–F. them–N] then–D. *23* the flame] flame–D. *28* that] thatt that–D. *30* spen] spare–F. *31* ton] touwn–?D. *33* doubtles] doubles–D.

105. V. *3* therby] therbe–D. *7* glose] golse–D. *9* spare] spre–D. *11* carre–M] carsse–?D, can so–F. *15* crosse] crusse–D.

106. VI. *1* lovve] lowe–D (*so elsewhere*). *4* well] will–D. our] or–D. *7* this] thes–D. *11* evell] well–F. *15* Alas] alas alas–D. *17* our] or–D. *18* oft] of–D. *22* them] then–D. *23* trowe] kowe=knowe–F.

107. VI. *7* reke] kepe–F. *12* hate] have–F. sumtyme] ontyme–F. *19* lede] live–F. *23* regnith] regnit–D. *26* by] be–D. *28* the] yt–F.

108. IX. *7* offence] a fence–D. *23* falshode] falsed–

conj. N. *24* an othe] a nothe–D. *29* agayn] a gayn–
D. *30* fayn] sayn–F.

109. XI. *11* abiecte] obiecte–F.

110. XII. *6* my] the–F. *7* methynks] methyncs–?D
(Wyatt).

111. XIV. *4* and] that–F. *17* Iye] yIe–D (Wyatt).

112. XV. *27* vnhappy] unhappe–F.

113. XVII. (W.)

114. XVII. *3* beate] boate–?D. *29* Ho] Lo–F. *30* In
comenant–D] incontinent–N. In covenant–F. *34*
be–N] *om.*–D.

115. XVIII. T. (Wyatt.)

116. XX.

117. XX. *1* syghe] syght–F.

118. XXI. *14* forthe] faithe–F. (*A line is drawn in the
manuscript after stanza five; the remaining stanzas
should perhaps be regarded as a separate poem.*)

119. XXI.

120. XXIII, XXXIII. (*Text follows second version except
for one or two spellings.*) *4* waies] was–D. *26*
sarwyes–XXIII] sorowys–XXXIII forgott] for nott–
XXIII, F. *30* Of–XXIII] With–XXXIII. *40* my] me–
XXIII, F.

121. XXIV (*two stanzas*), XXXVIII. *31* way–F] ways–D.

122. XXXII. T. *7* glyde–T] slyde–D. *8* face–T] place–
D. *11* on] vpon–T. *22* hope] both hope–T.

123. XLIII, LXXVII. *23–8 om.*–LXXVII. *29* Eche] The–
XLIII. *30* her–XLIII] his–LXXVII. *33* and] my–XLIII.
34 are dryven] ys turnd–XLIII. *35–46 om.*–XLIII. *46*
Armles] am left–N. *50* fayned] crafty–XLIII. *51* selie]
wyly–XLIII. *52* wise] young–XLIII. *53–8 om.*–
XLIII.

124. LI. *18* falshed] falsyed–F. *19* grame] game–D.

125. LI. *13* Me] my–D.

126. LII. *3* ys no–N] ys–D.

127. LIII. *3* payne–F] payns–D.

128. LIII.

129. LIV.

130. LIV.

131. LVIII.

132. LXIV. *2* or] and–F. *20* Do] To–D. *23* nedes] indes
(? nides)–D. *40* folysh] folys–D, sely–F. (W)

133. LXIX, T. *4* heale] salv–F. *8* thou] then–D.

134. LXX, T. *8* strayt it–T] strayter–?D. *22* v nto–?D
T] owt of–*orig.* D, F. *27* Encresse–D, T] Encresst–
F, Y. *34* fro] for–D. *40* Suche] your such–D.

135. LXXII. *5* still–?D.

136. LXXIII. *7* farre] faure–?D. *9* ouerlye] onlye–F.

137. LXXIII. *4* dedlye–F] delye–D. *8* vnto] into–F.
16 constraine] restraine–F, Y.

138. LXXIV. *12+* *line om.*

139. LXXV.

140. LXXV. *6* the–?D, that–F. *10* will not I] will I
not–F.

141. LXXV. *8* wrislye] werislye–D. *12* good or] gerdon–
F. *24* commedis] remedis–F. *31* her–F] our–D.
38 rehersall] so ferefull–F.

142. LXXVI. *7* purpose] purposed–F. *11* yt] that–F.
12 to endyght] tendyght–D. *14* her puissaunte] her
puisshaunte–D, for punisshmente–F. *17* yt] that–F.
renewe] renwe–D, renne–F. *22* thus] this–F. *24*
rudelye] kyndelye–F. *25* Redre] Rerdre–D. *31*
That] Yet–F. musing–*conj. Chambers*] moving–D.

143. LXXVII. *18 om.*–D] *conj.* Y.

144. LXXVII. *2* doth–M] hathe–D. forgett] forgott–?D.
4 frett] ffett–F. *16* be] are–F. *31* stroke–M] crueltie–D.

145. LXXVII. *3* morne] mone–F. *8* gro] goo–F.

146. LXXVII. *2* That shrynckith] and they mokith–F.
slendr] blinde–F. *4* peakes] payne–F.

147. LXXVIII. *2* scornefulnesse] scorenefulnesse–D. *9*
overthwarte] overtwawerte–D (*first* w *written over*
h). *15* setst–M] seiste–D. *21* foo] fooo–D. *29*
chaing–?D.

148. LXXVIII. *19* ware] want–F. *21* **A** thinckes athinckes–D. *27* eke] oke–F. *28* hom] have–**F.**] bente] lente–F.

149. LXXVIII. *2* remedye] comedye–F. *3* downe–F.] done–D.

150. LXXVIII. *17* ben done–N, F] bedon–D. *18* won] wo in–?D.

151. LXXVIII.

152. LXXIX. *8* to holde] is helde–F. *11* brute–D] beute–F. *14* ffo] ffu–D. *15* hardelye] frendelye–F. ere] are–D. *21* theye] thye–F. *22* wordes] woodes–?D.

153. LXXIX, T. *4* her] here–D. *7* not] nor–F. *14* to asswage] tasswage–D.

154. LXXIX. *3* bare] f bare–D. *7* dayes] daye–F. *8* werye] verye–D. *25* wich] w^t.–D, that–F.

155. LXXX. *30+ line om.*

156. LXXX. *33 word om.* *54* paynes that] paynes–F.

157. LXXXI.

158. LXXXI, A. *6* to] to to–D. *36* most hathe] must have–F. *39* wich] w^t.–D, that–F. *43* vniuste] oniuste–?D.

159. LXXXI, T. *6* or] ere–F.

160. LXXXI.

161. LXXXI. *15* a man] aman–D. *17* worldelie] wordelie–D.

162. LXXXII. *This poem is in a different handwriting and may be an imitation of Wyatt's 'patience' poems.*

163. LXXXII. *6* am] on–D. *12* that] what–F. *13* self] help–F. *27* Sustaine] Enflame–F. *29* wiche] livith–**F** (*the* w *has been written over* b, *the initial letter of the next word*). *32* burne] borurne–D.

164. LXXXIII. *32* liberte] librte–D.

165. LXXXIV. *23* flame] flames–F.

166. LXXXIV. *23* not] not and–D. *26* then] than–D.

167. LXXXV. *9* nor] not–F. *16* But I am–F] But am–D. *27* judge] jude–D. *40* I be] be–N.

POEMS FROM MINOR MANUSCRIPTS

168. H xxiii, T. *1* drynke] my drink–T. *2* suche ... wolde] would such Musick–T. *3* wears] it weares–T. *4* Innocencie] Pore innocence–T. *5* I iudge] iudge I–T. *6* assaulted] assaultes–T. *7* I am] am I–T.

169. H xxiii. *4* vnto] into–F.

170. P xxxii, T. *1* your] thy–T. *3* might ye befall] mought you fall–T. *8* so be but] very–T, and] *om.*–F.

171. P xxxii, T. *1* wonders] wonderous–T. *3* With ... cheare] Of liuely loke–T. expell] repell–T. *4* With ...lookes] With right good grace–T. *5* wordes] word–T. *6* The] Her–Y. *7* and ... chaunce] and these perchance–T. *8* the] with–T.

172. C, T. *1* in] within–T. *2* and] her foe–T. *5* Certes] Lo–T. do syeke] seke–T. *9* the best] best–T. lieth] lieth but–T. *10* out off daunger yet] better–T. *11* Rather then with] Than bide in–T. *12* Small is the pleasure where much payne we suffer–T. *13* Soner] Rather–T. it] *om.*–T. *15* And yet me thinkes although I liue and suffer–T. *16* Adwayting] I do but wait a–T. *17* Oft many thinges do happen in one houre–T. *18* me oppressed] oppressed me now–T. *20* vtterlye] wholy–T. *22* and] in–F, where–T. lengthe off] lengthes–T. *23* two ylles] these two euyls–T. *24* youe] *om.*–T. her] dothe–T. *25* Your aduise, yowe] What saye ye–T. best] the best–T. *26* cage in] cage–T. the] *om.*–F. to be] *om.*–T. *27* for] om.–T.

173. A lx, T. *8* Dearlye] Daily–T. *10* wofull] roofull–*Padelford*. *11* carefull–T] wofull–A. *14* ease–T] cause–A.

174. A lx, T. *2* guifte I] guifte whiche I–T, OA.

175. A ccxvi, T. *5* eyes] eyen–T, F. *9* list] lust–T, F. *21* trifling–T] tasting–A.

176. A ccxvi, T. *1* toppe] whele–T. *2* courtes estates] hye astate–T. *3* And vse my life in quietnesse eche

dele–T. *4* Vnknowen–T] Vnknowe–A. suche ...
ioyes] the wanton toyes–T. *5* so ... forthe] my time
shall slowly–T. *6* That] And–T. done] past–T. *7* I
... aged] Let me dye olde–T. *8* For–T] Ffrom–A.
8–10 For gripes of death doth he to hardly passe |
That knowen is to all: but to him selfe alas | He
dyeth vnknowen, dased with dreadfull face–T.

POEMS FROM BOOKS

77. V, T, Add. MS. 18752. *4* nothing but honesty] ye
not but honestly–T. *5 T omits refrain from each
stanza.* *9* The] This–T. *12* my–T] thy–V. *13* seyng]
sins–T. *17* offend–T] swarue–V. *18*–T] *om.* V. *19*
For syth you] But sins ye–T. know–T] knew–V. *21*
being] that am–T. *22* that–T, 18752] that I–V. *24*
neuer] not, ne–T.

178. T.
179. T.
180. T. *15* whom] whan–F.
181. T. *14* no] to–F.
182. T.
183. T.
184. T. *5* then] *om.*–F. *7* eke] *om.*–F. *11* my–N] me–T.
185. T.
186. T. *Not divided into stanzas.*
187. T.
188. T.
189. T. *The poem has been divided into stanzas and the
speech prefixes have been expanded.* *4* if] of–F. *7* and
rew my–T (*2nd ed.*)] alas, with–T. *26* should]
would–F. *27* An] A–F. *32 This line represents the
poet's comment.*
190. T.
191. T.
192. T.

193. T.
194. T.
195. T. *4* Indian] Inlian–F.

SATIRES

196. E (*after No. 74 above*), D LXXXV, C, P, A, T.
1–27–D] *om.*–E. *1* Myne owne–C] My nowne–D
7 or] and–F. *15* touche–C] twyche–D. me–C]
my--D. *19* frame–C] from–D. *27* That–C] thar–D.
28–A, C] *om.*–D, E. my wordes] wordes–A, my
worde–C. *29–30*–C] *om.* E, D, A. *29* And–C] Nor–
F. *31–51*–D] *om.*–E. *32* and] or–F. *38* highe–A, T]
him–D, C. dam] deme–C. *39* his–C] is–D. *40* do
not] donnot–D. *41* whar] when–F. *42* his–C] is–D.
43 suche–C] shuch–D. *45* lyon–C] lyond–D.
cowarde–C] cowardes–D. *50* Thopas–C] Thopias–
D, Topas–T. *53* laugheth] lawghes–D. *54* frowneth]
frownes–D. he is–D] is–E. *56* ever] neuer–D. *77*
could] wolld–D. *78* maist] may–D. *80* to hawke]
hawke–D. *85* these] theire–D. *90* with] what–D.
the] these–D. *92* owtewardly] vtterlye–D. *94* let-
teth] lettes–D. *96* beeste do so] bestes do–D.

197. E (*after No. 76 above*), D LXXXVII (*1–18 only*), A,
T. *1* and] or–D. *14* when her–D] wher–E. *19* quoth
she] *om.*–D. *25* delicates–T] the delicates–E. *43*
towny] townysshe–OE. *48* pourpose] poupose–E.
52 loked–T] loke–E. *55* tho the vnwise–Y] tho–E,
for the vnwise–T. *60* wonders] wondrous–Y. *89* set–
T] se–E. *108* backwards] backward–F. *112* in-
wards] inward–F.

198. E (*after No. 83 above*), A, T. *22* durt] dust–F.
24 moyster] moyste–E. *37* dayes–T] daye so–E.
69 be–T] by–E.

PSALMS

199. E (*after No. 93 above, lines 1–36 only*), A cxviii.
16 Bright as–N] Vpright all–E, upright as–A. *23* so
... untrue–*conj.* F] *om.*–E, A. *32* scaring] straunge–
A, straung–F. *37* eke] *om.*–F. *43* just ... honds–
conj. F] *om.*–A. *58* To] The–?A. *60* smokye]
smoking–F. *67* lust] list–F. *70–1 conj.*–M] *om.*–A.
72 seeme] sene–A. *99* anon] anow–F. *106* un-
twynde] be untwynde–*conj.* F.
The Argument. om.–E. *7* Innocence] Innocentes–A.

PENITENTIAL PSALMS

The Penitential Psalms appear in E (lxxxvi *et seq.*)
preceded by Surrey's sonnet and followed by No. 101.
They were published in 1549, but it would seem that
Wyatt's text was 'improved' after his death and these
readings have therefore been ignored. The title of the
1549 edition runs: 'Certayne Psalmes chosen out of the
Psalter of David commonlye called thee. vii. penyten-
tiall Psalmes, drawen into englysshe meter by Sir
Thomas Wyat knyght, whereunto is added a prologe
of the auctore before every psalme, very pleasant and
profettable to the godly reader.' The Penitential
Psalms appear also in A, and part of No. 201 has to
be supplied from that manuscript and from R.
200. *6* venemd–W] poyson–OE. *8* creeping–W]
sparplyd–OE. *10* moyst–W] warme–OE. launcyd–
W] launcyth–OE. *12* he–W] a–OE. *15* that–W]
whereoff–OE. had printyd–W] printyd–OE. *17* the
... cast–W] and owt off mynd clene cast–OE. *18* to–
W] the–OE. *20* ye–W] and ye–OE. forthwith–W]
anone–OE. *21* Vrye ... feld–W] vnder pretence off
victorye–OE. *22* I say–W] to go–OE. *24* for
enmy's–W] on the foes–?OE. *25* owt of dowt–W] all

alone–OE. *26* more ... or–W] he doth Love more
then–OE. he myndith–W] or god–OE (i), he lovth–
–OE (ii). *27* after–W] when–OE. *28* that lust–W]
this delyght–OE. *29* torn–W] tornd–OE. *30* from–
W] and–OE. *33* trecherye–W] gret–OE. *38* from–
W] how–OE. thretes alas–W] sore menace–OE. *42*
hete–W] colour–OE. *44* his–W] the–OE. *47* purpirll pall–W] pall–OE. *51* thynner ... cloth–W] a
thyn cloth–OE (i) a thyn vile cloth–OE (ii). *53*
faire hore–W] here his–OE. *54* knoing ... wykednes–
W] repentyng his excesse–OE. *57* taketh in hand–
W] hath taken in his hand–OE. *58* his ... save–W]
the plaintes and the cryis–OE. *64* did make–W]
mad–OE. *65* or–W] of–OE. *66* rof that–W] the
thing–OE. *70* seking ... conterpese–W] he tunes
his god to plese–OE.

201. *1* in–W] off–OE. *3* hope taken–W] cawght confort–OE. *5* marcy as the–W] in the same–OE.
6 wrechid–W] vs–OE. *13* open–W] knowlege–
OE. *15* largenes–W] length–OE. *17* provokt–W]
provoketh–?OE. *19* for recompence–W] prepare
agayne–OE. *22* more ... of–W] and have more
nede of the for–OE. *24* sekes–W] seksh–OE. *26*
fele–W] for–OE. *27* in–W] for–OE. onles ... me–
W] if ... me not–OE. *28–81* A] *missing in* E.
29 That] The–F. *38* shade–R] shadowe–A. *45*
thie] thyn–F. *55* rightwise–R] rightuous–A. *57*
Thie] Thyn–F. *59* R] *om.*–A. *75* suffers] sufferth–
R. *83* trapps–W] gy–OE. *84* sum–W] the–OE
(i), and–OE (ii). do–W] doth–OE. to my weping–W] vnto myn–OE. *92* ryches–W] glory–OE.
100 herd ... sen–W] pitid so to se–OE. *104*
the–W] bye–OE. yowr] your–OE, ?W. bait–W]
venim–OE. *105* made them–W] thei had–OE.
vsurpe] vsurpt–?E. *106* that so–W] that–OE. *109*
confusion's–W] confusion as–OE. *110* sugestion–
W] enterprise–OE.

202. *1* fevour–W] dolour–OE. *2* affter–W] affter the–
OE. the hete–W] thete–OE. *3* off] *om.*–F. faruour]
furuour–F, furour–A. *4* let ... behold–W] with
sobbyng multifold–OE. *5* sorowful–W] bet hyr–
?OE. *6* down rold–W] rold–OE. *14* beknoynge–W]
and knoleging–OE. *18* for to tremble–W] to be
adrad–OE. *21* So–OE] so him–*not* W. *32* straynid–
?W] strayning–?W, lowd–OE. agayne–W] lo–OE.
thus–W] thus oft–OE.

203. *7* and–W] that–OE. *8* within ... discharge–W]
vnder the mantell off mercy–OE. *9* and–W] oh–
OE. willfullness–W] forgiff–OE. *13* to ... dolour–
W] examplid there errour–OE. *14* was–W] did–OE.
execute–W] it extend–OE. *20* owght–W] nothing–
OE. *21* by cawse–W] that–OE. *22* and for to shew
my fawte have bene aferd–OE. *23* do–W] and–
OE. *24* feles] fells–E. *27* and–W] dyd–OE. *28* rage
... expresse–W] plaint that I by force expresse–
OE. *29* thy–W] and for thy–OE. was–W] hath–
OE. *31* priking–W] restles–OE. *37* from–W] to–
OE. *38* confesse–W] bemone–OE. *45* stormes–W]
wavis–OE. *59* iye] yIe–E. *64* lest–W] that lest–OE.
69 that–W] but that–OE. *70* hert–W] mynd–OE.
74 makth ... holdth–W] doth contynew–OE. *75*
your ... must–W] I say set all your glory yow
must–OE.

204. *1* This endid did our David hold his pece–OE.
2 abowt he–W] did seke–OE. *3* Did seke the Cave]
did seke the darke Cave–W, the darke Cave–OE (*W
neglected to delete* darke). *4* to–W] his to–OE. *5*
pees this pees that–W] marcy whereon he–OE.
6 sowle–W] hert for–OE. *7* mercyes plentifull hand]
mercy plenty full hand–W, mercy full hand–OE. *9*
as–W] and as–OE. *10* Fyndyng] Fyndith–F. *13* that–
W] and–OE. *14* A marble ymage–W] As marble
ymage–F, and ymage made–OE (i), an ymage–OE
(ii). *15* on hygh–W] lyfft vp–OE. *16* made as–?W]

semyng–OE. plaine ... sygh–W] syght to sobbe to
supp–OE. *17* that ... sendes–W] down from that
sonne dissendes–OE. *19* discends–R] distendes–E.
20 and with the luster on the cordes it glydes–OE.
25 affecte–W] desire–OE. *26* he ... off–W] off his
idolle–OE (i), erst he was off–OE (ii). *30* sure–W]
assurid–OE.

205. *2* in the be–W] be in the–OE. no alteration–W]
no such alterations–OE. *3* like as–W] as we–OE.
4 mesuryng–W] and mesuryng–OE. our–W] the–
OE. mutation–W] mutations–OE, F. *6* castigation–
W] castigations–OE. *8* famine and fire–W] derth
and of deth–OE, famine and of fire–F. *9* Stikkes
diepe–W] ar stykyt–OE. lo–W] now–OE. *12*
terror–W] fere–OE. *13* ferme–W] helthe–OE.
15 drede–W] fere–OE. *16* frailefull–W] sinfull–OE.
17 for why–W] by cawse–OE. above ... bownd–W]
ar clome above my hed–OE (i), above my hed
crowne–OE (ii). *19* to–W] a–OE. grownd–W]
down–OE. *20* By force wheroff the evill curid
skarris–OE *deleted line.* whilow plant–W] doth a
bow–OE. *21* and–W] that–OE. not well–W] evyll–
OE. *22* That ... is–W] Is festred–OE. *23* vnder
skyn–W] styll with sin–OE (i), styll within–OE (ii).
27 gruging–W] gnawyng–OE. *30* welth–W] helthe–
OE. *33* it ... forst–W] forcyd hath–OE. to crye
and–W] for to–OE. *38* hart–W] force–OE. quaile–
W] faile–OE. *41* my ... sure–W] Myn owne
veruues–OE. most–W] my–OE. *42* myn own vertus–OE] myn own acquaintance–*correction not by* W.
as frendes most sure–OE. *43* and–W] did–OE.
44 kyn–W] naturall kyn–OE. fardest gone–W] gone
farr off–OE. *47* reproche–W] deceyte–OE. *50*
knowyng ... hand–W] ffor that to the O Lord–OE.
51 I me dyrect thow shalt my helpe supplye–OE.
52 my–W] the–OE. in–W] off–OE. *53* to–W] to–
OE (i), off–OE (ii). *54* thou ... foos–W] myꞇ

enmys shold have–OE. *55* suche pleasant–W]
reioysing–OE. *59* my fawt confesse–W] confesse
my fawt–OE. *62* provokars–W] evill willers–OE.
63 hurt–W] harme–OE. *64* be bent–W] shall assent–
OE. *66* god–W] lord my–OE. seist–W] knowst–OE.
67 lord–W] god–OE. *68* be ... gone–W] nor be not
from me farr–OE.

206. *1* in–W] hathe–OE. *2* wind–W] shaad–OE.
3 shaad ... day–W] wynd restyth at myd day–
OE (i), rests at the mydes off–OE (ii). *7* still
myndes–W] sekys still–OE. *9* His fyngers strike
apon the sonour cordes–OE. *11* streme–F, &c.]
storme–E. discendes] distendes–F. *14* th'altryd–W]
his sensis sparplid–OE. *17* withowt–W] forth at–
OE. *18* terys–W] syghes–OE. syghes–W] terys–OE.
did strayne–W] pourd out–OE. *25* vp–W] had–OE.
30 stertyng–W] he stertes–OE. *31* His–W] With his–
OE.

207. *3* in–W] all–OE. *10* agayne–W] offttyms–OE.
17 is fixid fast–W] shall still remayne–OE. *26* shalt
... stable–W] hold ferme and fast thi word still
k–OE. *27* pure–W] stable–OE. *28* then–W] ame–
?OE. *29* I ame–W] to be–OE. *32* from my natyvite–
W] by corrupt nature–OE. *33* be ... alasse–W] yet
lo thou loves so the hertes trowgh in inward place–
OE. *38* not] no–E. led ... way–W] hath not led me
a way–OE. *45* thow–W] do thow–OE. *54* With
vpright spryte purgid from all vile lust–OE, F.
57 rendre to–W] retorne–OE. *58* my will–W] and
me–OE. *64* operation–W] repenta–OE. *70* owtward–
W] vttward–OE. *74* the lord lykyth–W] plesith
god–OE.

208. *1* Off–W] The–OE. *2* off grace–W] and grace–
OE. *4* did with the wonder astonne hym a space–
OE. *16* That–W] So–OE. his ... doth–W] doth
his graces to men–OE. *18* mesureles–W] this
mesureles–OE. to–W] and–OE. *25* David–W] our

David–OE. ponderd well–W] considerd this–OE.
27 derk ... hyde–W] sin had mad hym mis–OE.
29 he dare importune–W] Importunth he–OE.
209. *2* withowt impediment–W] withowten stopp or
lett–OE. *7* when–W] when so–OE, F (so *partially
deleted*). help my necessitye–W] ffor help vnto the–
OE. *14* brede–W] food–OE. *15* brede–W] foode–
OE. *16* plaintfull–W] plaints my–OE. *18* the–F]
thi–E. *19* As dispairate–W] I as dispairate–F, In
diepe dispaire–OE (*the line deleting these words
misses the initial* I). *23* ruyne lyff–W] lyve alone–OE,
pinyng–Fl, ruyne–A, kuyut–F. *25* was I–W] I ame–
OE. *28* provoke–W] assaut–OE. *30* In trowgh I
fownd no tast that myght me ples–OE. *32* from ...
rayne–W] haile downe from myn yIes–OE. *40* doth–
W] shall–OE. *41* frailte–W] misery–OE. all manekynd–W] euery man–OE. *43* ffynd–W] assynd–OE.
44 is–W] ffor–OE. *48* sins–W] the–OE. *50* in–
W] off–OE. *51* then–W] and so–OE. *52* thy ...
honour–W] shall honour thy glory–OE. *53* thy
grace–W] thou hast–OE. redemith–W] savid–OE.
thi–OE] this/thir–?W. *54* myghty] myght–E, myght
and–*conj.* F. *55* The lord hath his servauntes ioyes
estemid–OE (i), He hath his servauntes wishes so
estemid–OE (ii). *57* our discent–W] all mankynd–
OE. to be written–W] publysht me–OE. *58* consolation–W] comffor–OE. *62* vs–W] us men–OE. *63*
ar–E] as–F. *67* hys holy–W] thys holy to–OE.
68 hys–W] thys–OE. *70* bene gaderd–W] shall
range–OE (i), bene ranged–OE (ii). to–W] and–OE.
71 alone–W] that is–OE. *75* that–W] the–OE.
82 age] aye–F. *86* thi yeres extend–W] withouten
end–OE. *91* stablisht] stabisht–E.
210. *3* Ffor that he knew off hym were not exprest–OE.
4 that–W] by–OE. spryte–W] thing–OE. *17* he–W]
that he–OE. *20* all ... in–W] all reconpense as–OE.
22 wich–W] that–OE. *24* the ... fruyt–W] is fruyt

thereoff–OE. *27* glory–W] marcy–OE. *30* ponderd–
W] ponderth–OE, F. *31* knee–W] arme–OE.

211. 1 and from a–W] from–OE. *3* off darknes diepe–
W] where darknes doth–OE. *4* The have–W] To the
O Lord have–OE, To The–F. *9* that–W] but–OE.
is not–W] is–OE (i), it is–OE (ii). *11* thin ere–W] thi
sellff–OE. *12* Ffor lord–W] Ffor–OE. *13* And . . .
mercy–W] Thy natyff mercy to put–OE. *18* in thi
hand–W] mercy is with the–OE. *20* set my confydence–W] euer set my trust–OE. *22* eterne–W]
excellence–OE. *23* mercys–W] just–OE. alway
just–W] infallible–OE. *26* wachman lokyng–W]
wach that lokyth–OE. *27* by the–W] for his–OE.
28 Let–W] Let all–OE. vnto–W] in–OE alway–W]
I say–OE. *30* plentefful rannzome is with hym I
say–OE (i), rannzome comth–OE (ii). *31* shall
redeme–W] he shall rannzome–OE.

212. 2 did–W] hathe–OE. David–W] David into a
diepe as–OE. *5* confownd–W] resownd–OE. *9* full
. . . come–W] ple . . . e tyme was come–OE. *10* do
way–W] shake off–OE. *13* glint] glutt–F. *14* manne–
W] sinne–OE. *18* his sonne] his some–W, the deth–
OE. *19* From . . . me–W] of his dere sonne–OE.
20 My–W] our–OE. *21* can–W] may–OE. *23* and
sins–W] sins–OE. have–W] have then–OE. grace–
W] bonte–OE. *25* most do crave–W] aske hym
most–OE. *26* suyte . . . respect–W] forceable request–OE. *27* to the grave–W] with his ost–OE.

213. 2 answere to–W] supply thou–OE. *5* after thy–
W] for thyn own–OE. *7* off . . . and–W] accordyng
to just ryght in the–OE (i), off justice after suche
forme and–OE (ii). *8* thrall bond–W] bond–W.
9 his–W] thy–OE. *12* prykyng spurrs–W] suffrans
that–OE. *13* skante rysen–W] skantly rysn–OE.
15 foyld–W] soyld–F. *16* to . . . ryff–W] as man in
mortall stryff–OE. *17* me forst as ded–W] con-
strained me for–OE. *20* to–W] vnto the–OE.

21 dedes–W] workes–OE. *24* were–W] ar–OE. *25* did–W] doth–OE. *29* that I be layd–W] to make me seme–OE. *30* do–E] to–F. *32* I holly do–W] holly do I–OE. *33* and in thi hand–W] do me to know–OE. *36* Rydd–W] Dr–OE. *37* to–W] on–OE. me–W] bene–OE. *38* within–W] vnto–OE. *41* spryte vpryght] vpryght spryte–W, spryte shall guyde–OE. *43* lord shalt–W] shalt–OE. *46–9* There whilst thow shalt off thi benignite | Confound my foos and them distroy that seke | To hurt my lyff by theyre iniquite | Thus (*orig.* Sins) I thi servant humbly the besek–OE.

DOUBTFUL POEMS

214. D xl. *15* thus ... swaru'd] thys to asward–D *17* avow] avoe–D. *21* thou] tho–D.

215. D xl. *2* fflyght] fflyth–D. *23* now] yow–?D.

216. D xlii, T. *Rollins prints another version from Ashmole MS. 48. T omits the refrain in each stanza and has many variants. I have adopted some spellings from T.*

217. D xlvii, A ccxvii. *Printed by Nott as Wyatt's.* *1* thoughte–A] thoughtes–?D. *8* had had–A] had–D. *10* But yett] And–A. *11* Whereffor] Thearfore–A. do] must–A. *13* mowt well] mowt wyell–D, well moght–A. *16* Ioynd] Iond–D, Joynd'e–A. *17* Whereffor ... do] Whearby ... must–A. *18* Sence crewell will doth me so use–A.

218. H xxiv.

219. H xxiv. *7* stryf] servys–F.

220. P xxxiii, *Nugae Antiquae.* *1* myn eyes] my neyes–P.

221. P xxxiii, *Nugae Antiquae.*

222. A ccxvi, xxix.

223. A ccxvii, H, T. (*T version in thirteen lines among anonymous poems.*)

224. V. *2* mystres] mysters–V. *20* Though] Thouth–V.
23 part I] part–V.

225. V. *4* hart] my hart–V. *15* Askyng–M] And
kyng–V. *24* breake] breaket–V.

226. V. *8* to] with–V (*Chambers gives several other
minor variants from* A Boke of Balettes=B).

227. V, B, Add. MS. 18752. *2* this–B] my–V. *3* loue–
B] ioy–V. blinde–B] bind–V. *4* Except her–B] For
lacke of–V. I am now–B] now am I–V. *6* her–B]
his–V. *7* meanes–B] paynes–V. *15–20*–B] *om.*–V.

228. V.

229. A cv. *7* myrth] myrt–A. *12* from] for–A.

No. 166 also appears in *A Gorgeous Gallery of
Gallant Inventions* (1578) and may not be Wyatt's.
Line 5 reads 'Wherunto I may wel like' and Rollins
conj. that 'like' is a misprint for 'link'.

GLOSSARY

(References are to the numbers of poems)

Accomberd: encumbered, overwhelmed
Acited: summoned (8)
Affects: affections, passions
Again: against
Ainst: against
Algate: in every way
Allowance: praise
Ambs-as: double ace
Among: amidst
Apaire: impair, injure (35)
Armeles: defenceless
Assays: trials
Astart: escape
Ataced: silenced
Auysing: gazing at

Ban: curse
Bearing in hand: deceptions (14)
Bekinde: by kind, by its nature
Borde (Boorde): jest
Borow: pledge, security
Bote: remedy
Boteles: bootless, in vain
Bowght: circuit
Breade: breadth
Brenning: burning
Brute: reputation
Bygone: ornamented

Calcars: astrologers
Carefull: full of care
Cater: caterer
Ceace: seize
Chase: chose
Chave: chaff, provender, livelihood
Chaw: chew
Chepe: merchandise, bargain
Clattering: chattering
Clyve: cliff
Complysyth: accomplisheth
Convey: steal
Crysped: curled
Cure: care

Daskard: dastard
Daunger: subjection
Departed: separated
Depert: divide, separate, allot
Discus: set free
Dressyd: risen
Dryve: defer
During: enduring

Elonged: distant from
Entremete: interpose
Esterte: escape
Estew: avoidance (cf. eschew)

Fantasy: love
Fett: fetch
Fonds: play the fool
Force, no: no matter
Forger: liar
Forse: waterfall.
Frame (N): good condition (8)
Frame (V): deceive (16)

Gadlyng: fellow
Gaynward: towards, facing (97)
Glede: fire
Grame: sorrow
Grave: engrave, carve
Grownder: causer
Groyns: groans, grunts
Gruging: grudging, murmuring, vexing (205)

Happe: luck
Hardiness: boldness
Hay: hunting-net
Heins: refuge
Hiere: reward
Hold: prison
Howgy: huge

Incontinent: immediately

Jeopretie: jeopardy

Kant: portion
Kappurs: colt's
Kest: cast (*dial.*)

Layes: lairs

Lese: lose; speak evil of
Let: prevent
Lever: preferable, rather
Lynn: cease

Mak: mate
Mew: cage
Myschief: sorrow

Narr: nearer
Noppy: nappy, foaming
Not: ne wot, not know

Overlye: supreme
Overthwart: perverse, cross

Passe on: mind
Paysithe: weighs
Peakes: foolish fellows
Pere: appear
Piery: precious stone
Pirrye: squall
Poyntes: punctuates, hesitates (208)
Prese: press, crowd
Preseth: presseth, hastens
Pressed (Prest): ready
Pressions: pressures (8.T. *passions*)
Pretence: defence (212)
Price: bargain
Private: deprived of
Propose: purpose
Purpose: conversation

Quaint: cunning

Rabates: abates
Rathe: early, soon
Rayne: rein, restraint
Recheles: reckless, heedless
Recure: remedy
Reke: reck
Repayre: adorn
Repulse: bit
Restore: restoration
Retourneable: capable of being returned
Revert: turn away
Revoulsid: drawn away (141)
Rof: took
Ruell: rule

Saffry: savoury
Samble: assembly
Scantt: scarce, hardly
Semblable: like
Semblaunt: appearance, countenance
Seson: seize on, embrace
Shapen: shaped
Shitt (Shytt): shut (120); excluded (3)
Shright: shriek, shrieked
Sitteth: suits, fits
Slipper: slippery
Small: slim (37)
Solaine: solitary
Sonour: sonorous
Sours: source (94): flight (101)
Sparplid: diffused

Sperkling: flashing, scattering, lively (?)
Spill: kill
Steaming: flaming
Sterve: die
Stock: tree-trunk
Straynably: violently
Styk: hesitate
Sythens: since

Tho: then (91)
Trace: way of life
Traced: lured (8)
Train: deceit, enterprise
Trayed: betrayed (Reading of D. E has *tryed*. 45)
Trusse: quiver

Unquyt: without penalty
Unsparred: unbarred
Untwind: untwine

Vaileth: availeth
Vnto: until
Vre: use

Waker: watchful
Wanhope: despair
Wealth: well-being, happiness
Wenyng: weening, supposing
Wered: worn

Whereby: wherefore

Withsaue: preserve
Witsaue: vouchsafe
Wonders: wondrously
Worth, in: in good part
Wrislye: shrivelled
Wry: veil

Yede: went
Yere, to: for this year
Ywys: certainly, indeed

Zins: five

INDEX OF FIRST LINES

289